Pniniad

Marc Szeftel's Belgian passport, 1953

Pniniad

Vladimir Nabokov and Marc Szeftel

GALYA DIMENT

A McLellan Book

University of Washington Press

SEATTLE AND LONDON

This book is published with the assistance of a grant from the McLellan Endowed Series Fund, established through the generosity of Martha McCleary McLellan and Mary McLellan Williams.

Library of Congress Cataloging-in-Publication Data
Diment, Galya.
    Pniniad : Vladimir Nabokov and Marc Szeftel / Galya Diment.
      p.   cm.
    Includes bibliographical references and index.
    ISBN 0-295-97634-9 (alk. paper)
    1. Nabokov, Vladimir Vladimirovich, 1899–1977. Pnin.   2. Nabokov, Vladimir Vladimirovich, 1899–1977—Friends and associates.   3. Russian Americans—New York (State)—Ithaca—Biography.   4. College teachers—New York (State)—Ithaca—Biography.   5. Cornell University—Biography.   6. Russians in literature.   7. Szeftel, Marc.   I. Title.
PS3527.A15P5936   1997   97–10871
813'.54—dc21   CIP

Marc Szeftel's passport (facing title page) courtesy of Division of Manuscripts and University Archives at Suzzallo and Allen Libraries, University of Washington

Jacket drawing courtesy of Milton Glaser. Copyright © 1956 by Milton Glaser

To Rami, Mara, and Sasha
as well as to my
Vitebsk-born father

Now a question addressed to myself. Why do I spend so much time on this daily personal conversation . . . ? The question provides some of the answer: it is a substitute for the absent conversation. . . . This is number one. Number two is in a different perspective: I hope to be read by those who will look for my contact after I am gone. And finally, writing itself is appealing. . . . I am not Nabokov. . . . Anything [he] wrote had literary value; as to my writing, it may have little or even none. But it may have some, and this may be enough to be read.

—Marc Szeftel, Diary, February 18, 1978

Contents

Acknowledgments

I am grateful to the Graduate School Fund of the University of Washington for the 1992 Summer Research Grant which allowed me to start working on this book, and for the Fund's 1993 Addendum to the same grant, which paid for travel to Ithaca in the fall of 1993.

Special thanks go to Brian Boyd, D. Barton Johnson, and Daniel Waugh, who answered my questions and offered suggestions throughout my work on the manuscript and then readily agreed to critique the manuscript once it was ready, providing volumes of useful commentary without which this book would have been so much poorer. Dan Waugh was also instrumental in making me undertake this study, for it was he who alerted me to the existence of Marc Szeftel's archive at the Suzzallo Library of the University of Washington.

I am also grateful to Robert Alter and an anonymous reader, whose evaluations of my manuscript for the University of Washington Press were very helpful and deeply gratifying. Robert Alter was among the first people who knew about my project back when I was still only contemplating it, and his encouragement and support at the time were invaluable.

My heartfelt thanks and gratitude also go to:

Marc Szeftel's family: especially Kitty Szeftel, who kindly and patiently spent many hours with me, both in person and on the phone, as well as Sophie Tatiana Keller, Marc Watson Szeftel, Daniel and Linda Crouse, Flora Sheffield, William Nemerever, and Donald Keller for their friendliness and eagerness to cooperate with my project, and for all the information they provided.

My colleagues at the University of Washington: In addition to the late Donald Treadgold and Imre Boba, I thank Jack Haney, Willis Konick, Jim Augerot, Karl Kramer, Nora Holdsworth, Larry Lerner, and Peter Sugar, who shared their reminiscences with me, and, in some instances, served as consultants in matters where my own expertise was not sufficient; Hillel Kieval for materials on Jewish history, and help with Hebrew; and George Klim and Katarzyna Dziwirek for assisting me with Polish.

Other fellow Nabokovians: Vladimir Alexandrov, for his early enthusiasm about the project and his encouragement; and Gene Barabtarlo and Stephen Jan Parker, for their readiness and willingness to share expertise, reminiscences, and advice.

Other colleagues and friends: among them Beth Holmgren and Madeline Levine, who enlightened me on Polish intellectual history.

People at Cornell and in Ithaca, who readily provided sought-after information in interviews and/or letters: M. H. Abrams, Gardner Clark, Peter Kahn, James McConkey, Charlotte Fogel, Walter M. Pintner, John Marcham, Knight Biggerstaff, Beatrice MacLeod, Milton Cowan, Gould P. Colman, William Brown, Milton Barnett, Dorothy Staller, and Marianne R. Marsh, Administrative Manager in the Department of English, who went beyond the call of duty to help me locate people I needed.

Nabokov's and Szeftel's other colleagues, friends or students who responded to my inquiries in a most helpful fashion: Robert M. Adams, Vera S. Dunham, Franklin A. Walker, Daniel Matuszewski, R. E. Johnson, Gustave Alef, Charles Timberlake, John C. Cairns, Florence Clark, Lee Croft, George Gibian, John Trueman, and the late Harry Levin.

I am also grateful to Steven Rudy for commenting on chapter 2 of the present study, sharing his thoughts on Roman Jakobson and Jakobson's collaboration with Szeftel and Nabokov, as well as for granting me permission, on behalf of The Roman Jakobson and Krystina Pomorska Jakobson Foundation, Inc., to publish for the first time Roman Jakobson's letters to Marc Szeftel. In addition, Alison Jolly was extremely helpful in commenting on the parts of this book which dealt with Nabokov's relationship with her father, Morris Bishop, and in making it possible for me to quote from Morris Bishop's unpublished letters.

I would like to thank Dmitri Nabokov, who allowed me to publish his father's and mother's letters to Szeftel; John Marcham, who permitted me to quote from his father's unpublished reminiscences; Paul Gates, James McConkey, Stephen Jan Parker, and Charles Nicol, who agreed to let me quote from their letters to Marc Szeftel; and *Cornell Magazine,* which granted me permission to reprint Marc Szeftel's 1980 article, "Lolita at Cornell."

Further gratitude and thanks go to:

Naomi Pascal, associate director and editor-in-chief of the University of Washington Press, herself a former student of Professor Nabokov and life-long admirer of the writer Nabokov, for believing in the project in its earliest stages. Also Gretchen Van Meter, editor at the UW Press, for her painstaking yet sensible and sensitive copyediting.

The administration and staff of the Division of Manuscripts and University Archives at Suzzallo and Allen Libraries of the University of Washington—Karyl Winn, Kerry Bartels, Nan Cohen, Janet Ness, and, in particular, Gary Lundell—for all their enthusiasm about the project and help with Szeftel's archive, as well as for permission to publish some of the archive's materials.

The administration and staff of the Department of Rare and Manuscript Collections of Carl A. Kroch Library at Cornell University, and in particular Gould P. Colman, the University Archivist at the time, for their generous and courteous service and advice.

Fred Bauman, Reference Librarian in the Manuscript Division of the Library of Congress for his help with obtaining permission for me to review Nabokov's "Notes for Pnin's Life," which are kept there.

The administration and staff of Holland Library at the Washington State University at Pullman, and, in particular, John F. Guido and Siegfried Vogt, for sharing with me the catalogue of Marc Szeftel's library, which Kitty Szeftel had donated to them after Marc Szeftel's death, and for helping me to locate some of the books that were not immediately available on the library shelves.

My research assistants, Yelena Furman and Dana Sherry, graduate students in the department and both astute readers of Nabokov, for their help with letter writing, bibliographic research, and photocopying.

And, of course, my husband Rami, and my daughters Mara and Sasha, for all their love, help, and support, as well as for the meaning they give to my life.

Parts of chapter 3 appeared in *The Nabokovian* as "Pnin Revisited, Or What's in the Name(s)" (Fall 1993), and are reprinted here with that journal's permission. Portions of the Introduction and chapter 2 are featured in an article published in *Nabokov Studies* ("Timofey Pnin, Vladimir Nabokov, and Marc Szeftel," 1996) and are, likewise, reprinted here with that journal's permission.

Pniniad

Introduction

Whether because I have known Nabokov at close hand or because of my interest in his creative process, he seems to fascinate me as a person and as a writer, although his writing leaves me cold, in spite of all its virtuosity and even beauty.

—Marc Szeftel

This is a book about two very different people whose paths might never have crossed had not tumultuous revolutions and wars redirected and reshaped their lives. The name of Marc Szeftel, a Russian historian and Nabokov's longtime colleague at Cornell University, is familiar to many Nabokov specialists because he is often cited as the prototype for one of Nabokov's most memorable protagonists, Timofey Pnin. Both Andrew Field and Brian Boyd in their biographies make direct connections between Pnin and Szeftel, Andrew Field claiming that the writer actually confessed to him ("while riding in the elevator of the Montreux Palace") that Szeftel had served as the source for the character, and Boyd simply stating that "[m]any have identified Marc Szeftel . . . as Nabokov's model for Pnin."[1]

When Szeftel left Cornell in 1961, he went directly to the University of Washington and thereafter spent the rest of his life in Seattle. Upon Szeftel's death in 1985, his widow, Kitty Szeftel, gave his archive, including numerous diaries and letters, to the university's Suzzallo Library. *Pniniad* draws heavily on previously unpublished materials found in the archive, as well as on personal interviews with Nabokov's and Szeftel's colleagues, family, and friends.

My purpose in this book is twofold. First, I intend a study of *Pnin*, its origins, and its sources, for it is my strong opinion that Marc Szeftel had a serious impact on the novel. Second, and even more important, I also believe that much can be gained from exploring Szeftel's and Nabokov's relationship, from examining their lives as they intersected, for between the two of them, Nabokov and Szeftel embodied immeasurably more than one literary work. They personified the complexity and variety of Russian émigré experience in Europe and the United States, its ethnic, social and religious diversity, its triumphs and its failures. *Pniniad* is, in many ways, my attempt to use Pnin's émigré creator and Pnin's émigré model as a vehicle to illuminate at least some dark corners of this fascinating cultural terrain.

Nabokov's and Szeftel's were clearly contrasting personalities: Szeftel was anything but playful and fun loving. Though history and literature were his first loves (he studied law in Poland and Belgium mainly to oblige his father, who wanted him to be a "practical" man), he lacked Nabokov's literary sophistication, sensitivity, and fanciful imagination.[2] He also came from a markedly different social background than either Nabokov, the heir to Russian aristocrats and statesmen, or even Nabokov's wife, who, like Szeftel, was Jewish. Unlike Véra, who was born into a prosperous bourgeois St. Petersburg family, Marc Szeftel spent his childhood in small Jewish towns within the Pale of Settlement, where his father worked as a photographer and the family's income was very modest.

As Szeftel himself remarked in his diary, he and Nabokov were in no way intimate friends. Szeftel admired and envied Nabokov, whose Russian novels he had read when still in Europe (unlike Nabokov, who settled in Berlin, Szeftel spent the European part of his exile in Poland and Belgium). He joined the faculty of Cornell in 1945, three years before Nabokov did. Nabokov was familiar with Szeftel's work on *The Lay of Igor's Campaign,* in which Szeftel collaborated with Roman Jakobson, his former colleague at the École Libre des Hautes Études in New York. "It is on the whole an admirable work," Nabokov wrote to Wilson in 1948, commenting on *La Geste Du Prince Igor,* "Szeftel's and Jakobson's studies being especially brilliant."[3] In the early fifties, Szeftel, Nabokov, and Jakobson attempted to collaborate on an English-language study of the epic, but the project eventually fell through. Szeftel tried to get close to Nabokov but sensed that the writer was deliberately creating an insurmountable distance between them. Their mutual colleagues sometimes felt that Nabokov's attitude towards his fellow émigré was "patronizing . . . even dismissive."[4]

Nabokov probably viewed Szeftel as, in many ways, a caricature of himself. Nabokov's command of English was vastly superior to Szeftel's, yet, to those close to him, Nabokov often complained that he spoke merely "imitation" and "pidgin" English[5] which was "stiffish" and "artificial."[6] While he was a more exciting lecturer than Szeftel, he knew he was not so flamboyant or interactive and spontaneous as some other Cornell professors (Harry Caplan, a professor of Classics, for example). "He was utterly helpless without the prepared text," Nabokov would say about Pnin,[7] and in the writer's mind, this description probably applied as easily to himself as it did to Szeftel, for Nabokov lamented "think[ing] like a genius . . . writ[ing] like a distinguished author, and . . . speak[ing] like a child."[8]

Ironically, Szeftel too saw himself as a caricature of Nabokov, for he viewed the other man as embodying the professional fulfillment and success he felt had eluded him. This occasioned both admiration and resentment that sometimes exploded into anger. Like Pnin, Szeftel was more than accustomed to failure, and he envied Nabokov his background, his published books, his seemingly robust health, and his considerable reputation.[9] He even envied Nabokov his wife, for Véra Nabokov clearly fit Marc Szeftel's ideal of a perfect and loyal female companion who devotes herself to making sure her cerebral husband can concentrate solely on his work (a luxury Szeftel always wanted, but felt he never had).

In the ultimate manifestation of "Nabokov envy," Szeftel, a historian, even attempted to share in the other man's glory by writing a literary study of Nabokov's wildly successful *Lolita.* In 1963, when already in Seattle, Szeftel wrote to Nabokov in Switzerland, informing him that he had "a rough draft of a study about your *Lolita* and would like to complete it." "I feel," he added, "that to do it I need the script of its film version. Would it be too much to ask you to send it to me to Seattle . . . "[10]

It *was,* apparently, too much. One can only imagine what Nabokov felt when he learned that his character, his "poor Pnin," was planning to write a study of the creator's best-selling novel.[11] What we do know is that, in response to his request, Szeftel got a brief note from Véra informing him that Nabokov regretted he could not send him the screenplay and offering no explanation as to why.[12] Szeftel felt insulted and betrayed, both by the abrupt refusal and by the fact that Vladimir Nabokov did not deem it worth his while to write to his old collaborator and colleague himself. Szeftel never again attempted to communicate with Nabokov. He also never wrote his full-length study of *Lolita.*

How important is Szeftel to our understanding of *Pnin?* I suspect some critics and readers may feel a bit queasy—as I myself often do, and as Nabokov always did—about bringing "real life" and fiction too close together.[13] In order to appreciate *Pnin* as a novel, one, of course, does not need to be aware of Szeftel's possible impact on it. If one, however, is interested in the writer's "workshop," in how *Pnin* came into being, Szeftel may be very important. There are, after all, strong biographical correspondences that are hard to discount as merely accidental. Thus, both Pnin and Szeftel were born in February, both studied sociology, both got their university degrees in 1925 in Eastern European capitals (Pnin in Prague, and Szeftel in Warsaw), and both devoted much of their lives to an unfinished study of what Nabokov called in his novel the "great work on Old Russia, a wonderful dream mixture of folklore, poetry, social history, and *petite histoire*" (*Pnin*, 39), which I believe is an obvious, albeit not spelled out, reference to *The Lay of Igor's Campaign* (Slovo o polku Igoreve, 12th century), a famous Russian epic.[14]

I believe that bringing Szeftel into our analysis of the novel can actually help to answer some of the hotly debated questions and long-standing riddles in *Pnin* and its history, such as the reasons for Nabokov's change of heart about the book's ending, or the intricacies of the relationship between *Pnin*'s narrator and its protagonist. I also believe that knowing the particulars of Szeftel's life and academic career can help one understand why Nabokov may have changed certain "facts" of Pnin's existence between *The New Yorker* version of the work and its final book form.

And yet it was, in my opinion, not the biography but the "notion" of Marc Szeftel that served as an inspiration for the novel.[15] Alfred Appel remembers how he told Nabokov about some of the funnier problems that Szeftel's students experienced while trying to decipher the notes of what they thought was Szeftel's incomprehensible English: "Nabokov laughed at the story until tears streamed down his face . . . but then . . . mused with warm appreciation: 'What an innocent man.' "[16] It was Szeftel's legendary "foreignness," his naïveté, his imperfect English (according to Field, Nabokov even told Szeftel that he spoke "ugly English"),[17] his old-worldliness, his unrelieved seriousness in academic pursuits, as well as his dignity in the face of disrespect and even ridicule, that could make the "notion" of Szeftel so attractive to Nabokov as he was fashioning his fictional Russian lecturer in a small American college.

In Szeftel's diaries there exists no direct acknowledgment that he was aware of Nabokov's using him as a prototype for Pnin. And yet Szeftel's widow, Kitty Szeftel, says she immediately recognized her husband in Pnin when the first installment came out in *The New Yorker* in 1953, and that "[Marc] seemed to agree with me, and I think he more or less took it as a compliment."[18] Szeftel's former student at the University of Washington, Daniel C. Matuszewski, also recalls that "Dr. Szeftel was proud of his relationship with Nabokov [and] happy to confirm that he was at least one of the models for the figure of Pnin."[19] That Szeftel took his association with Pnin as a compliment and was pleased to acknowledge it on special occasions should not come as a surprise. Szeftel liked the novel very much (the only Nabokov novel, he felt, where the writer's "soul . . . shows itself" most profoundly), and Pnin happened to be his favorite character in all of Nabokov.[20] Like Desdemona, the maid of the Clements, from whom Pnin rented a room, and like Liza Bogolepov, Pnin's one-time wife, Szeftel actually thought that Nabokov's protagonist was "a saint" (*Pnin*, 40, 184).[21]

It may appear puzzling, then, that Szeftel never recorded in his diary the strong suspicion or even conviction that Pnin was largely based on his very own character. While we will never know for sure Szeftel's reasons for the omission, the fact that he intended the diary to be read by others after his death suggests a plausible answer. Having experienced a lion's share of disrespect and even humiliation in his life, Szeftel appears to have been extremely sensitive about his posthumous public image and reputation.[22] A link to Pnin would not have been helpful in this respect, for regardless of what he himself thought of Pnin, Szeftel also undoubtedly knew that many interpreted the character as a caricature of a failed scholar and a socially awkward individual.

This may also explain why, in public, Szeftel frequently chose to implicate others, rather than himself, as having inspired Nabokov's portrayal of Pnin. While such a thing was hard to do convincingly at Cornell, where Pnin's indebtedness to Szeftel was a commonly held belief, at the University of Washington, where Szeftel started teaching in 1961, the situation was somewhat different. Fortunately for Szeftel, yet another professor at Washington in the sixties was, in the minds of many, a "perfect Pnin." Yuri (George) Ivask, a poet of some repute and a professor of Russian literature, was legendary for his antics, absent-mindedness, and funny English. Once, during a seminar, he was asked by his graduate students to explain the difference between Akhmatova and Annensky as poets. Searching for words, he asked them for the proper verb to describe hurting one's finger with a needle. "Pricking it," came the response. "That's it!" Ivask allegedly said. "Akhmatova had a bigger prick than Annensky."[23]

Since Ivask also knew Nabokov, it was widely rumored on campus that the writer most likely fashioned Pnin after him.[24] Willis Konick, a professor of Comparative Literature at the University of Washington, remembers having coffee once with Yuri Ivask when, in all confidence, Ivask told him that Pnin was actually modeled on Szeftel. A week later, while eating lunch with Szeftel, Konick was in turn assured by Szeftel that it was definitely Ivask who served as the prototype for Nabokov's character. Szeftel's and Ivask's designating each other as real-life Pnins was apparently so routine a practice that quite a few people knew about it.[25]

In his diary Szeftel also consistently implicates someone else as having served as the prototype for Pnin, but here it is no longer Ivask but Vladimir Nabokov himself. "People often asked me," Szeftel typically wrote in his diary in 1970, "who Pnin was, who he was modeled after. He is modeled after more than one man and he is, of course, not an exact copy of Nabokov himself but he does have Nabokov's traits."[26] While Szeftel's publicly stated opinion that Ivask had served as the prototype for Nabokov's character may have been more calculated than sincere, his privately expressed belief in the autobiographical dimensions of Pnin is probably genuine.

In his 1986 revised biography of Nabokov, Andrew Field cites Nabokov's description of a typically "Pninian" moment that allegedly took place between Nabokov and Marc Szeftel (again, interestingly enough, while "riding an elevator," but this time at Cornell) during the period when *Pnin* was appearing in installments in *The New Yorker*: "Szeftel gave a deep sigh and said 'Ve arre all Pnins!' 'He had forgotten that I was writing that book and did not see that he was a character speaking to his author!"[27] And yet Szeftel probably saw more than either Field or Nabokov were willing to credit him for. Marc Szeftel simply divined that, as a possible prototype for Pnin, he was in good company with the author himself.

Arthur Mizener, a prominent Americanist and Nabokov's and Szeftel's one-time colleague at Cornell, divined it too, and thus became the first person of whom I am aware to describe publicly the character of Pnin as a fictional combination of Marc Szeftel and Vladimir Nabokov. Nabokov, wrote Mizener in 1977 in the *Cornell Alumni News*, "had an unlimited supply of sympathy for simple souls such as the professor of Russian history [i.e., Szeftel] on whom Pnin was modeled. Perhaps he recognized in Pnin's model something of the simplicity—even innocence—that underlay the wonderful intelligence and great sophistication of his own mind."[28]

Mizener's belief that Pnin had features recognizable in both Szeftel and Nabokov has been shared by many former colleagues of both men. Robert M. Adams, a widely published scholar and critic of English literature who taught at Cornell in the 1950s, while not doubting that "Szeftel did serve in some ways as a model for Pnin," also suggests that "Nabokov himself provided much of the material for Pnin—exaggerated and fantasized, of course."[29] The late Harry Levin, a renowned Harvard Comparativist who was among the Nabokovs' earliest and closest friends in the United States, proposed a similar explanation: "The character drawn by our friend Volodya was essentially a composite. . . . [S]ome of it may have come from within the author himself. He was, of course, too debonaire to become 'a Pnin-like figure.' But he retained a humorous attitude toward the way he fitted [into] American academic life."[30] Similarly, to Peter Kahn, a Cornell art history professor who knew both men quite well, Pnin was "clearly an amalgam of several Cornell types—all European, first of all [Nabokov] himself, [then] a lot of Marc [Szeftel]."[31] Another long-time colleague, M. H. Abrams, an eminent scholar of English Romanticism, thinks he remembers the writer actually acknowledging that "Pnin was more Nabokov himself than any other person."[32] Former students of Nabokov appear equally willing to trace the character, at least partially, back to its creator. Thus, Ross Wetzsteon tells us that Nabokov "was considered a kind of Pnin-figure" on the Cornell campus, while Julian Moynahan suggests that the "Pninian" combination of personal and academic traits characterized Nabokov as well, but in his case was "raised to the level of towering genius."[33]

In "The Double Pnin," Ambrose Gordon introduces what I consider a very useful paradigm for Pnin's character—Pnin as the Exile and Pnin as the Alien.[34] "Funny Pnin" is the eternal Alien, a pathetic foreigner with faulty English and premature dentures (inherited, doubtless, directly from Nabokov himself), whom the Cockerells of this world crave to ridicule. "Sad Pnin" is the eternal Exile, a Leopold Bloom-like figure, who can be poignant, dignified, and, in the long run, morally superior to those who are on more familiar terms with the world around them.

It appears that at first Nabokov did not much care for his protagonist and was prepared to part with him without ceremony: as late as 1954 Nabokov still fully intended to close his novel with Pnin's demise. "Poor Pnin dies," he explained to a potential publisher, "with everything unsettled and uncompleted, including the book Pnin had been writing all his life."[35] As he was fleshing out his initial design, however, it was probably the discovery of the dignified 'Exile' in Pnin—and of the awkward 'Alien' in himself—that made him change the ending. There is a certain delicious irony in the possibility that Marc Szeftel, at the time he was uttering his seemingly quintessential "Pninian" thought in the Cornell elevator about the universal nature of Pnin, was, for once, more perceptive about the nature of the book, its protagonist, and even its creator than was Nabokov himself.

A few words should be said about the book's focus and organization. Since *Pniniad* is partially based on materials found in Marc Szeftel's archive at the University of Washington, and since Szeftel's life and personality are much less known than Nabokov's, I devote more attention to him than to his more illustrious one-time colleague. (I am sure Szeftel would have liked that!) Chapters are organized in chronological order (Nabokov, probably, would not have liked that!), starting with Szeftel's early life, and ending with his final years in Seattle. Chapters 2 through 5 proceed from the time when Szeftel's and Nabokov's lives touched each other, resulting in their professional relationship at Cornell, Nabokov's writing of *Pnin*, and Szeftel's interest in *Lolita*. Relevant archival materials can be found in the Appendixes. These include Szeftel's autobiographical writings and his talks or published essays relating to Nabokov, as well as correspondence of interest, including letters he exchanged with both Nabokov and Roman Jakobson.

Since Szeftel's English usage is one of the subjects discussed in this book, I have striven to preserve the flavor of his written English by retaining his orthography, syntax, and punctuation in all quoted materials, including those interspersing my own text. I have made corrections [in brackets], some of them employing "the flare of a 'sic!' " (*Pnin*, 143), only in cases of obvious typos. Where Szeftel's meaning might be misconstrued as a result of this or that verbal or grammatical inaccuracy, I have tried to clarify [again, in brackets]. Unless otherwise noted, all translations from the Russian are mine. For purposes of transliteration, I have used the Library of Congress system except in the case of well-known Russian names, which I have rendered in their familiar spellings.[36]

1 / Marc Szeftel's Odyssey:
An Alien and an Exile

Who am I, after all? A Jew? A Russian? A Pole? A Belgian? A French? An American? All of the above . . . ? Or, simply, a man?

It pains me sometimes that I am not totally "genuine" in any-thing: it would have been better to belong to one culture but to belong to it fully.

—Marc Szeftel

The circumstances surrounding Marc (Moïse) Szeftel's birth and early life could not have differed more from Nabokov's. Szeftel's immediate ancestors on both sides came from densely populated Jewish areas in south-western parts of the Russian Empire, the territories of today's Poland, Lithua-nia, Ukraine, and Belorussia.[1] This was the notorious "Pale of Settlement," the only lands where Jews were authorized to live prior to 1917. By 1897, five years before Szeftel was born, nearly five million Jews—or roughly 99 per-cent of the total Jewish population of imperial Russia—lived in numerous Jewish settlements (*shtetls*) or small towns within the Pale.[2] The remaining one percent (among them the family of Vladimir Nabokov's future wife, Véra Slonim, as well as some of Marc Szeftel's own relatives) managed—through conversion, capital, good connections, or exceptional talents—to leave the Pale behind and settle in St. Petersburg, Moscow, or other large urban centers.

Szeftel was born on February 10, 1902, in Starokonstantinov (Old Constan-tine), a small Ukrainian town on the river Sluch which is generally believed to have been founded in the fifteenth century. Situated on the southern border of what used to be the province of Volhynia, Starokonstantinov appears to have had close to 25,000 inhabitants at the time of Szeftel's birth, most of them Jewish.[3] While even smaller in size in the nineteenth century,[4] Starokonstantinov could boast several famous Jewish scholars and literary men, among them Abraham Ber Gottlober, teacher and writer, who was born there in 1811, and Abraham Goldfaden (1840–1908), the Yiddish playwright and poet who became widely recognized as the founder of the Yid-dish theater.[5]

Like many towns within the Pale, Starokonstantinov had a visible Chris-tian population as well, not just Ukrainian but also Russian. Thus most of the teachers at the gymnasium Marc attended were Russian, and so were some of the students, several of whom became his friends. Russian Christian-ity may have been, in fact, literally next door to the Szeftels' household: a former neighbor on Aleksandrovskaia street, one of the two largest streets in town, remembered that the Szeftels' house stood next to a "Russian Ortho-dox church which for some reason was called 'Green.' "[6] Szeftel himself places the church a bit farther away. He also recalls that the church simulta-neously repelled and intrigued him: "Its modest inside made upon me the impression of darkness and disorder and it did not appeal to my childish mind. But we children used to run up and down the wooden belfry next to the church. Once I even ventured to stir the great bell of the belfry to see how it worked."[7]

At the turn of the century, Starokonstantinov was apparently a typical Jewish town and, as such, had a diverse Jewish population. There were, to be sure, fervently religious Orthodox and Hassidic Jews, for whom "the Bible was a daily paper," to use Maurice Samuel's phrase.[8] Their households were usually prolific and poor, and they spoke exclusively Yiddish. But there also existed a rapidly growing, largely secularized middle-class segment of the Jewish population. Uriel and Anna Szeftel, Marc's parents, definitely be-longed to that group, for, according to their son, the family chose "a middle way of life, half-Gentile, half-Jewish":

> The family language was Russian. . . . Russian books were read, as well
> as Russian newspapers. Most of our acquaintances were Jewish . . . but
> there were only a few people among them with strong Jewish cultural
> interests. I attended synagogue with my father on the three great
> holidays of the year. We never missed the celebration of Passover at
> home, and occasionally observed the Purim customs or the Hanukkah
> customs, but my father kept his business open on Saturday, and rarely
> attended synagogue on the Sabbath, and our cooking at home was not
> according to ritual.[9]

His father insisted, however, that his two sons should study Hebrew, and there were weekly lessons at home.[10] The secular nature of the family also determined its relatively small size, which, to everyone's despair, became even smaller when Marc's beloved younger sister, Tania, died suddenly in 1917, when she was eight years old. The only other sibling, Marc's younger brother, Arthur, had different interests and temperament, and the two were not particularly close.

Marc Szeftel's father was a photographer, and in the family pictures that his sons brought with them to the United States, most of them made in their father's own studio, Uriel Szeftel appears just as Marc describes him—a handsome and intelligent-looking man, who bears a strong resemblance to a popular turn-of-the-century Russian writer, Leonid Andreev.[11] That Uriel Szeftel did not look particularly Jewish—something in which his son took a certain pride, as he also did in what he thought was his own rather "unJewish" appearance—could not, however, protect him or his family from the fear of anti-Jewish pogroms. The ever-present prospect of yet another incident of violence against Jews in the area seems to account, at least partially, for the family's frequent moves. When Marc was a year old, there occurred one of the bloodiest massacres of Jews in Kishinev (April 19, 1903), and over the next three years pogroms happened with sadistic regularity throughout the Pale, claiming by the end of the period more than 3,000 Jewish lives. In 1905, for example, in the southern provinces of Russia which bordered on Volhynia, where the Szeftels lived, pogroms accounted for 62 percent of all Jewish deaths.[12]

In Szeftel's recollections of his childhood, one would be hard pressed to find the same "Arcadian," idyllic tonality that distinguishes Vladimir Nabokov's childhood memories. "There is nothing interesting [I can say] about my childhood," Szeftel records at one point in his diary. "It is a myth that childhood is a carefree, happy period of one's life. Maybe for others it was but not according to my memories. How many tears and disappointments there were! And this feeling of powerlessness connected with childhood."[13] "Powerlessness" was never a word Nabokov associated with childhood. Quite the contrary: as a child, Nabokov tells us again and again in *Speak, Memory,* he felt strong and confident, in full control of the universe around him. But then, Nabokov's universe was vastly different from Szeftel's. Starokonstantinov was a far cry from St. Petersburg, the majestic Northern capital, where Vladimir Nabokov had been born three years prior to Marc Szeftel.

Marc Szeftel cites lack of opportunity for Jews as the reason for his family's move from Starokonstantinov. But Flora Sheffield, Arthur Szeftel's widow, is convinced that she heard from her parents-in-law that the family had been "escaping the pogroms in Russia."[14] There was no significant violence in the area at that time, but rumors of impending pogroms were always rampant. Either in 1911 or 1912 (Szeftel is not clear on that point), the family moved to Lublin, a much bigger town in Poland where nearly 40,000 Jews comprised 40 percent of the entire population.[15] Poland, which was then a very reluctant part of the Russian empire, had its own history of anti-Jewish riots, but in the early 1900s, its pogroms were neither as frequent nor as violent as those in Russia.[16]

And yet, with years, Marc Szeftel came to feel that Polish anti-Semitism, while not then as murderous as the Russian or Ukrainian variant, was if anything even more pervasive: "The rejection of Jews by most Poles cut across all class lines; while I could identify to an extent with educated Russians, I could not do so with cultured Poles."[17] Partially because of this anti-Semitism and also due to the renewed fear of possible pogroms deriving from political instability in Poland, in 1914 the family attempted to move again. They went first to the Russian town of Smolensk, where Marc's maternal uncle lived, but within two weeks it became clear that they could not stay.[18] Even though Smolensk had a Jewish population, it was not within the Pale, and Uriel Szeftel discovered he did not have adequate business prospects to persuade the local authorities to make an exception for him and his family. So they settled in Vitebsk, a town very close to Smolensk but in Belorussia rather than Russia, and thus well within the Pale. Marc's maternal aunt lived there, and Anna Szeftel herself had spent several years in Vitebsk as a child.

Outside of Russia, Vitebsk is undoubtedly one of the best known of former Jewish centers, its fame largely owing to Marc Chagall, who was born near there and immortalized the town in his paintings. Chagall (who, at the time the Szeftels arrived, was actually in Vitebsk, having just returned from Paris, getting married to Bella Rosenfeld, and on his way to Petrograd)[19] described Vitebsk alternately as "a place like no other; a strange town, an unhappy town, a boring town . . . [with] [d]ozens, hundreds of synagogues, butcher shops, people in the streets,"[20] and as "my beloved city [whose] breath . . . I kept transferring from one canvas to the other."[21] It was in this "strange" Vitebsk, that Marc Szeftel, as he would recall later, began to feel more at ease with his identity as a "Russian Jew":

> The one meaningful novelty was the good Russian spoken by my Jewish schoolmates in Vitebsk. In Lublin my friends spoke Polish or

Yiddish among themselves; at the time I spoke neither, and because of my Russian language I associated mainly with [Russian] Orthodox boys. By contrast, in Vitebsk I was among Jewish boys almost exclusively. I found this natural, and at that point, if asked whether I was "Jewish," I would reply "yes" without hesitation—my legal status, especially, made it obvious. However, I would also have answered "yes" when asked if I was Russian, because of language and schooling. There was no conflict in loyalties in my mind between the Jewish and the Russian.[22]

It was also in Vitebsk that Szeftel began to master Yiddish and became interested in writers like Peretz and Sholom Aleichem. Yet the stay there was too brief to have a lasting effect on the boy's sense of who he was. Uriel Szeftel's business prospects were probably no better in Vitebsk than they had been in Smolensk, and since the situation in Poland had stabilized, by August 1916 Marc Szeftel found himself back in Lublin. His parents had decided to cast the family's lot with Poland: Marc was to learn Polish and enter a Polish gymnasium, since Russian gymnasiums had all but disappeared as a result of Poland's surge towards independence. He did so, and three years of Lublin gymnasium were followed by six years at the University of Warsaw. In both places he felt that, despite his good Polish language skills and his genuine interest in the country's history and culture, he was never allowed to forget that he was a Jew and an outsider.[23]

At first, Uriel Szeftel put significant pressure on his son to become a doctor, something that Marc, who wanted to study history and literature, felt absolutely no inclination to do. Since the Szeftel clan had a long tradition of lawyers in the family (several of his uncles as well as his maternal grandfather were lawyers), the two eventually settled on law as a compromise. This seemed a practical choice in more senses than one: not only did lawyers make a good living in Poland but it was also incomparably easier for a Jew (once he became a Polish subject) to practice law than to obtain a job teaching at a university.

Little is known about Marc Szeftel's life in Warsaw. The surviving chunk of his autobiography breaks at that point, and there are also very few mentions of the period in his diaries. In one retrospective entry, Szeftel actually voices his own astonishment at "how vaguely I remember these years."[24] In another entry he complains that while living in Warsaw he never visited other Polish towns such as Cracow, Lwow, or Wilno, mostly because of "the fear of anti-Semitism which . . . was pervasive and aggressive."[25] Other materials found in the archive allow for but a sketchy outline of what was likely one of the more painful (and thus probably almost deliberately forgotten) periods of his early life. What we do know is that the whole family moved to Warsaw in 1919, and in 1920, when he was eighteen years old, Marc Szeftel married Ryfka Carkes (some documents list her maiden name as Carkies, while the Russian spelling of the name is Tsarkes), who was five years his senior. Marc Szeftel would later tell his second wife that Ryfka's parents, with whom he was staying at the time, "sort of made him feel that he was obligated to marry this girl."[26] It was a religious Jewish ceremony and Szeftel received a dowry from his wife's family in the amount of 50,000 German marks.

We also know that in 1922, whether alone or with his wife, Marc Szeftel spent three weeks in Bad Kissingen, Germany.[27] How Szeftel spent the next three years (outside of his studies at the University of Warsaw) is unclear. It is also unclear whether Ryfka Szeftel's apparent mental and emotional instability became immediately obvious. Flora Sheffield seems to remember that the two lived together for only one year.[28] Kitty Szeftel believes she was told by her husband that his first marriage "was never consummated."[29] But in a legal document, prepared most likely in the early thirties, Szeftel states that he lived with Ryfka's family, first "as a fiancé" and then "as a husband," from 1920 to 1925.[30] Be that as it may, in 1925, the same year Marc Szeftel graduated from the University of Warsaw with a degree in law (and the same year Vladimir and Véra Nabokov were married in neighboring Germany, and Nabokov's first novel was written in Berlin), Ryfka Szeftel was committed to a mental institution with the diagnosis of schizophrenia.[31]

In 1930, when Szeftel and his parents were already residing in Belgium, he started annulment proceedings on the grounds of Ryfka's unfitness for married life. Religious Jewish laws in Poland at the time demanded permission of 100 rabbis in cases of annulment. For the next ten years, Marc Szeftel strove to obtain the necessary permissions and to put together enough money to pay not only the rabbis, who often wanted large fees for their services, but also his wife's family, who requested, as part of the settlement, 40,000 Belgian franks, of which 20,000 were to pay for Ryfka Szeftel's treatment.[32]

The financial burden was so severe that Szeftel appears to have seriously contemplated changing faiths, so that his annulment or divorce could be done in accordance with the laws of Catholicism.[33] Despite his father's insistence that Marc had obtained a "practical" degree, Szeftel still had little money of his own. Not being a Polish or Belgian subject, he could not practice law in these countries. Instead, he held only low-paying temporary jobs, such as being a "stagiaire" (trainee) in a law firm or working as a bookkeeper in the diamond-polishing business of his uncle, Solomon Nemerever. The husband of Marc's paternal aunt, Nemerever was a well-to-do entrepreneur who had emigrated to Belgium prior to World War I, and who had been directly responsible for arranging the visas and paying the way for the Szeftels to settle in Antwerp.

Solomon Nemerever's son, William, who was almost twenty years younger than Marc, remembers his cousin as a learned but somewhat impatient and intolerant young man who did not like his bookkeeping job and did not perform his duties too well. In his diary, Szeftel has nothing good to say about the work environment in which he found himself. The incessant noise made by numerous diamond-polishing machines was apparently so overwhelming that, in the evenings, he would try to get away from all sound by going to one of the city's parks and simply "listen[ing] . . . to silence with rapture."[34]

Solomon Nemerever, who, according to his son, was every bit as opinionated and strong-headed as his nephew (albeit not as well educated), had little patience for what he perceived as the young Szeftel's "snotty" attitude. The two of them clashed harshly and frequently.[35] Finally, according to Flora Sheffield, the two men virtually stopped talking to each other. She remembers that, soon afterward, Marc either quit his job or was let go,[36] but Szeftel himself recorded in his diary that his job at his uncle's plant lasted for eleven years, which would cover most of his stay in Belgium.[37]

Notwithstanding Marc's disagreements with his uncle, the Szeftels' general existence in Antwerp appears to have been quite comfortable. For the first time in their lives the family felt relatively free from the burden of anti-Semitism and the physical dangers associated with it. With the help of Marc's brother Arthur, who also worked for Solomon Nemerever, the Szeftels bought a house in the Jewish quarter of the city. It was a fairly large dwelling, and Uriel and Anna Szeftel let out two of its three floors to supplement the income received from Uriel Szeftel's photography business, which was located on the ground floor.[38]

Early in his stay in Antwerp, Marc Szeftel developed an interest in the history of Belgian Jews and even published several articles on the subject in a local Yiddish paper. History remained the discipline he wanted most to pursue, and he finally got his wish in 1934, when he enrolled in the graduate program in history of law at the Université Libre in Brussels. He had entered that university in 1932, intending to get his doctorate in law, which would have enabled him to open a legal practice once he became a Belgian subject. However, between 1932 and 1934, when he got his degree, the Belgian emigration laws changed significantly. By 1934 ten years were required, rather than five, to become a naturalized citizen. That gave Szeftel a long-sought excuse to switch from law to history, albeit the history of law.

For most of the time he studied in Brussels, Szeftel continued living with his parents in Antwerp, commuting daily by train since it was only a half-hour ride. His brother, who was married by then, resided in Brussels. According to Flora Sheffield, Marc would stop by their place now and then to get a bite to eat. It was also around this time that, according to Kitty Szeftel, Marc Szeftel became "romantically interested in a Catholic girl"[39] and even wrote to the Archbishop of Malines (Mechelen), asking him whether a marriage between a Catholic and a Jew would be "legitimate" from the point of view of the Belgian Catholic Church. The Archbishop assured him that such a marriage would indeed be valid. It turned out to be all for naught, however, since the girl's family apparently had no intention of letting her marry a Jew.[40]

When Szeftel switched to history, he became a student of Alexander Eck, an émigré from Russia who had received his degree in Slavic philology and history from the University of Warsaw in 1898. Vera S. Dunham, a prominent American Slavist who was also Eck's student at the time, remembers Marc Szeftel as "a bit difficult, very bright, stubborn, imaginative, creative":

> What I remember about Marc most vividly at that time was his closeness to Alexander Eck. Marc was not self-effacing. Au contraire. He was quiet and proud and secretive. Yes, strange because not young, although . . . sort of ageless. Strangely careful. At school, in seminars and consultation hours, we frequently sat together . . . sometimes poring over Richard Hakluyt and the other early British explorers and traders in a very strange land. What I shared with Marc most of all was the *uncomfortable* but great gift from Alexander Eck. He taught us deeply and forever after to search for *documentation* and to attempt to decipher and evaluate it. Just this commitment made you a historian, and Marc became verily Eck's disciple.[41]

In the obituary that Marc Szeftel wrote upon Eck's death in 1953, he stressed Eck's excellence as a teacher and a scholar: "As a teacher Eck was a rigorous master of the scholarly method. His lectures were perfectly organized and delivered with sober elegance in impeccable French. In his seminars he always insisted on an intensive interpretation of texts." He also emphasized his mentor's bravery and political activism: "The war of 1914 found Eck joining the French Foreign Legion together with many Russian revolutionaries abroad. . . . World War II meant for Professor Eck resumption of military duty, in spite of being sixty-three years of age. He served first in the Military intelligence of the French Armée de l'Orient, and later in the British Intelligence Service, where he earned several awards. . . ."[42] Dunham was similarly impressed with Eck's heroism: "Alexander Eck was a hero. Truly. . . . Having served in the first World War, he took off to fight Hitler."[43] Privately, in his diaries, Szeftel later complained that his esteemed teacher had lacked tolerance and tact.[44]

In 1938, the year he became a Belgian citizen, Szeftel was stunned by Hitler's occupation of Austria. In his diary thirty years later, he wrote: "I remember having followed the events minute by minute, in front of a newspapers shop on Pelikanstreet in Antwerp. When I read about the 2 hour ultimatum to [Austrian Chancellor Kurt von] Schuschnigg, my knees bent under me, so strong was the shock (a realization that the Germans will move in, with nobody to stop them!). . . . I had my knees bending under me in the same fashion only once [more], when in 1945 . . . I saw in the paper a headline on the atom bomb dropped on Hiroshima."[45] Szeftel's panic was shared by thousands of other European Jews at the time. Immediately following the occupation, or the *Anschluss,* as it came to be known, Vienna Jews reportedly "were committing suicide at the rate of two hundred per day."[46] The ones who chose not to were rounded up and taken to the Dachau and Buchenwald concentration camps.

Szeftel spent a year prior to Hitler's invasion of Belgium living by himself in Brussels and assisting Eck in teaching Russian philology and history at the Université Libre. Like his Warsaw period, the days and months following the invasion are scarcely mentioned or commented upon in Marc Szeftel's diaries. Vera Dunham can easily understand why: "Certain memories—because of pain, perhaps—resist elaboration. Our world—Marc's and mine when we were so young—literally and figuratively exploded in the Blitzkrieg."[47] Szeftel himself confided to his diary that his war past was "painful to recall."[48] There was much pain for the Szeftel family during the period of the invasion, and Szeftel's sister-in-law, Flora Sheffield, is still greatly troubled when she recounts the events that took place in the late spring of 1940.

When a German invasion of Belgium began to look more and more imminent and daily bombardments made life in Brussels dangerous, Flora Sheffield and her husband rented a small house in La Panne, very near the French border. They did not have a car, and on May 12, 1940, the day of the invasion, Arthur Szeftel managed to find a taxi driver who agreed to take them across the border the following morning. According to Sheffield, they asked their relatives to come to La Panne, and, since the family was large (in addition to Arthur's brother and parents, there were also his wife's relatives), Arthur Szeftel also bought four tickets for a bus that went into France. When Marc Szeftel arrived on May 12, his brother gave him a bus ticket, as well as 3,000 Belgian marks, so that Marc could leave for France the same day. On the morning of May 13, Flora's family were all there, but Arthur's parents had not yet come. The taxi was large, with additional seats in the back, and it could accommodate nine people, including the driver. Even without Arthur's parents, there were already eight passengers: Flora, Arthur, their one-and-a-half-year-old son Paul, Flora's father, her sister, and her aunt, uncle, and cousin. Flora Sheffield recounts what occurred next:

> We were ready to leave and my in-laws haven't come yet. . . . When we were all seated in the car, they came, my father and mother-in-law. The car had something wrong with it, it had no starter, so somebody had to push us to get started. We got one gallon of gas in order to get over the border. My mother-in-law and father-in-law were in their seventies. My husband did not know what to do. They could not get in the car. My husband gave them two tickets on the bus ride to get into France. Also they, can you imagine, they pushed that car, and that was the last we saw of them. We know that they got over the border. Two old people, and my mother-in-law was an angel, but she was so scared. She had lived through pogroms in Russia and anti-Semitism in Poland, and in Belgium she was free, and now she had to flee again. . . . What I know about them is that they got into France and were so scared that they went back to Antwerp; that was their home, they had a house there. Then, after a while, seeing that they could not stay in Antwerp, they both came to France. I don't know how they came, but they did.[49]

In 1941, when they were already in the United States, Flora and Arthur (who had changed their last name to "Sheffield" to give it an Anglo-Saxon ring) got a letter from Uriel Szeftel informing them that he was dying in a Lyon hospital[50] and that his wife had disappeared from their apartment in Lyon during a Nazi sweep through France. According to Flora Sheffield, the news devastated both her and her husband: "My husband was very sick, here, in the United States on account of that; I think he never could forgive himself that he couldn't help his parents. He had shock treatments, and everything: he was very sick. . . . "[51] Marc Szeftel, apparently, could not forgive his brother either. After the war he told his wife Kitty that, on the day of the invasion, he had left for France fully convinced that his parents were leaving Belgium the following day, in the taxi Arthur and Flora had hired.[52]

While his brother and sister-in-law were staying in Aix-en-Provence, waiting for Flora's American-born sister to arrange their American visas, and while his parents were shuttling in panic between Lyon and Antwerp (and the Nabokovs were heading toward the United States aboard the ship chartered by a Jewish rescue organization in New York—the ship left France on May 19),[53] Marc Szeftel, unaware of what was happening with the rest of his family, was making his way, much of it on foot and under frequent bombardments, to the south of France.

Much later, in a letter to the *Cornell Daily Sun,* where an article about him was to appear in 1961, Marc Szeftel summarized what happened to him in France:

> When France collapsed in June 1940, looking for an opportunity to leave France, I joined a group of Polish soldiers bound for England. The formation, however, was not allowed to leave by the French Government (acting on German orders), was demobilized and put into a labor camp. Before going to the camp a group of us tried to cross the Spanish border, was turned back and sent to the camp. I stayed there for 2 years, helped many Poles to leave the camp, and finally escaped from it with the help of Belgians and left France for the U.S.A. through Spain and Portugal (the trip from Lisbon to New York took more than 5 weeks).[54]

The details of the two years he spent in France are also rather sketchy. The family legend, as related to me by Szeftel's stepson, Daniel Crouse, and his wife, Linda, has it that, while in France, Marc Szeftel was in three different camps, and that in one of them he posed as a Polish priest. About to be discovered, he allegedly revealed his Jewish identity to one of the prisoners, and with the help of other Poles in the camp, was smuggled out in a bread truck.[55] Daniel Crouse found the story so fascinating that he often pleaded with his stepfather to sell it to Hollywood: "I said just do it. I always felt he missed the boat there. The kind of courage it took to survive . . . His was a much better story than the ones made into movies in those days."[56]

Kitty Szeftel's version of the years her late husband spent in France prior to coming to the United States is somewhat less Hollywoodish. She remembers Szeftel telling her that as soon as he made his way to Provence he fell in with a group of Poles who were determined to cross the Pyrenees into Spain.[57] Telling them that he was Polish as well, and identifying himself by a simple Polish name (which she does not remember), Szeftel joined them in trying to cross the border but was caught and sent to a detention camp not far from Marseille.[58]

In the camp, Szeftel stuck to his assumed name and Polish identity. He later told Kitty Szeftel that in order to avoid praying at the camp's Catholic Church, he pretended to have a personal confessor in Marseille, and was allowed to visit him on weekends (it was still early in the war, and French camps were no match to Hitler's or Stalin's).[59] It appears to have been not a total pretense, however, for in his diary Szeftel records at least one instance when he actually used a personal confessor:

> There was a Dominican convent near Place St. Ferréol, where, I was told, there was a priest, still young but losing his sight, of strong spiritual impact on any one who would meet him. *Father Perrin!* . . . It was Summer 1941. A statute was issued enjoining registration of Jews. I was myself hidden as a Roman Catholic Pole in Camp Ste. Marthe, but I looked for spiritual support and reassurance that the best of the Christians were on my side.

When Szeftel asked the priest whether it was "a sin not to obey the registration order," Father Perrin reportedly replied: "[T]his statute is not a fair statute. If one punishes a thief for being a thief, it is just. To punish him for being a Jew is unjust."[60] Szeftel's belief in the basic goodness of "the best among the Christians" was thus confirmed. Szeftel met other French clergymen at the convent as well, of which one, Father Cohen, was of particular interest to him, since he was a convert from Judaism.[61]

On his weekend visits to Marseille, Szeftel, according to his wife, established contacts with several members of the Belgian and Polish "underground," which proved useful not only to him but also to other prisoners whom he apparently helped to escape from the camp. On one such visit he also bumped into an old acquaintance from Belgium who knew Arthur's address in New York. Subsequently, Szeftel contacted his brother, who, according to Flora Sheffield, eventually sent him money and arranged for the American visa.[62] When all his documents were in order, Marc Szeftel used another weekend pass and enlisted the help of his underground friends to make his escape. He took a train through France, Spain, and Portugal. From one of the stops along the way, Szeftel sent a card to the commandant of the camp, informing him that one of his prisoners had no intention of coming back.[63] In the autumn of 1942, two years behind the Nabokovs, Marc Szeftel arrived in New York. After thwarted attempts to make permanent homes in Russia, Poland, Belgium and France, this forty-year-old refugee, bachelor, and orphan got one more try to do so, and one more country to do it in.

2 / Colleagues and Collaborators
Szeftel and Nabokov at Cornell

Nabokov was my colleague at Cornell University, and there we met frequently. We had a very good relationship, but we never had an intimate friendship. Nabokov avoids that kind of friendship, having Vera is enough for him, and it also contradicts his essential ego-centricity.

Marc Szeftel

Almost as soon as Szeftel arrived in the United States, he found a position teaching Russian and French history at the École Libre des Hautes Études à New York, the "university in exile" founded by refugee French and Belgian scholars in the United States. His colleague at the École was Roman Jakobson, a founder of the Prague Linguistic Circle and the preeminent figure in the Formalist and Structuralist movements which had yet to be accepted by American academe. Other colleagues included Henri Grégoire, an authority on Byzantium, whom Szeftel had known in Brussels, and Claude Lévi-Strauss, the pioneer of structural anthropology and of the structural study of myth.

In 1943, Szeftel got involved in a projected study of the most famous medieval Russian epic, *The Lay of Igor's Campaign,* which, in the opinion of the vast majority of scholars, occupies the same place in Russian literary and cultural history as does *Beowulf* in English, or the *Chanson de Roland* in French. *The Lay* deals with a disastrous 1185 campaign by Prince Igor of Novgorod-Seversk against the Polovtsy, a nomadic Turkic tribe that inhabited the steppe of southern Russia. The volume was to contain exhaustive linguistic and historical commentaries, the latter being the responsibility of Marc Szeftel and George Vernadsky, a prominent Russian medievalist at Yale. It was during the work for this volume that Szeftel became friends with Roman Jakobson, who did the linguistic commentary for the study, translated the epic into modern Russian, and wrote a long essay arguing for the epic's authenticity.[1] The book, *La Geste Du Prince Igor': Épopée Russe du Douzième Siècle,* was published in 1948.[2]

Szeftel was to characterize his relationship with Jakobson during the war as "very close," and Jakobson's numerous letters and postcards to Szeftel from that period do not contradict that notion.[3] The two men appear, however, to have been rather formal with each other, always using in their correspondence a polite and respectful Russian *Vy* (You) instead of a more familiar *ty* (thee). In 1946 Szeftel and Jakobson collaborated once again, this time for an article on "The Vseslav Epos," a *bylina* or epic narrative traceable to as far back as the eleventh century but first published only in the eighteenth.[4]

Jack Haney, a professor of medieval Russian literature at the University of Washington, whose colleague Szeftel was in the 1960s, considers Szeftel's historical commentary on "Vseslav" to be "Marc's best work . . . a remarkable historical bit of sleuthing. . . . It is . . . one work that is inevitably quoted by medievalists." According to Haney, Szeftel often complained that while he had done most of the research for the Vseslav study, Jakobson received most of the accolades.[5] In the diary, too, one can feel Szeftel's resentment towards Jakobson and some envy of his success—not unlike the feelings he was to develop towards Nabokov. And yet, as with Nabokov, Szeftel also tries to give his more famous colleague sufficient credit. Thus he records in his diary that Jakobson always impressed him as a truly tireless worker: "We were writing . . . at his home. We had a leisurely supper, with a long rest afterwards, and then sat down to the final session at around 9 P.M. At 12 P.M. (may be even 1 A.M.) I could not continue, but Jakobson, a night worker, was full of pep. I was forcing myself and becoming irritable, because of extreme fatigue. Jakobson did not understand: 'What is the matter?' he was asking. Finally, at 2 A.M. I took leave, most of the article having been finished."[6]

Despite these and similar academic pursuits as a historian while at the École, Marc Szeftel constantly worried that European history was not a good specialization if he wanted to teach in an American university. In April of 1943, he got a letter from Mikhail Karpovich of Harvard which only strengthened his apprehensions. Responding to Szeftel's question about possible academic jobs, Karpovich told him that jobs during the war were extremely scarce since academic budgets were being cut everywhere. Karpovich also informed Szeftel that Russian history was not even taught at many universities, and it might be thus easier for Szeftel to find a job teaching Russian language.[7] Discouraged by this and similar assessments of the academic situation, Szeftel decided to change his field altogether. Consequently, when in 1943 he got a fellowship from the Belgian-American Educational Foundation, he chose to use the money to go back to graduate school to study sociology at Columbia. He spent two years there, fully intending to get another Ph.D. even though he soon discovered that he "did not have at all 'the sociological mind' " and that, in general, he had no respect for sociology as a discipline.[8] In May of 1944 Szeftel compiled a list of all sociology departments in the country and the research interests of their faculty. He started with Harvard, where he discovered an ex-compatriot (this early notation also provides a glimpse of Szeftel's English at the time): "Pitirim SOROKIN.—'Leaves from a Russian Diary.' In U.S.A. began in Minnesota where he wrote 'Sociology of Revolution' . . . Came in Harvard in 1931. conservatism. Pretty excentric in his behaviour and sociology. . . . More recently, tendency toward mysticism. . . . Bitter, incisive critic of other people's work."[9] During his studies at Columbia, Szeftel continued to lecture on Russian and French history at the École Libre. He also now taught sociology at Bard College and from time to time substituted as a sociology teacher at Yeshiva College. In the fall of 1945, however, an unexpected offer from Cornell to assume a position as an assistant professor of Russian history put an abrupt end to Szeftel's budding career as a sociologist.

Prior to 1945, the last (and only) person to teach Russian history at Cornell was Philip Mosely, who had been appointed as assistant professor in 1939, when the Department of History decided to expand into a new field.[10] By all accounts, Mosely was a very successful teacher and a promising scholar. And yet, according to Frederick George Marcham, who taught English history in the same department, Mosely's senior colleagues were not happy with his frequent travels abroad, which necessitated hiring replacements while he was gone.[11] A couple of years later, when Columbia made the Russian historian a better offer, the department refused to make it worth Mosely's while to stay at Cornell, despite significant pressure from university president Edmund Ezra Day.[12] Soon Mosely was gone, and with him, all through the war, the subject of Russian history.

As soon as the war ended, the department picked up its belated search for Philip Mosely's replacement. They began to compile a long list of possible candidates: David Hecht from Ohio, Lantzeff at Wellesley, Mazour at Nevada, Harry Howard at Miami University, C. B. O'Brien from Overseas Organizational History Division.[13] Then someone mentioned Szeftel. That Szeftel was eventually hired by Cornell is somewhat surprising, given that he was still a relatively obscure scholar, since his studies on *The Lay* and the

Vseslav epos had not yet appeared in print. The fact that Szeftel was Jewish adds another curious dimension to the departmental decision.

Historically, Cornell's policy toward accepting or employing Jews, while generally discriminatory, had been no worse, and in some instances slightly better, than that of the other Ivy League schools.[14] One such "positive" instance occurred when Sage Chapel was dedicated in 1875 and Cornell took a rather brave step towards religious and cultural tolerance by setting forth that, in addition to Christian clergy, the chapel would also open its doors to visiting ministers of all faiths, including Jews. (It is also true, however, that having made this generous determination, the university waited for twenty-one years before inviting the first Jew, Rabbi E. G. Hirsh, to pray there.)[15] In the early years of the twentieth century, however, things got worse. According to Morris Bishop, a professor of Romance literature and the official Cornell "historian"—and the very same Morris Bishop who became Nabokov's closest friend on campus—by 1907 the Cornell fraternities "ceased, generally, to enroll Jewish members."[16]

As late as the 1940s the Ivy League schools, including Cornell, were still not particularly generous when it came to hiring or accepting Jews.[17] Thus in 1945, the same year that Szeftel was appointed, a Yale history professor, writing to a colleague at Cornell to recommend someone for a vacant position in modern European history, felt compelled to notify him that the candidate was not Jewish: "His father was an Italian Swiss . . . his mother comes from old American stock dating back to Colonial times . . . he is married to a Texas woman. I mention all this because I think the impression got around that [R.] is a Jew and this hurt him, doubly unfairly, in academic preferment."[18]

Cornilus deKiewiet, to whom this letter was addressed and who in 1945 became dean of the Arts College, apparently was himself not above raising the issue of a candidate's Jewishness at departmental meetings. Szeftel remembers one such occasion which occurred soon after he joined the department: "[W]hen we discussed candidates in the Department, [d]eKiewiet observed concerning one of them: 'She is Jewish!' 'No,' answered [Paul] Gates (the Chairman), who was completely innocent in these matters. . . . 'It is obvious,' answered [d]eKiewiet (the name was Rosenberg or Goldstein)."[19]

And yet, M. H. Abrams, one of the best-known Cornell scholars, who, while Jewish, was also hired by the university in 1945, feels that 1945 was in many ways the beginning of a new era in Cornell's professional relationship with Jews. With the university faculty stripped down because of the war economy and war losses, "gates opened," according to Abrams, and Cornell, for the first time in its history, started to hire "without any regard to ethnic origin." Abrams also feels that able Jewish scholars began to be promoted at a faster rate than before: he himself was tenured within three years of getting his job at Cornell.[20]

It is important to note that Szeftel recorded in his diary that he did not feel any anti-Semitism, while at Cornell, especially of the magnitude he had been used to in Ukraine and Poland. It is also true, however, that he often wondered whether his colleagues even knew he was Jewish: "When I joined the Cornell Department of History, I was the only Jewish member of it. . . . Did they know of my Jewishness? I doubt it . . . "[21] He was probably right: as late as 1993, Knight Biggerstaff, a professor emeritus of Chinese history and, during Szeftel's last years at Cornell, his chair, was genuinely surprised to hear that Marc Szeftel was a Jew.[22] In the final analysis, we shall probably never know whether it was a sign of the changing times or of Szeftel's "un-Jewish" appearance (he was, after all, like his father: blonde with regular, delicate features) and his rare and thus not easily identifiable Jewish name that helped him avoid being "hurt" in "academic preferment." One thing is clear, though: even if his colleagues did not mind or did not necessarily know that he was Jewish, they did notice right away that Szeftel was different.

"Marc Szeftel [was] a man of Polish birth [sic]," writes Marcham in his reminiscences. "His health was not robust; his war-time experience had weakened him. He was a refugee bringing with him a large part of his European inheritance, and thus in outlook a person far more strange— foreign, shall I say,—than anyone who had previously been a member of our department."[23] "Strange" and "foreign" are surprising words for a department which had at least three other foreigners—Marcham himself was English, and so was M. L. W. Laistner, a professor of ancient history, while deKiewiet was Dutch. The department also had its reasonable share of "strange" people, beginning with Laistner, the departmental chair at the time of Szeftel's hiring, who could be quite bizarre. A bachelor who lived with his aging mother, Laistner was apparently so fearful of women that in 1935 he flatly opposed the university's attempt to pull the faculty of history into one department solely because, as he told his colleagues, "he could not bear the thought of . . . employing a woman stenographer. That any female, however gifted, should become associated with the department in any way was a notion that stirred him to violence."[24] On one occasion, Gould P. Colman, the now-retired Cornell archivist who was in the 1950s a graduate student in the department, witnessed just such an outburst when Laistner, upon seeing a new graduate student in his office, screamed "Get out! Get out!" apparently for no other reason than that the student happened to be female.[25]

According to several people interviewed for this book, the department also had a flamboyant eccentric from Kansas, Curtis Nettels, who taught American history and vocally expressed his passionate hatred for England. This, understandably, complicated even further the dynamics in a department where two members were English. Another member of the department, Karl Stephenson, was a severe alcoholic who repeatedly endangered his life and eventually committed suicide. And yet, as Marcham indicates, it was Marc Szeftel who was immediately perceived by the others as being the misfit. Even the physical arrangement of the department seemed to underscore Szeftel's "alien" status. According to Colman and Biggerstaff, Szeftel's office in Boardman Hall (which exists no more, having been razed in 1958 to give way to Olin Library) was situated a whole floor up from the eight or nine other offices of the history department.[26]

Szeftel's life outside the department appears to have been just as lonely. Beatrice MacLeod—whose house the Nabokovs would rent in 1953, while she and her husband, a professor of psychology at Cornell, were away in Michigan—met Szeftel on a social occasion soon after he arrived at Cornell. This was either at Telluride House, the Cornell guest quarters where Beatrice MacLeod served as executive secretary, or in a friend's house. She remembers Szeftel as "a small man, a little eccentric, odd. Obviously not American. He had none of the social graces one adopts as a born American moving into Academia." She also remembers that he was very ill at ease that evening.[27]

A year after Szeftel began to teach in the department, offering such courses as "Russian Revolution," "Soviet Period," and, for a more advanced audience, "Intellectual History of Modern Russia,"[28] he faced his first true adversity when deKiewiet, who was a dean by then, accused him during a faculty meeting of poor teaching and bad English. The charge was apparently based on the complaints of some students, whose names or number deKiewiet refused to divulge. While some of their mutual colleagues were stunned by deKiewiet's rude manner and sprang to Szeftel's defense ("For Szeftel was clearly the most insecure person," writes Marcham, "in consequence of his health and his recent wartime background"), the harm was done, and the reputation stuck.[29]

Whether Szeftel was really such a bad teacher and whether his English was really all that incomprehensible are hard questions to determine now. But from talking to people whom he taught in those years, one gets a strong impression that these accusations were largely unjust. Thus, to Frank Walker, who took every Russian history course Szeftel offered, Szeftel was "the most intellectually stimulating professor I had ever encountered."[30] Milton Barnett, who studied with Szeftel in 1947–50, also found him an "intellectually interesting" teacher who "offered unusual insights," and "showed enormous interest in students who were responsive."[31] Other former Cornell students interviewed for this book expressed similar sentiments.[32] Kitty Szeftel, who took a class from her husband-to-be before they married in 1949, insists that the "imperfection" of Szeftel's English during these early Cornell years has been vastly exaggerated: "His English was excellent. Some of his students at Cornell complained because he used words that they had to go and look up in the dictionary." She also believes that it was the difficult nature of his courses and his demanding attitude toward students that made some of them sour and discontent.[33]

Szeftel's daughter, Sophie Tatiana Keller, has another explanation for occasional hostility toward Szeftel from his Cornell students. According to her, Szeftel "hated the whole fraternity/football scene very violently. He used to call students involved in it 'animals,' and he would say in Europe they won't be allowed in the door. He would take great delight in making fools of them in class, and cutting them down to shreds in front of everybody. He would come home and regale us with these tales at dinner. He really enjoyed it, so I am sure he embittered quite a few people." Unlike her mother, Sophie Titiana Keller also believes that Szeftel's English could pose a legitimate problem for his students: "Some of them were not used to his accent. His English was very charming and very idiosyncratic. It was difficult for them to adjust to that. He used a great many words that were sort of a dictionary vocabulary. . . . He also didn't always complete his sentences and his grammar was not perfect."[34]

On August 28, 1947, Marc Szeftel received a letter from Morris Bishop informing him that they both were "on a Committee to do something about a Professor of Russian Literature."[35] Two weeks earlier, in a letter to Blanche Knopf of the Knopf publishing house, Bishop had remarked: "By the way, I am concerned with finding a Professor of Russian Literature. What I want is a man who will suck the students into his classes by personality and by a creative attitude towards literature. We have enough footnoters around; if literature is to compete with science, it must be presented as a means to wisdom and as an upbuilder of life. The only person I have in mind is Vladimir Nabokov. Do you know of some wonderful fellow?" Blanche Knopf did not.[36] In September of the same year Bishop wrote to Nabokov directly: "We need at Cornell a Professor of Russian Literature, to replace Professor Ernest Simmons, whom we lost to Columbia. The Dean has asked me to look around. . . . As an old admirer of your work, I think first of you."[37]

Both Andrew Field and Brian Boyd in their biographies of Nabokov attribute the initial interest in Nabokov as a candidate for the job to Morris Bishop, who happened to have seen a feature about him in a publicity brochure from Wellesley, where Nabokov was teaching at the time.[38] Bishop, as he mentioned in the letter cited above, also knew and admired Nabokov's publications in the *Atlantic Monthly* and *The New Yorker*, magazines in which Bishop occasionally published his own light verse. Yet, according to Milton Cowan, a professor of linguistics, it was he, and not Bishop, who first drew everyone's attention to Nabokov as a possible candidate.

When Cowan was named director of the Division of Modern Languages in 1945, his appointment was accompanied by a sizable grant from the Rockefeller Foundation for the purpose of setting up a new arrangement between language teaching and literature. Before the war, literature professors often had to handle beginning language classes and complained that they had no time to teach their subject. The new arrangement would create a Division of Literature and would put descriptive linguists in charge of language courses, thus allowing literature people to deal with literature.

The same year Cowan was appointed, Ernest Simmons, who was the head of the Russian Department at Cornell, moved to Columbia and took his other departmental colleagues with him. According to Cowan, Simmons's move virtually "wiped [Cornell] out on Russian." Around that time, as they were looking for Simmons's replacement, Gordon Fairbanks, who was a general descriptive linguist working with Indo-European languages, showed Cowan a copy of Nabokov's *The Real Life of Sebastian Knight*. Cowan read it, was intrigued by the novel, and suggested to Bishop and others that, if a real specialist could not be found, Nabokov would do nicely because, being a writer, he might attract more students. The rest, as they say, is history.[39]

Nabokov was interviewed at Cornell in October of 1947. It was then that he first met Marc Szeftel, who was still on the hiring committee.[40] Soon thereafter he was offered the job, which he accepted. For a while, however, Nabokov appears to have been confused as to his title. In a February 1948 letter to William Forbes, a fellow lepidopterist, Nabokov wrote that he was hired as Associate Professor and Chairman of the Russian Department,[41] but in the 1948 *Directory of Cornell Faculty, Offices, and Employees* he is listed as "Associate Prof. Romance Languages," while in the 1949 edition of the same *Directory* he is, indeed, "Associate Prof. Chairman of Department of Russian Literature."[42]

According to Cowan, Nabokov was never offered the chairmanship of the Russian department for the simple reason that such a department no longer existed. All languages were now under the umbrella of the Division of Modern Languages. Since the Division of Literature was still in the works (once created it lasted for only two years and was abandoned later as a bad idea), and since Bishop was also a "literary figure," the committee decided to put Nabokov, at least temporarily, with Bishop in the Department of Romance Languages. It was also the committee which, in Nabokov's absence, submitted the listing for the 1948 *Directory,* while it was Nabokov himself, still apparently believing that he was chairing the nonexistent department, who provided the information for the listing in 1949.[43]

There was apparently also some confusion as to which courses Nabokov was going to teach his first year, and it fell to Marc Szeftel to clear things up. Szeftel wrote to Nabokov in February of 1948 and described Nabokov's teaching load. Nabokov objected that Morris Bishop had never discussed his teaching the "Introduction to Literature" course, and that only Russian literature was his specialty. By the end of March, the issue was settled in Nabokov's favor, and he was given another course in Russian literature instead of the general survey.[44]

Even though Szeftel may have been somewhat resentful that Nabokov was made an associate professor despite a lack of advanced academic degrees, while he himself was still an assistant professor, Szeftel was generally delighted to have Nabokov on board. They were both émigrés, they both liked Russian literature, and, like Szeftel, Nabokov's wife was Jewish. In April, prompted by Jakobson,[45] he sent Nabokov *La Geste Du Price Igor'*, and got a grateful response: "I am laid up with a bad cold and your book with its mass of fascinating information is a boon and a blessing."[46] During the summer, while in New York, Szeftel visited Mark Aldanov, who was then editor of *Novyi zhurnal* (The new journal) and knew Nabokov. "Szeftel was here and was telling me about you," Aldanov wrote to Nabokov soon after. "All the good news. I myself have not read everything you have published in the past two years. . . "[47] Szeftel, on the other hand, did, and was probably full of praise. It sounded, in short, like the beginning of a beautiful friendship.

There is considerable disagreement among former colleagues who knew both Szeftel and Nabokov as to which man was, in the long run, more successful in adjusting to the American system of education. Thus Gardner Clark, a professor of Russian Economics and one of Szeftel's few close friends on campus, thinks that "Szeftel didn't adapt to the American teaching scene as well as Nabokov did."[48] But Milton Cowan believes it was the other way around, and that Nabokov "did not really belong in an academic institution," while Szeftel did.[49]

Since many of us now hold an image of Nabokov as a very popular lecturer, it may come as a surprise that, when Cornell hired him, many were actually apprehensive that it would not work out. "It was all irregular," Bishop recalled in 1970. "His only critical work was his study of Gogol, which was regarded as brilliant but eccentric. . . . He had no record of graduate study, no advanced degree."[50] As Cowan puts it, "Nabokov simply did not fit into an academic picture. . . . He was a square peg in a round hole or a round peg in a square hole, whichever you want. He didn't fit and I think he was kind of proud of that."[51]

Nabokov's way of teaching could indeed be unorthodox. His wife Véra was at his side at all times: carrying his briefcase, poking him when in his oblivion he would forget to acknowledge a colleague walking down the hall,[52] taking students' attendance, grading papers, assisting during lectures, sometimes even reading Nabokov's meticulous lecture notes to the students when her husband was indisposed.[53] Several colleagues who observed the Nabokovs' "synchronized" teaching were amazed at how smooth the performance was. Szeftel remembers that "while [Vladimir] was busy in reading to the students his lectures, [Véra], at the mention of a name, was writing it on the blackboard (to relieve V. V. of this drudgery, and to allow him uninterrupted performance)."[54] Peter Kahn recalls a lecture he attended where "Véra had these notes on cards and she would hand them to him . . . He would expect a particular note and she had it ready . . . So obviously they must have rehearsed or something."[55]

As is well known by now, Nabokov's exam questions could also be untraditional. To students used to broad and abstract categories, Nabokov's preoccupation with seemingly meaningless details often appeared incomprehensible ("What color was the bottle containing the arsenic with which Emma [Bovary] poisoned herself?"[56] "What morsels of food were left on William Price's breakfast plate on the morning when he left for London?").[57] A man who held "strong opinions" as a teacher, too, Nabokov was usually tolerant of only one interpretation of any given work: his own. Stephen Jan Parker, who was Nabokov's student at Cornell in 1950s, remembers that Professor Nabokov "convinced his students that they were required to adopt his literary approach for purposes of examinations and term papers. It was thus a universal practice for the students in Goldwin Smith B Lecture Hall at Cornell University to copy down assiduously each of his utterances."[58]

Nabokov also did not like being publicly argued with or interrupted by students. James McConkey, a writer and a professor of English Literature who inherited the "European Novel" course after Nabokov left Cornell, remembers seeing Nabokov, "his whole face flushed and red," running out of the classroom where he was lecturing and into the office of the Division of Literature. Nabokov appeared to be so agitated that McConkey actually worried that "he was going to have a stroke or something.... He was stammering.... I thought he might fall over." Apparently, this "Pninian-size rage" was occasioned by one of the students' pointed question as to whether, if Professor Nabokov refused to discuss Dostoevsky in his lectures, the student himself could do so.[59] When Nabokov reached the chairman's office, McConkey heard him shouting that "he wanted this boy expelled, he wanted him kicked out of the University, it was just impertinent."[60]

Nabokov was also enraged by how Russian was taught at Cornell. Despite all his efforts—and, apparently, Szeftel's full support—Véra was not hired to teach Russian (according to Szeftel, her Russian was deemed to be "too literary" and "not contemporary enough"). The general linguists who taught Russian—like Gordon Fairbanks, immortalized as Leonard Blorenge of *Pnin*—were, in the opinion of the Nabokovs as well as Szeftel, often incompetent language teachers. "You just wait," Véra allegedly told Szeftel. "Fairbanks . . . will transform Russian in such a way that soon you and I will cease to understand it!" Nabokov suggested to Szeftel that one day Fairbanks would be so successful in convincing everyone that only he knew what Russian ought to be like, that "in a hundred years or so, they will attribute everything I wrote in Russian to Fairbanks." Szeftel further recalls a "sharp conversation" that took place between Milton Cowan and Nabokov concerning Fairbanks and his virtually non-existent Russian: "Nabokov ran into my office after their conversation very agitated . . . and read me, out of his notebook, what he told Cowan." One of the outcomes of that confrontation was Nabokov's refusal to come to Cowan's annual reception that year. Véra did come, however, and when Szeftel asked her why her husband was not there, she reportedly replied: "Everything has its limits."[61]

Though some students may have found Nabokov's teaching methods funny or unusual, and some of his colleagues no doubt thought his behavior exasperating, Nabokov gradually became an exciting presence on campus and a very popular professor whose classes were packed. As one student remembered recently, "Whether correcting a translation ('Emma's head is not shaped like an egg; the skin of her face has the appearance of an eggshell'), soliciting chauffeuring help ('My son is playing soccer this weekend'), admonishing us to become rereaders or dissecting the European fiction that we studied, he was always an easy listen."[62] Nabokov's lectures were not only interestingly original but were also marked by what Szeftel calls "an actor's delivery": "No gesticulation, but emphasis distributed adroitly, and modulations of voice."[63] Milton Cowan is the first one to admit that the risk Cornell took paid off: "When we brought him here we didn't know what we were getting, and I am not sure we always knew what we were getting after he was here . . . but we were lucky we had him. Nabokov gave to Cornell as much as it gave him."[64]

Nabokov developed a reputation for being reclusive soon after he started teaching at Cornell. "Long before he retired to the sixth floor of the Montreux Palace," recalls Robert M. Adams, "he was an isolated, intricately introspective person."[65] Many had a sense that Nabokov did not have any desire for real friendships, that Véra was somehow all that he needed, and that even the Bishops, who were the Nabokovs' most frequent companions at Cornell, were in no way their intimate friends. M. H. Abrams often wondered whether it was even realistically possible to stay very close to Nabokov: "He was very touchy. You were apt to say something with the best of intentions that he would take amiss."[66] James McConkey found it extremely difficult to see the real man behind the playful mask Nabokov always put on in public: "Nabokov might ask you, for example, what you thought of a certain segment of a soap opera, and if you said to him that you wouldn't dream of watching . . . such a soap opera, he would show shock at your fastidious smugness, your superiority to such an art form—but if you showed interest he would attack you for being vulgar."[67]

Despite the common émigré background he shared with Nabokov, Szeftel was no more successful in trying to get close to Nabokov than were others.

Szeftel even felt that his attempts to befriend Nabokov were strongly discouraged: "Our friendship was not to be. Whenever I told him that we almost never saw each other he would respond: 'But we both know what we are working on!' From his point of view, it seems, a contact was not necessary."[68] Szeftel also recalls that Avgusta Jaryc, another Russian who was a language instructor in the Division of Modern Languages, once asked him if he thought Nabokov had a "soul."[69]

Thus contrary to Szeftel's expectations, the arrival of the Nabokovs did not make his social life more lively or his circle of friends any wider. It was apparently around this time that Szeftel, now a man of forty-six, began to think even more seriously about getting married again.[70] Gardner Clark, who, like Nabokov, started teaching at Cornell in 1948, remembers sitting in a restaurant in College Town with Szeftel and noticing William Forbes, the lepidopterist who had been among the first people Nabokov contacted when he was hired by Cornell. Forbes, also known on campus as "pink Jesus" because of his pink skin and dirty white beard, was a bachelor of almost sixty-five, and on that day he was sitting in the corner eating all by himself. Clark recalls jokingly remarking to Szeftel: "Marc, that's what you will look like in ten years if you don't get married." Szeftel, according to Clark, was visibly stunned.[71] Within six months of this conversation he was married.

Kitty Crouse came from a distinguished and influential Utica family, well known in upstate New York. Kitty's father, Nellis Maynard Crouse, who had done advanced graduate work at Cornell, was a historian, a specialist in French colonization, and an author of several books on the subject. A divorcee in her thirties with a young son, Kitty Crouse worked as a secretary in the Department of Economics at Cornell during the war, but as soon as the war ended, she went back to school to get her degree. She found herself in Marc Szeftel's course.

It was probably not love at first sight. Daniel Crouse remembers an earlier suitor, ten years his mother's junior, who had been "crazy about her, crazy about me," but whom Kitty was afraid to marry because of the difference in age. He maintains that she was "on a rebound" from that relationship when she met Szeftel. Kitty herself believes she was immediately predisposed to find her husband-to-be appealing because he was everything her first husband was not. In her mind, Szeftel was a lot like her father, whom she revered: a mature man, an intellectual, and a historian to boot. She also thought he was good-looking.

Szeftel's side of the story is harder to put together since in the diary he never talks about his feelings for Kitty prior to the marriage, or what went into his decision. It is clear that he was lonely and more than ready to acquire a family. It is also very likely that, in addition to her own personality, Kitty's influential family was a definite plus, and so was a learned, Cornell-educated father-in-law. Daniel Crouse believes that his mother's money also played a serious role in Szeftel's decision but, given Daniel Crouse and Szeftel's complicated and frequently antagonistic relationship, it is possible that this opinion is at least somewhat colored by filial jealousy and resentment.

The wedding took place on June 18, 1949. Kitty vaguely remembers that the Nabokovs were there, which is a good possibility since they did not leave Ithaca till four days later when they headed for a writers' conference in Salt Lake City.[72] Later that year Szeftel adopted Daniel, but the boy, twelve years old at the time, never wanted to bear his stepfather's name. He said he was too fond of his grandfather, who had lost his own two sons in a train accident, to trade the name Crouse for any other name, particularly for one he could not even pronounce.[73] Szeftel, no doubt, was hurt. Soon after their marriage Marc and Kitty Szeftel bought a house at 115 Oak Hill Road, where they lived and raised their children (in addition to Daniel, Sophie Tatiana was born in 1951, and Marc Watson was born in 1954) until the family left for Seattle in 1961.

Nabokov spent part of his first year at Cornell dealing with the same *Lay of Igor's Campaign* that Szeftel and Jakobson had worked on several years earlier. He wanted to teach the epic in his class, but Samuel Cross's English translation as found in *La Geste Du Prince Igor'* did not satisfy him. Nabokov quickly translated the poem for his class, and that inspired him to attempt a much more careful line-by-line translation of the work.[74]

When Roman Jakobson learned from Szeftel that Nabokov was full of praise for many aspects of *La Geste Du Prince Igor'*, he got permission from the editor of the *American Anthropologist* to solicit a review from Nabokov. The review was to appear in the spring 1949 issue of the journal, and the deadline for submission was December 15, 1948.[75] Late in October, Jakobson enthusiastically responded to "the excellent news that Nabokov will review our book in the *American Anthropologist* and that he is translating the Slovo [i.e., the Lay] into English."[76] A month later he wrote to inquire, among other things, "how it is with Nabokov's review."[77] Around the same time, Nabokov wrote to Edmund Wilson: "I know the *La Geste* volume well,— and am, as a matter of fact, reviewing it for the *American Anthropologist.*"[78]

Several days later, Nabokov wrote to Wilson again, telling him that his review of the book "is so good that it would be a pity to bury it in the Anthropologist (gratis)." He intended, instead, to send it to *The New Yorker*.[79] Nabokov apparently did not inform either Szeftel or Jakobson about his decision, for as late as the end of January, Jakobson reminded Szeftel to ask Nabokov "not to forget about the American Anthropologist."[80] Nabokov sent the review to *The New Yorker* on February 10.[81] It never appeared.[82] This less-than-perfect beginning of the Nabokov-Jakobson professional relationship was portentous.

Nabokov, Szeftel, and Jakobson agreed to collaborate on an English edition of *The Lay of Igor's Campaign* around the same time that Nabokov was asked to write the review. Nabokov was to provide a new translation and Szeftel and Jakobson would revise and expand their previous historical and literary commentary.[83] In subsequent years Nabokov and Jakobson had numerous occasions to discuss the project while Nabokov was visiting Harvard, occasionally guest-lecturing in the Slavic Department, of which Roman Jakobson was by then the most prominent member.[84] In December of 1952, Jakobson informed his two collaborators that the Bollingen Foundation was interested in issuing an advance contract for the volume.[85] The publisher was offering to pay all three equally, since they agreed to be "editors with equal responsibility," but Jakobson felt that Nabokov should get more for his translation and thus was asking Bollingen "whether Nabokov's translation could not be remunerated additionally."[86] Nabokov appeared to be happy with the arrangement, and he wrote in a letter to Harry Levin in May of 1953: "Bollingen has bought for a handsome sum my 'Igor' and Roman's comments. Roman arranged the whole matter with wonderful charm."[87] The curious omission here of any mention of Marc Szeftel's participation in the project is conspicuous.

In July of 1953 they signed a contract according to which Nabokov was to receive $1,000, and Szeftel and Jakobson, $500 each. Half of the sum was to be paid immediately, and the other half upon the presentation of the manuscript. The manuscript was to be delivered to the publisher by May 1, 1954.[88] By March 1954, Szeftel was beginning to get worried: "I have seen Nabokov very little lately. All our contact with regard to Igor is represented by two telephone conversations due to my initiative. I know he is very busy, meeting deadlines, but I do not know much of his work on Igor. We have a tentative appointment in the beginning of May to discuss the Igor problems."[89] Nabokov and Szeftel did get together at some point that year, and

Nabokov read the translation "loudly [i.e., aloud] to me (very well) in a personal meeting."[90] Later Nabokov gave Szeftel a copy of his translation. Szeftel wrote numerous comments, corrections, and observations concerning historical accuracy[91] most of which Nabokov apparently "readily" accepted and incorporated into the text.[92]

The deadline for the manuscript submission had come and gone, but the volume was nowhere near completion. These were extremely busy years for at least two of the collaborators. Nabokov was working intensively on both *Pnin* and *Lolita* as well as translating his published autobiography into Russian and preparing his commentary for *Eugene Onegin*. Jakobson was equally preoccupied with his numerous projects. Much to Szeftel's disappointment—and somewhat to the detriment of his academic advancement—*The Lay of Igor's Campaign* was put on a long hold. The next event that directly affected its fate did not happen till the spring of 1957.

As early as 1950, after he had finally realized that the Russian department and his chairmanship of it were not to be, Nabokov inquired of Jakobson whether there was any possibility of a job for him at Harvard. He cited the "poor preparation" his students were receiving from their Russian language instructors and the "very small enrollment" in Russian literature courses he taught.[93] There were no vacancies at the time, and Nabokov had to stay at Cornell. Seven years later, just around the time when *Pnin* was being published by Doubleday, Nabokov finally got his chance to try for a job at Harvard. Harry Levin, a very good friend of Nabokov, was chairing the Department of Modern Languages, which included Slavic, and he proposed Nabokov for the vacancy in the program.

Szeftel learned of what happened next from Jakobson. Jakobson, according to Szeftel, "respected N[abokov] as a writer" but wanted the position for Vsevolod Setchkarev. Another influential voice in the department, Mikhail Karpovich, was also less than enthusiastic about Nabokov's candidacy and, according to Szeftel, even "testified against N[abokov]'s appointment before the ad hoc committee" appointed to study the hiring situation in the department. Both Jakobson and Karpovich believed that the job should go to someone with a Ph.D. and with a more disciplined training in Russian literature. In a now famous statement, Jakobson replied to Levin's assertion that Nabokov was a great Russian writer—and this is Marc Szeftel's version of his answer—"I do respect very much the elephant, but would you give him the chair of Zoology?"[94] Szeftel, probably following Jakobson, believed that Nabokov learned about what happened from Levin. The result, according to Szeftel, was devastating both for the Nabokov-Jakobson relationship and for their mutual project:

> The upshot was N.'s great hate for Jakobson . . . , to such an extent that he canceled all cooperation with J. on the *Slovo o polku Igoreve*, the English edition of which was then being prepared by the three of us, and would not refer to J. otherwise [than] as "bolshevik agent," a very nasty way of action and a dangerous one for J. (this was in Joseph McCarthy times).[95] N. himself never went to the Soviet Union, out of rigid intransigence, while J. made several scholarly trips to Moscow, but I cannot believe that N. used his epithet with any degree of sincerity. This was vindictiveness, an obvious vindictiveness. And as K[arpovich] did not display much activity to thwart J.'s opposition, N. spread his dislike also to K., whom he called [an] "old fox" (*staraia lisa*)[96]. . . .
> [I]n his anger N. even wanted to put both J. and K. in an 'inferno' of one of his novels (*ia eshche ikh vyvedu v odnom iz moikh romanov*). . . .
> Out of spite, N. went still further. I have not heard him before this incident ever express any doubts as to the *Slovo*'s authenticity. . . .
> Now, as J. adhered fanatically to the thesis of authenticity, N. began to look for arguments against it. . . . I . . . told about it to J. whose answer was "Let him try to attack the authenticity, he will be crushed! . . . "
> N.'s break with J. took the shape of a letter in which N. objected to J.'s trips to the Soviet Union in no uncertain terms. He called me up before he wrote the letter, announcing his decision and suggesting to me, gently, that if I want it, we could work on Igor, the two of us, independently from J. This I could not do.[97]

Nabokov's angry letter to Jakobson, written on April 14, 1957, read in part: "After a careful examination of my conscience, I have come to the conclusion that I cannot collaborate with you in the proposed English-language edition of the SLOVO. Frankly, I am unable to stomach your little trips to totalitarian countries, even if these trips are prompted merely by scientific consideration."[98] There was no mention of what had transpired at Harvard several weeks earlier.[99] Szeftel's reasons for declining Nabokov's offer were honorable—he felt he owed it to Jakobson not to abandon the project, since it was Jakobson who had introduced him to the complex world of the epic back in 1943, while they were together at the École, and who had invited him to participate in the earlier study. He also felt that he had a much more solid friendship with Jakobson than with Nabokov.

Szeftel and Jakobson never finished their volume, although the project was not laid to rest until 1982, the year of Jakobson's death.[100] Nabokov had published his translation independently in 1960.[101] Much to Szeftel's distress, there was no acknowledgment given in it either to him or to Jakobson for the help and comments they had offered.[102]

3 / Pnin

The real virtue of this book is in its sweetness. It is very funny. It creates a type-hero, in this case The Eternal Refugee ... [The] hero who is at one level absurd is simultaneously endowed with dignity and moral grace. This is a remarkable feat.

—Pamela Hansford Johnson

Pnin as we read it is funny and pathetic simultaneously or by turns, but by the time we reach its last page it is neither: it is exhilarating.

—Ambrose Gordon, Jr.

The first chapter of *Pnin* was actually written in the Pacific Northwest, the same Pacific Northwest that would become Marc Szeftel's home upon leaving Cornell. Nabokov could have not foreseen this ironic twist of events, but, as a believer in fate's wise orchestration of "coincidences," he probably reflected on it in later years. The coincidence is slightly imperfect, though: *Pnin* was begun in Ashland, Oregon; Szeftel ended up five hundred miles farther north, in Seattle, Washington.

We do not know for sure when it first occurred to Nabokov to create this fictional Russian professor, but we may know why he called him "Pnin." The surname is rather uncommon and has been interpreted to mean various things: anything from the Russian *pen* (a stump), because "many American characters in the book stumble over it,"[1] to English 'pain' ("It is no accident," writes Boyd, "that the book's risible name ... almost spells 'pain' ").[2] Most critics agree, however, that Pnin probably owes his name to the late eighteenth-century Russian publicist and minor poet Ivan Petrovich Pnin, an illegitimate son of Prince P. N. Repnin (it was a common practice for illegitimate children to inherit only a part of their fathers' last names). Interestingly enough, while, as far as we know, Nabokov himself never suggested a connection between the protagonist of his novel and Ivan Pnin, Nabokov's sister did. After two chapters of *Pnin* were published in *The New Yorker,* Elena Sikorskaia wrote to her brother in the spring of 1955: "I came into contact with the sweet and charming Pnin only for one moment and am already dreaming about meeting him again. By the way: Ivan Petrovich Pnin (1773–1805) was, so it seems, a good poet."[3]

While critics generally agree on the origins of Timofey Pnin's name, they often differ as to Nabokov's reasons for such a linkage. Julian Connolly, for example, suggested in 1981 that Nabokov may have wanted to emphasize that Timofey Pnin, not unlike his real-life namesake, is both dispossessed (in his case, not of his father but of his fatherland) and noble (if not in origin, then in spirit).[4] Andrew Field drew a connection between Ivan and Timofey in a different way by linking the title of Ivan Pnin's most famous work, *The Wail of Innocence* (Vopl' nevinnosti, otvergaemoi zakonami, 1801) to Timofey Pnin's innocent nature and penchant for wailing.[5] Gennadi Barabtarlo, on the other hand, doubts that themes of illegitimacy, innocence, dispossession, or nobility have anything to do with the name-borrowing, since he believes that Nabokov often used real names merely to provide, in Nabokov's own words, "a definite, specific historical frame."[6]

Barabtarlo also goes on to suggest that, "since Ivan Pnin is the only known bearer of that name and does not seem to have been married, Timofey Pnin's origin is doubly fictitious."[7] But Ivan Pnin did, in fact, marry and procreate. His son, Petr Ivanovich Pnin, was born in 1803, became a minor artist, spent several years studying in Italy, and is said to have died of cholera in Naples in 1837. This information can be found in a book published in 1950 in Russia which can possibly shed some light on why Ivan and Timofey Pnin came to be related through the magic of Nabokov's fiction.

The book is Vladimir Orlov's *Russkie prosvetiteli 1790s–1800s–kh godov* (Russian enlighteners, 1790s–1800s), and it focuses on several minor men of letters of the post-Radishchev[8] era. In a chapter devoted to Ivan Pnin, Orlov provides a rather detailed biographical sketch of the man and discusses, among other things, Pnin's illegitimate birth and the practice of truncating last names for children born out of wedlock.[9] The year the book came out, it was purchased by many American university libraries, among them Harvard, where Nabokov was doing his research while on leave from Cornell during the spring of 1953.[10]

It was a logical book for Nabokov to consult. He was working on his commentary to *Eugene Onegin*, and, while at Harvard, he looked at a great number of books connected with the period immediately preceding Pushkin and with the authors (Radishchev among them) who could have affected Pushkin's body of knowledge and his political sensibilities. Nabokov's extensive research at the time is confirmed by a number of letters he sent to friends and colleagues, among them a letter to Henry Allen Moe, of the Guggenheim Foundation, written in March of 1953: "I have devoted two months to research at the Widener Library for my 'Eugene Onegin', and have found more fascinating material than I expected or hoped."[11] Szeftel quotes Nabokov's statement that, while at Harvard, he "read all the books in Pushkin's library."[12]

The chronology of Nabokov's library research and the first appearance of Nabokov's famous protagonist is suggestive. Several days after he finished his work at Widener, Nabokov left for Arizona and then Oregon, where, in June of 1953, Pnin was born as a fictional character. If Orlov's book did make its way to Nabokov at Harvard, as I suspect it did, it was probably instrumental in furnishing Nabokov not only with a name for his character but also with the relevant information about the real-life Pnin. Thus he could learn (if he did not know already) that Ivan was an illegitimate son of Prince Repnin and that he, in turn, had a son.[13] The latter may have indeed been of some importance. Barabtarlo is quite right when he alludes to Nabokov's craving for a "definite, specific historical frame," and Ivan's son could in many ways provide this "frame": he could have had children, grandchildren, and great-grandchildren all the way up to Timofey's father, Dr. Pavel Pnin, "an eye specialist of considerable repute [who] had once had the honor of treating Leo Tolstoy for a case of conjunctivitis" (*Pnin*, 21).[14]

But even more important is the book's title—*Russkie prosvetiteli* (Russian enlighteners)—insofar as it may actually suggest one of the reasons Nabokov's protagonist got to share Pnin's name. If we characterize Ivan Pnin not as a minor publicist or a minor poet but as a minor "Russian enlightener," then his relationship to Timofey Pnin becomes quite straightforward, for what is Pnin if not a minor "Russian enlightener" of American students? And how truly Nabokovian to parody not only actual people but also actual titles.

Nabokov did not at first take the novel very seriously; it was his "little book," as he described it to Katharine White in September 1953.[15] He was, at the time, fully engrossed in *Lolita*. Composing funny scenes from the life of a very Russian émigré teaching in a very American small college must have served as a refreshing reprieve, or a "brief sunny escape," as he himself called it.[16] Brian Boyd believes that there were financial considerations as well: knowing that *Lolita* would be hard to place because of its uncomfortable subject matter, Nabokov wanted to write something that would be sufficiently light, entertaining, and an easy sell.[17] Marc Szeftel appears to corroborate this point of view by recording in his diary that Nabokov talked of the serialized *Pnin* as an excellent financial opportunity: "The 'New Yorker' paid N[abokov] extremely well (he told me that this source of income practically was equal to his salary of that time) and he was not eager to cut the series short (*Zhalko, eto doinaia korova* [Would be a pity: it's a good milk cow]), but at a certain moment he had to make out of it a novel."[18]

Sending his first story about Pnin from Ashland to *The New Yorker* in the summer of 1953, Nabokov characterized his protagonist to the editor as "not a very nice person but . . . fun." Boyd, who quotes the letter, finds the remark "curious" and "decidedly out of keeping with [Nabokov's] later admiration" for the protagonist.[19] In *Strong Opinions,* Nabokov would claim that the design of the whole of *Pnin* "was complete in my mind when I composed the first chapter,"[20] but he was probably overstating the case in order to argue with the critics who suggested that the novel, pieced together from published stories, did not have a carefully conceived overall structure.[21] More likely, at that early point in the history of *Pnin,* Nabokov did not really know for sure what he was going to do with his "fun" character: Pnin was largely a profitable vehicle for amusing vignettes and endless comedies of error. Unlike *Lolita,* the "serious" novel, which had been thoroughly planned and structured before its composition, the "light-hearted" *Pnin* may have been planning and structuring itself in the process of coming into being.[22]

1953 was a good year to send a story about a Russian American to *The New Yorker.* It was the year of Stalin's death and Beria's arrest, and the magazine had an unusual amount of material devoted to things Russian. Pnin was, therefore, not the only Russian émigré to be portrayed in the pages of *The New Yorker* that year. He shared the space with the likes of Alexis Lawrence Romanoff, who, like Nabokov, came from a noble family, left Russia after the revolution, and was a Cornell professor. A specialist in chemical embryology, Professor Romanoff apparently had affinities not only with Nabokov but also with Pnin, for, if we are to believe Eugene Kinkead, the author of the lengthy profile on Romanoff, he possessed "an oppressive social timidity that ma[de] him ill at ease in large gatherings, even of people with interests similar to his."[23]

The heightened interest in post-Stalin Russia continued through the next two years as well. In 1955 *The New Yorker* published what was probably the only sonnet in any language ever composed about Omsk, a town in Western Siberia. Written by Richmond Lattimore, it concluded with the following

five lines: ". . . . And when, in 1917/the army of the Bolsheviks drew near,/the
town was full of western refugees,/who fled on east, and strewed the way
between/with dead from cold, fear, hunger, and disease."[24] Refugees themselves who had made it all the way to the United States also continued to be
in vogue, and in 1955 Pnin cohabited the pages of *The New Yorker* with,
among others, Roman Vishniac, a Russian Jew and zoologist, better known
now for his photographs of pre-war Jewish life in Poland, whose grandfather
was "one of the first Jews to be granted the legal right to live and work in
Moscow," and whose father "was Russia's leading manufacturer of umbrel-
las and parasols."[25]

"Pnin" the story, which was to be the first chapter of *Pnin* the book,
appeared in the November 28, 1953, issue of *The New Yorker*. When one
compares the story with the later chapter, the most striking difference is in
the dates that serve as landmarks of Pnin's existence. In the earlier version,
Pnin graduates from the University of Prague in 1920 (as opposed to 1925;
Pnin, 11) and finishes the first year of studying English in his new country in
1945 (as opposed to 1941; *Pnin*, 16).[26] Nor is his birthday mentioned in the
story. The paragraph in *Pnin* which reads: "And now, in the park of
Whitchurch, Pnin felt what he had felt already on August 10, 1942, and
February 15 (his birthday), 1937, and May 18, 1929, and July 4, 1920" (*Pnin*,
21), appears in the story as: "And now, in the park of Whitchurch, Pnin felt
what he had felt already on August 10, 1942, and May 18, 1937, and May 18,
1929, and July 4, 1920."[27] The later revisions have the effect of bringing Pnin
much nearer to Marc Szeftel, who graduated from the University of Warsaw
in 1925, and came to the United States soon after the war started rather than
during its final year. Szeftel's and Pnin's birthdays also eventually ended up
being suspiciously close, for Szeftel was born on February 10. This closeness
appears even more remarkable when one realizes that, in chapter 3, which
takes place in 1953, Pnin's birthday falls on Tuesday. In fact, February 15 that
year was a Sunday, and it was February 10, and thus Szeftel's birthday, that
fell on Tuesday.[28] Did Nabokov, for a brief moment, actually confuse the
character and his colleague, and look up the wrong date in the 1953 calendar?[29] (Kitty Szeftel believes that the Nabokovs were annually invited to
Marc's birthday parties and, therefore, would have been likely to know his
birthday.)[30]

Nabokov sent the second installment to *The New Yorker* in February 1954,
but it was rejected as too "unpleasant," largely because of his portrayal of
Eric and Liza Wind and their brand of psychoanalysis. This verdict pro-

voked Nabokov to object to the editor that this " 'unpleasant' quality of Chapter 2 is a special trait of my work in general; you just did not notice in Chapter 1 the same nastiness, the same 'realism' and the same pathos,"[31] thus almost suggesting that he had been as nasty to Pnin in chapter 1 as he was to Pnin's ex-wife in chapter 2.

By February 1954, Nabokov did already have a more or less general outline for the book: "ten chapters of unequal length . . . the insecurity of Pnin's job becomes evident. . . . Liza . . . returns for a while to Pnin. . . . Pnin finds himself solely responsible for the welfare of Liza's boy. Then, at the end of the novel, I, V. N., arrive in person to Waindell College to lecture on Russian literature, while poor Pnin dies, with everything unsettled and uncompleted." He also intended to finish the book in June.[32] Although many details in the finished novel were already present in this outline, the end was still curiously different from that of the *Pnin* we know. It is as if, at that point, Nabokov felt that when the series in *The New Yorker* ended and the chapters were made into the novel, he should do to his "milk cow" what one does when no more milk is available or needed—slaughter it. He was, in short, still prepared to treat Pnin with "the same nastiness, the same realism and the same pathos" as he did his many other characters.

The second story to have been accepted by *The New Yorker*, "Pnin's Day" (chapter 3), came out in 1955, issued by coincidence on Nabokov's birthday, April 23. It had yet another curiously different "landmark" of Pnin's existence. In the story, Pnin starts teaching at Waindell College in 1948 (i.e., the same year that Nabokov himself started teaching at Cornell),[33] while in the novel, once again, Pnin's lifeline parallels Szeftel's, and he is said to have joined the college in 1945 (*Pnin*, 50, 62). The last two published chapters, "Victor Meets Pnin" (chapter 4) and "Pnin Gives a Party" (chapter 6), were brought out in rapid succession that same year, in the October 15 and November 12 issues.

The history of *Pnin*, first as a series and then as a novel, accounts, in my opinion, for much of its peculiar duality, which the critic Ambrose Gordon underscores so well when he distinguishes between the Alien and the Exile in Pnin. Pnin-the-Alien, destined to die "with everything unsettled," belongs to the series, which was supposed to entertain *The New Yorker* readers and leave them craving more. As Nabokov began putting it all together as a unified work of fiction, something—or someone—apparently, persuaded him to keep the protagonist alive.[34] Thus Pnin-the-Exile, who survives and even triumphs in the end, already belongs to the novel, which had to become more than merely the sum of the published vignettes. It should not come as a surprise, then, that Nabokov's characterization of his protagonist changed so dramatically from 1953 to 1955. In 1953, while trying to sell his first Pnin story to *The New Yorker,* the writer, as we have seen, described his character as "not a very nice person." In 1955, shopping for a publisher for his novel, Nabokov already portrayed Pnin as: "A man of great moral courage, a pure man, a scholar and a staunch friend, serenely wise, faithful to a single love [who] never descends from a high plane of life characterized by authenticity and integrity."[35]

Gordon is not the only critic to emphasize the essential duality of Pnin's character. David H. Richter similarly distinguishes between Pnin-as-a-clown in the initial chapters, and Pnin-as-a-hero at the book's closure: "At the outset, we watch a clown's performances detachedly; the reader may be genuinely disappointed that Pnin's ultimate disaster is withheld. But as the innocent and suffering protagonist is further revealed, we are more likely to feel a keen pang of pity at his anticipated misfortunes."[36] This interesting duality—the serial Pnin versus the novelistic Pnin, the clownishly "fun" but unpleasant character versus the "man of great moral courage," the Alien versus the Exile—may also explain both the book's final strengths and its weaknesses. If the story of Timofey Pnin had been first written as a novel, the work would likely have been deprived of at least some of its intriguingly ambiguous complexity. It is also possible, however, that the protagonist's funny and courageous traits would have been better balanced, making *Pnin* less vulnerable to the kind of devastating criticism that Kingsley Amis leveled against the novel in 1957, when he called it "this limp, tasteless salad of Joyce, Chaplin, Mary McCarthy and of course Nabokov (who should know better)."[37]

While the constantly failing, Chaplinesque Pnin may strike some as a direct antithesis to the successful Nabokov, it is quite obvious that the character and his maker had important traits and tastes in common. After all, Pnin's reflections on Russian literature, like his comments on *Anna Karenina* (or *Anna Karenin,* as Nabokov would have it) and his attacks on Freudianism, are taken almost verbatim from Nabokov's own lectures.[38] (Joseph Frank even called his review of Nabokov's *Lectures on Russian Literature* "The Lectures of Professor Pnin," and suggested that the majority of Nabokov's students probably found Professor Nabokov "as endearingly nutty as his own Professor Pnin.")[39] Nabokov also apparently acknowledged to Andrew Field that "Pnin's interest in gestures was really his own."[40] Furthermore, despite the changes discussed above, Nabokov's and Pnin's lives still partially revolved around the same important dates: thus, both landed in the United States in 1940 and became American citizens in 1945. (They also are almost the same age—Pnin is a year older than Nabokov, having been born in 1898.)[41] Pnin likewise inherited Nabokov's love for Pushkin and Lermontov, his distaste for noise, his very own dental plates,[42] his inability (through most of the novel) to drive a car, and his intolerance of the petty banality or "poshlost'," which in the novel is ably represented by the other Russians on campus—Oleg and Serafima Komarov.[43] What makes these parallels of Nabokov and Pnin confusing to some is the fact that, in the book, another character seems to bear a much more "logical" resemblance to the author: namely, VN, the book's dramatized narrator.

In his introduction to the English translation of *Dar* (*The Gift*), Nabokov characteristically warns his readers against conflating real-life authors with their fictionalized second selves and narrators. "I am not," he wrote, "and never was, Fyodor Godunov-Cherdyntsev . . . , I never wooed Zina Mertz, and never worried about the poet Koncheyev."[44] He also, obviously, never consulted Pnin's father about his infected eye, never slept with Liza Bogolepov, or was privy to Cockerell's Pnin impersonation. And yet, the narrator's identification with the author of *Pnin* is unusually close. We do learn, for example, that, like Nabokov himself, VN is Vladimir Vladimirovich, that he was born in St. Petersburg in the spring of 1899, that he lived on Morskaya ulitsa and attended a liberal gymnasium. We also find out that, like the author, the narrator enjoys butterflies and is "a prominent Anglo-Russian writer" (*Pnin*, 140). Furthermore, even Nabokov himself appeared to have encouraged the blurring of the lines between his authorial and his fictionalized selves. "[A]t the end of the novel," he explained to Pascal Covici, an editor at Viking Press (which, having bought the original rights to *Pnin*, would eventually decline to publish the novel), "I, V. N., arrive in person to Waindell College to lecture on Russian literature."[45] He later wrote to the same editor: "It is an absolute necessity for me . . . to introduce 'myself' in Ch. 7."[46]

As a result, many critics tend to follow what they think is Nabokov's lead and to identify the narrator of *Pnin* simply as Nabokov. "Aristocratic, poised, successful in love and work," writes Boyd, "narrator Nabokov could not be less like poor awkward Pnin."[47] Likewise, Charles Nicol, while acknowledging the existence of so-called purists who may think otherwise, maintains that the narrator's name should be the same as the author's.[48] Yet it was not accidental, it seems to me, that in a letter to the editor cited above, Nabokov did put quotation marks around "myself." The narrator in *Pnin* is of course largely autobiographical—but so is Fyodor in *Dar.* "I was as arrogant as I was shy," the narrator says at one point, reminiscing about his past meetings with Timofey Pnin (*Pnin,* 178). But what we get in the book is only the narrator's "arrogant" side, Nabokov's own superego-ish "public" image, which was often created by those (Szeftel among them) who, being accustomed to Pnin-like failures, mythologized Nabokov's successes.[49]

Pnin is, in fact, all about perceptions.[50] In the same letter where he calls Pnin a "man of great moral courage, a pure man," Nabokov also takes pains to describe how others in the book perceive him: "[H]andicapped and hemmed in by his incapability to learn a language, he seems a figure of fun to many an average intellectual."[51] Even though Nabokov himself obviously had no "incapability" when it came to English, and also liked to define himself as "an indivisible monist,"[52] Pnin and VN can be actually seen as two representations of his own public personality: an old one from the forties, that of an obscure and seemingly eccentric Russian lecturer with a hard-to-pronounce name teaching an odd language in a small women's college; and a newer one from the fifties, that of a respected Cornell professor, a polished intellectual, and a successful author to boot.[53] The old image also belonged to an "Alien," since for a large part of the forties Nabokov was still a stateless, passportless refugee,[54] while in the fifties he was already a dignified "Exile" with American citizenship.[55]

Other critics have commented as well on this possible manifestation of Nabokov's autobiographical duality. Thus, according to David Cowart, both Pnin and VN, "are parody Nabokovs: one the maladroit exile and perpetual clown, the other suave ladies' man and successful academic. . . . The author is living the examined life by critiquing, if not 'exorcising,' two facets of his own personality."[56] Chapter 5 of *Pnin* is particularly interesting in this respect. It takes place at "The Pines," a summer house near "Onkwedo," "in one of the fairest of New England's fair states" (*Pnin,* 111),[57] which is a fictional metamorphosis of Mikhail Karpovich's "dacha" in West Wardsboro, Vermont, frequented every summer in the 1940s and 1950s by numerous fellow Slavists.[58] Both Pnin and VN, or "Vladimir Vladimirovich," as he is referred to here, make their appearance at "The Pines"—Pnin in person, VN but in spirit and also, obviously, as the narrator. "This was the first time Pnin was coming to The Pines," VN as the narrator tells us, "but I had been there before" (*Pnin,*

117). According to Boyd, the Nabokovs visited Karpovich's summer cottage in 1940, soon after their arrival to the United States, and then again in 1942.[59] Both times Nabokov was still his "Pninian" public self—a recent émigré just trying to penetrate American academe. In his novel, however, Nabokov could also allow himself to revisit the place already in his "new, improved" image— as a successful "VN," whose dazzling reputation makes the Pnins of this world envious.

I suspect the earlier incarnation of plans for *Pnin* intended even more emphasis on the interplay between these two public perceptions, and this interplay may also explain why, according to the 1954 plan, Pnin was destined to die at the end of the novel. It would have been, after all, a simple case of art imitating life: in America, while, in his own eyes, Nabokov never really changed, in the eyes of others, he began as a caricature-like Pnin but ended up as a larger-than-life VN. It stood to reason, therefore, that as soon as VN came to Waindell, Pnin had to disappear.

It is, in my opinion, largely through Marc Szeftel that Pnin eventually gained not only more years to live but also more independence from both VN and Nabokov. That Pnin can be simultaneously recognizable as both Nabokov and Szeftel should not come as a surprise since, as I have mentioned in the introduction, Nabokov most likely viewed Szeftel the same way he viewed Pnin—as a caricature of himself. It is probably because Nabokov became aware of the dangers of emphasizing the caricatural aspects of Pnin that Marc Szeftel appears to have acquired an increasingly important role for the book. It seems to me that the "humanized" Pnin is, in many ways, the "Szeftelized" Pnin.

To be sure, some elements of this "Szeftelization" were already present in the early version of the novel. When, upon reading the stories in *The New Yorker*, Kitty Szeftel recognized her husband in Nabokov's protagonist, she was mostly struck by Pnin's and Szeftel's common problems in adjusting to American life, academic and otherwise, their shared background in sociology, their inability to drive a car (like Véra, Kitty Szeftel was her husband's personal chauffeur), and by the fact that the two experienced a similar predicament of trying to build a relationship with a stepson. Their stepsons, Daniel Crouse and Victor Wind, were even the same age (twelve) when they first entered Marc Szeftel's and Timofey Pnin's respective real and fictional lives.[60] Most of Szeftel's and Nabokov's colleagues recognized Szeftel in Pnin on the evidence of less intimate acquaintance: his "funny" English, his isolation, proverbial bad luck, social awkwardness, slow academic advancement (like Timofey Pnin, at fifty-five a rather "mature" assistant professor, Szeftel for a number of years was easily one of the oldest assistant professors on his campus), and relative obscurity as a scholar.

But as Nabokov was getting to know Szeftel better during their work on *The Lay*, and simultaneously trying to make his protagonist less of a caricature, Pnin increasingly embodied traits of Szeftel, and, as we have seen, even Pnin's life gradually assumed much of the chronology of Szeftel's life. By late 1955 the merging of Szeftel and Pnin appears to have been almost complete, for it was really Szeftel whom Nabokov described to a potential publisher as his Pnin: "a scholar" and "a pure man," full of both "authenticity" and "integrity," yet also an insecure and "humorless" individual (*Pnin*, 80), whose "alien" personality and faulty English made him a butt of jokes and ridicule which even Nabokov himself could not always resist.

The final *Pnin* version provided even more that could be easily recognizable as Szeftel's fictional biography. In addition to the changed dates and chapter 5, it featured the description (not available in *The New Yorker*, since chapter 2 was also rejected) of Pnin's ten years of work on "The great work on Old Russia" (*Pnin*, 39), which echoed Szeftel's work on *The Lay of Igor's Campaign*.[61] Ten years is exactly the amount of time that Szeftel had spent working on the epic by 1953, first with Roman Jakobson, and then with Jakobson and Nabokov. So by the time both Kitty Szeftel and her husband's colleagues read the full book, there was even less doubt in their minds that Pnin was indeed modeled after Marc Szeftel. Some of them, as Boyd tells us, "even reproach[ed] Nabokov for cruelly mocking Szeftel in the person of Pnin."[62]

Nabokov, of course, could argue if he wished to (and, at least according to M. H. Abrams, he probably did), that he was mocking himself "in the person of Pnin" as "cruelly" as he was mocking Szeftel.[63] Yet even those who were inclined to believe him could not help but be aware of the huge difference that separated the two men. To use one of Nabokov's favorite metaphors, during his fifteen years in the States, Nabokov had managed to evolve, in the eyes of others, from an awkward caterpillar (Pnin) to a spectacular butterfly (VN). Szeftel, on the other hand, was incapable of a similar metamorphosis. He was doomed to remain Pnin. Szeftel's doom, however, may have proved to be Pnin's blessing: as a quasi Nabokov, that is, as the alien public persona of the early period in his American life, Pnin had to disappear as soon as VN replaced him; but as a quasi Szeftel, he could exist on his own and thus survive.

As a quasi Szeftel, Pnin could also claim a larger share of our sympathy and our pity. One of the most fascinating aspects of Nabokov's possible "Szeftelization" of Timofey Pnin is his attempt to give his non-Jewish protagonist a certain "Jewish dimension" by linking his early life to that of Mira Belochkin and her father. That, in turn, leads to the most moving and poignant instance of Pnin's humanity, as revealed in his reflections on Mira's tragic fate:

> In order to exist rationally, Pnin had taught himself, during the last ten years, never to remember Mira Belochkin—not because, in itself, the evocation of a youthful love affair, banal and brief, threatened his peace of mind . . . , but because, if one were quite sincere with oneself, no conscience, and hence no consciousness, could be expected to subsist in a world where such things as Mira's death were possible. One had to forget—because one could not live with the thought that this graceful, fragile, tender young woman with those eyes, that smile, those gardens and snows in the background, had been brought in a cattle car to an extermination camp and killed by an injection of phenol into the heart, into the gentle heart one had heard beating under one's lips in the dusk of the past. And since the exact form of her death had not been recorded, Mira kept dying a great number of deaths in one's mind, and undergoing a great number of resurrections, only to die again and again, led away by a trained nurse, inoculated with filth, tetanus bacilli, broken glass, gassed in a sham shower bath with prussic acid, burned alive in a pit on a gasoline-soaked pile of beechwood. (*Pnin*, 135)

Nabokov, obviously, had his own strong feelings on the subject of concentration camps, and this powerful description reflects them. In 1946, upon becoming aware of the true scope of the atrocities committed by the Nazis, Nabokov revealed the full measure of his pain and indignation when he wrote to his sister: "My love, as much as I may want sometimes to hide in my little ivory tower, there are things which wound too deeply—like the German atrocities, burning children in crematorium ovens, children as delightful and precious as yours and mine. I retreat into myself but there I find such hatred towards the Germans, towards concentration camps, towards tyranny of all kind that as an escape ce n'est pas grand'chose."[64] A year earlier he had discovered that his own brother Sergei died in a concentration camp near Hamburg, where he had been taken because of his homosexuality and his outspokenness.[65] Nabokov's very emotional and personal response to the Nazis' war crimes was probably also further deepened by a realization that, if his family's last-minute escape from France had not been successful, his own wife and son could have been interned as Jews and sent to an extermination camp. (I strongly suspect that it is Nabokov's own pain, caused by this particular realization, that feeds Krug's agony after the tragic loss of his wife and son in *Bend Sinister.*)

And yet it was Marc Szeftel whose experience of having a beloved Jewish woman perish in a concentration camp approximated most closely that of Pnin. Szeftel's thoughts of his mother's death brimmed with agony and incomprehension: "My mother was killed by Germans when she was 70 years old! By clean-cut, neat, 'decent' Germans, most likely ... Well-dressed, well-shaved, disciplined beasts, friends of dogs and birds, admirers of flowers and sentimental Lieder . . . There is nothing worse in nature than a two-legged animalistic beast! (*Khuzhe dvunogogo zhivotnogo zveria v prirode net!*)."[66]

According to Kitty Szeftel, Marc Szeftel tried once again in the early 1950s to find out which camp his mother had been sent to and what had happened to her, but, unlike Pnin, he did not find an investigator in Washington who was able to supply him with any relevant information.[67] Szeftel almost never talked about his mother to his wife and children (it was too painful for him, they felt), but in his diary he confessed that when he prayed it was not to God—his feelings about religion were always ambivalent—but to her.[68] We will obviously never know whether Szeftel ever revealed that to Nabokov, but in the novel we do find an uncanny echo of that practice: "[Pnin] did not believe in an autocratic God. He did believe, dimly, in a democracy of ghosts. The souls of the dead, perhaps, formed committees, and these, in continuous session, attended to the destinies of the quick" (*Pnin,* 136).[69]

Lucy Maddox is right to call *Pnin* one of Nabokov's "self-conscious, convoluted novels," but *Pnin,* in my opinion, goes beyond the scope of his other novels in that its self-consciousness extends not only to creating a narrative but also to creating a character.[70] Pnin starts out as a known "type" but ends up as an enigma. As in no other novel preceding *Pnin,* with the possible exception of *Invitation to a Beheading,* Nabokov here creates a protagonist as the "other": someone who at the end is much more "unknow-able" to the narrator, and even to the author himself, than he was in the beginning. Marc Szeftel may have been at least partially responsible for that

dimension of Pnin. I also believe that Szeftel's possible role in aiding Nabokov's fleshing out of *Pnin*'s protagonist can throw more light on one of the
most discussed and unresolved critical issues regarding the novel: namely,
the reliability of the narrator, who purports to know many details of Pnin's
inner and outer life which he was not privy to observe firsthand.

Our belief in the narrator's omniscience is undermined by Pnin himself,
who disputes many "facts" about his past as described by the narrator. Thus
Pnin insists that Pnin Sr. "never displayed him to his patients," as the
narrator claims he had done when the young VN found himself in need of
an eye specialist. VN further remembered the doctor had expressed particular pride that day over his son's achievements in algebra, but according to
Pnin "his marks in algebra had always been poor." Pnin also rejects the
narrator's claim that, as a young man, Timofey had acted the role of the
cuckolded husband in an amateur production of Arthur Schnitzler's *Liebelei*,
and eventually goes so far as to admonish a mutual friend not to believe a
single word the narrator says: "He makes up everything. He once invented
that we were schoolmates in Russia and cribbed at examinations. He is a
dreadful inventor (*on uzhasnïy vïdumshchik*)" (*Pnin*, 180, 185).

Lucy Maddox calls the narrator of *Pnin* "the paradox[ically] unreliable
first-person omniscient narrator,"[71] and this interplay between the narrator,
who pretends to know all, and the protagonist, who pleads with us not to
believe anything the narrator says, is well summarized by Michael Wood:

> *Pnin* is a mild-mannered book... but the textual quandary here is
> deeper than anything in *Lolita*. Whom are we to believe? The narrator,
> surely. This is his story, we are in the habit of believing narrators unless
> broad hints tell us not to, and people do quite often wish to hide their
> pasts, or pieces of their past. On the other hand, what possible interest
> could Pnin have in lying about his marks in algebra, and is there any-
> thing in the novel to suggest that he lies at all? Many of his problems
> proceed from his scrupulous, awkward directness, and in the end it
> makes most sense to believe Pnin in spite of the stacked narrative odds.[72]

Wood goes on to suggest that while the narrator is in perfect control of
the caricature-like, "invented" Pnin, the human, believable Pnin, or, as
Wood calls him, "*our* Pnin, the human creature who has been evoked in the
spaces and against the designs of this narrative," walks out of the novel
appearing to be no longer dependent on what the narrator says or thinks of

him.[73] Numerous critics share Wood's sense of Pnin's independence at the end of the novel. Thus Andrew Field suggests that "the narrative movement in *Pnin* is the flight of a character from his author" in which he finally succeeds.[74] Michael Long likewise asserts that Pnin "elud[es] his predatory pursuer at the end,"[75] and Julian Connolly believes that Pnin, in leaving everyone, including the narrator, behind, "moves on to a higher plane—his path is that of a spiral."[76] Much has also been made of the "poetic justice" that befalls the narrator at the end of the novel: the very dubious pleasure of Cockerell's company and "a British breakfast of depressing kidney and fish" (*Pnin*, 191).[77]

The most dramatic declaration of Pnin's independence and VN's "just deserts" comes from Charles Nicol, who, as I mentioned earlier, calls the narrator simply "Nabokov." Nicol actually goes as far as to describe the two men as antagonists and their relationship as a struggle between the "devilish" narrator and the innocent protagonist, in which Pnin "has confronted Nabokov and won."[78] Nicol thus stops just short of suggesting—as Paul Grams, for example, does—that the narrator is "the evil designer" whom Pnin evokes in chapter 1.[79] "It stood to reason," Pnin was supposedly thinking back then, "that if the evil designer—the destroyer of minds, the friend of fever—had concealed the key of the pattern with such monstrous care, that key must be as precious as life itself and, when found, would regain for Timofey Pnin his everyday health, his everyday world; and this lucid—alas, too lucid—thought forced him to persevere in the struggle" (*Pnin*, 23–24). Finding that key, then, or wresting it away from the narrator (the destroyer of Pnin's mind, or, at least, of its complexity) becomes Pnin's plight. It is the plight of a person, fictional or otherwise, who wants to cease being an invented buffoon and a cliché and insists on his right to be a dignified and respected individual.

Such was precisely the plight of Marc Szeftel. Andrew Field summarizes Nabokov's and Szeftel's colleagues' assessment of the Pninian qualities in Szeftel as follows: "a whimsical manner, fabulous absentmindedness, and a certain eccentric manner with the English language." He also states that "Marc Szeftel was, like Timofey Pnin, a victim of campus politics and could not get a promotion at Cornell."[80] Many of these impressions appear, however, to be based more on the "myth" of Szeftel than the reality. Szeftel could come across as the classical absentminded professor because he struck many, especially a younger generation, as so different from themselves. But he was punctual and, unless sick, never missed his lectures. He was, likewise, not known for losing exam papers or not turning in grades, and, by all accounts, he performed as a serious and conscientious advisor to his graduate students. And while it is true that Szeftel himself often noted that his organizational skills left a lot to be desired,[81] throughout his life he strenuously attempted to structure his existence by making regular lists of things he needed to do. His "eccentric" English too, though problematic, was probably not so off-putting as Field would have us believe.[82]

As to Szeftel's promotion, whereas no one will argue that it was painfully slow and that for several years he was among the oldest assistant professors on campus, by 1961, when Szeftel left Cornell for the University of Washington, he was assuredly a full professor. Probably because he was embarrassed at having been such an old assistant professor, in his own resumés and official university biographies, Szeftel liked to lump all his titles together, stating that from 1945 to 1961 he had been "Asst., Assoc & Full Prof. Russian History. Cornell University."[83] Yet we can safely assume that he was promoted to associate professor in 1951 (since he is first identified as Associate Professor of History in the 1951–52 *Directory of Faculty and Staff*), and became a full professor in 1956 (an entry in his diary, dated February 24, 1956, discusses the upcoming departmental vote on his promotion, and he is also listed as full professor for the first time in the 1956–57 *Directory*). It should also be noted that many people at Cornell whom I interviewed in 1993, and several of whom Field had interviewed for his biography, were apparently not aware of Szeftel's final rank at Cornell. Some even believed that he had never gotten his tenure. This may help to explain another legend that Field appears to have picked up at Cornell: that of Nabokov's protesting the nonrenewal of Szeftel's contract.[84]

Szeftel was also not totally obscure as a scholar. By 1956, when *Pnin* appeared as a book, Szeftel had published two studies and eleven articles. *La Geste Du Prince Igor'*, published in 1948, earned him considerable respect from fellow Slavists, as did the second work he produced jointly with Roman Jakobson, a study on the Vseslav Epos.[85] Medieval Russian historians are rarely among the campus stars anywhere, even if their contributions to the field are much more substantial than Szeftel's. In large Departments of History (or, for that matter, Literature), Russian specialties have often been academic Cinderellas. Both Nabokov and Szeftel became aware of this situation soon after they joined American academe, and I strongly suspect that Pnin's interest in the Cinderella fairy tale stems, at least partially, from his sense of affinity with this neglected stepdaughter.[86]

Thus Szeftel—like Pnin—had the odds cruelly stacked against him. He was a serious scholar and, in all probability, a caring teacher, but the Cockerells of this world—and, most likely, many of Szeftel's own colleagues— often needed to be dazzled in order to be impressed. Some also probably enjoyed having Szeftel around because, like Pnin, he was an easy person to feel superior to—a foreigner, teaching an obscure subject in heavily accented English and possessing no talent for witty small talk at faculty cocktail parties. Of his past, little was known and little was sought to be known. Few appear to have been cognizant of, or willing to consider, that Szeftel had good reasons to be one of the oldest assistant professors on campus: His academic career had been rudely interrupted by the war, the gloomy reality of possible extinction as a Jew, the internment camp, and emigration. Few of Szeftel's American-born colleagues could claim obstacles to their careers as harsh, but little of that went into creating the myth of Marc Szeftel. One of the people who *could* recognize and appreciate these hardships was Vladimir Nabokov, and, in his own inimitable way, he did just that.

While Nabokov was always aware of the irreconcilable differences in their personalities and actively discouraged Szeftel from seeking a closer friendship (and while he was not always above joining the others in laughing at Szeftel), his appreciation of Szeftel's history and pain appears to have become more pronounced as the fifties progressed and he became better acquainted with his colleague's past. Pnin's ultimate triumph over—and escape from—Cockerell and even VN may have been directly influenced by Szeftel's own human triumph in the eyes of Vladimir Nabokov. The "notion" of Szeftel could also have aided the relationship between the narrator and the protagonist: just as Szeftel's colleagues, including to a large extent Nabokov himself, could never be reliable narrators of Marc Szeftel's life because they could or would see only what was funny, entertaining, and superficial, so most of Pnin's fictional colleagues, including VN, were in no way competent or reliable judges of the "real" Pnin.

Having walked out of one book, it took Pnin five years to walk into another. In *Pale Fire*, Pnin reappeared as a tenured professor and "the Head of the bloated Russian department" at Wordsmith University ("New Wye, Appalachia, USA").[87] We easily recognize him here, for Pnin apparently continues to be "humorless," reportedly provoking one of his colleagues (John Shade) to exclaim: "How odd that Russian intellectuals should lack all sense of humor when they have such marvelous humorists as Gogol,

Dostoevski, Chekhov, Zoshchenko, and those joint authors of genius Ilf and Petrov."[88] Pnin is also described by the book's commentator/narrator, Charles Kinbote, as "a farcical pedant of whom the less said the better,"[89] but since Kinbote is awesomely unreliable, his comment serves only to reinforce Pnin's image as the opposite of Kinbote's own. Therefore, Pnin, we are safe to assume, is still "a pure man . . . characterized by authenticity and integrity." Something is new, though, about the old protagonist, for when we meet Pnin in person in the university library, he is a picture of peaceful contentment: he wears a "Hawaiian shirt" and "an ironic expression on his face."[90] Pnin makes his physical appearance in the very last segment of the novel, which Nabokov was finishing in the fall of 1961, at the very same time that Marc Szeftel (who, we must admit, was not given to wearing Hawaiian shirts) started teaching at *his* new place—the University of Washington. It was probably just a coincidence, but of the kind that Nabokov, again, might have appreciated.

4 / Szeftel in Search of Success
Lolita

[Nabokov] ... told me a month after the novel came out ...
from Putnam: "Someone I know, a homosexual, informed me
that *Lolita* had cured him of that vice." This is easy to understand: the passion for Lolita destroys Humbert Humbert; it's his
cross, his fate. "Yes, in my novel fate is everything," confirmed
Nabokov when I expressed this opinion to him.

In Nabokov's work one can detect a strong motif of a double, so
I asked him whether this motif is also present in *Lolita*. He
answered: "Yes, the mirror reflection is always there" ("Da,
zerkal'noe otrazhenie vsegda u menia est").

Lolita is a weak novel, but an excellently written book.

—Marc Szeftel

As the Pnin stories were appearing in *The New Yorker,* Nabokov
sent the magazine's literary editor, Katharine White, the manuscript of
Lolita, hoping that she might decide to publish some chapters of this novel
as well. He wanted both the manuscript and the author's identity to be kept
in secret and beseeched White to make sure that "there would be no leaks."[1]
One can only imagine, then, how shocked and angry Nabokov was when the
August 27, 1955, issue of *The New Yorker* carried a story by Dorothy Parker
about a widowed mother and a daughter who compete for the love of the
same man. The daughter's name was Lolita, and so was the title of the story.
Parker's "Lolita" could easily appear to Nabokov as a parody of his own
novel. Far from being "sexy," Parker's heroine "was of no color at all ... and
her hair, so fine that it seemed sparse, grew straight." The man who is
attracted to her is described as an "older" man—here over thirty. Surprisingly enough, they get married and live happily ever after, much to the
consternation of Lolita's mother, who wanted her son-in-law all for herself.[2]
Upon seeing the story, Nabokov sent several incensed letters to White demanding an explanation. The editor assured him it was a pure coincidence,
and Nabokov eventually dropped the issue.[3]

Coincidence or not, this little-known episode underscores the problems Nabokov was facing with *Lolita* at the time.[4] There was the issue of his artistic vanity: since Nabokov had not been successful in finding an American publisher brave enough to call *Lolita* its own and had had to settle for a minor French publisher with a dubious reputation (Olympia Press), he could readily have construed Parker's story as a manifestation of mockery. But his reaction probably went much deeper. In 1953 and 1954 he had shown his manuscript to several friends and editors and was basically relying on their good will, for it was essential that both the novel and the identity of its author be kept secret lest his storyline be "scooped" or his job at Cornell endangered. Seeing Parker's story in *The New Yorker,* he doubtless thought his worst fears were being realized, that her "Lolita" was just the tip of an iceberg, that many more people had read his manuscript, knew that it was his, and were going to talk about it. All that would of course change in 1958, when the Putnam edition gave *Lolita* and its author true legitimacy and status, but in 1955 Nabokov's fears were reasonable.

Marc Szeftel liked to think that he had "witnessed Lolita's conception".... One afternoon N. told me at the Library: 'You remember my 'Volshebnik' [*The Enchanter*]? Now I make out of it a 2 volume novel, with action in the U.S., and I call it 'Lolita.' No more was ever ... said about it until the publication of the book."[5] Olympia Press brought out *Lolita* in the autumn of 1955. The publication went largely unnoticed until Graham Greene pronounced it one of the three best books of that year. Greene's praise proved to be a mixed blessing, for it led to the novel's initial notoriety. Responding to Greene, John Gordon, a conservative English critic, called *Lolita* "the filthiest book I have ever read. Sheer unrestrained pornography." Gordon also stated that people who might want to publish or sell *Lolita* in England "would certainly go to prison."[6] By March 1956 the identity of the author was no longer a secret, and the next year witnessed numerous bans, legal actions, and public uproars.

Szeftel, who borrowed a copy of the novel in October 1956 from Avgusta Jaryc,[7] vividly remembers Nabokov's showing him a full-page ad for *Lolita* in a magazine while bashfully covering, with his other hand, an ad on the opposite page for a book with an explicitly sexual subject ("as if the two advertisements belonged to the same kind of interest," notes Szeftel).[8] This and similar pairings were of major concern to Nabokov, who complained to Wilson in 1956: "In the same issue of the [New York Times] *Book Review* [where *Lolita* was discussed] there is a nice advertisement of Books on Sex, with patients 'telling their case histories in their own words.' I am extremely irritated by the turn my nymphet's destiny is taking, but although I foreglimpsed the situation, I have no inkling how to act, nor do I know even what kind of assistance or defense I can expect in our times when crusades are definitely *vieux jeu.*"[9]

Marc Szeftel remembers that Véra Nabokov was even more upset than her husband when it came to *Lolita*'s reputation as an "amoral" novel: "Vera Evseevna was indignant that in one of the Soviet magazines it was stated that Vladimir Vladimirovich had written a novel about 'degrading a young girl.' The note was anonymous but V. E. said she knew who wrote it and would never forgive that person.... V. E. emphasized a different theme in the novel: 'How can they not see that the girl was left all alone, without a single close relative in this world?' "[10]

Even many otherwise broad-minded intellectuals, including Nabokov's own friends, were either scandalized by the novel or uneasy about it. The example of Edmund Wilson is well known. "I like [*Lolita*] less than anything else of yours I have read," Wilson wrote to Nabokov in 1954. "Nasty subjects may make fine books; but I don't feel you have got away with this."[11] William Styron recalls that after the Olympia Press edition came out, he went to Hiram Haydn, the editor-in-chief at Random House, to suggest that they might want to publish *Lolita* because it was such a masterpiece. Haydn, usually "a sophisticated and rather scholarly man," reacted with great vehemence: "Hiram rose from his desk, his face actually blue with rage. 'That loathsome novel will be published over my dead body!' he roared." Haydn then proceeded to tell Styron "that he, Hiram Haydn, had a daughter the age of the victim of Humbert Humbert's disgusting lust, and when my own daughter was that age perhaps I'd understand the hatred a man might feel for *Lolita*."[12] He was, apparently, not the only outraged parent. Marc Szeftel's daughter vividly remembers how, upon the publication of *Lolita*, her mother told her father: "Well, I am certainly not going to let Tanechka walk past this man's house to school anymore!" Only six at the time and quite alarmed, Tanechka asked her parents how, then, she should be going to school now. Kitty Szeftel laughed and said she was only kidding. The daughter feels, however, that her mother's indignation about the book was genuine.[13]

Both Vladimir and Véra Nabokov were probably even further distressed by the reaction of their closest friend on campus, Morris Bishop. According to M. H. Abrams, Bishop "had warned Nabokov never to publish *Lolita* because he would get fired."[14] Bishop's daughter, Alison Jolly, remembers that there was an early period when her father "deliberately did not read *Lolita* in case he had to defend Nabokov to the trustees. He wanted to be able to say, dismissively, 'I have not bothered to look at the new book but the overall stature of Nabokov is immense. He should certainly continue as a Cornell professor.' "[15] Bishop also reportedly told Szeftel as soon as the novel came out: "I would not like to have to defend him, would you?"[16] When Bishop finally read the novel, he did not care for it at all. "Nabokov's *Pnin* is a shimmering delight. His *Lolita* is not," he wrote to his daughter in 1957.[17]

Bishop's concern over *Lolita* appears to have been twofold: on the one hand, he truly did not want any harm to come his friend's way; on the other, a staunch patriot of Cornell, he also did not want the university's reputation to suffer as a result of Nabokov's notoriety. Milton Cowan feels that it was Bishop's anxiety over Cornell's reputation that made him dislike *Lolita:* "He was shuddering in his shoes for Cornell, dear old Cornell."[18] Cornell's reaction to Nabokov's novel was indeed a source of great anxiety to Bishop. "[Nabokov] is doing his best to make a giant scandal of it," Bishop wrote to Alison Jolly in May of 1957, "but the scandal has not yet penetrated to the Cornell Alumni."[19] Marc Szeftel thought that Bishop's attitude towards *Lolita* was further complicated by the fact that, while Bishop kept saying that he merely "feared American puritanism," he himself appeared to be leery of the eroticism of *Lolita,* condemning several passages in the novel as "pornography."[20] M. H. Abrams agrees with Szeftel: "Morris Bishop could tell off-color jokes as well as the next man but he was, in many ways, puritanical about public literature. I think he genuinely felt *Lolita* was not the kind of thing one should publish."[21] Alison Jolly also agrees with this assessment of her father's reaction, but hastens to add: "From our present perspective, we were then prudish, uptight and ignorant. From a 50's perspective, however, the modern era would seem revoltingly degenerate in our daily newspaper diet of child abuse. My father and others critical of *Lolita* shared the views of a very much wider public."[22]

In August of 1958, G. P. Putnam's and Sons printed the first American edition of *Lolita.* Its success exceeded everyone's expectations, and for many weeks it vied with Boris Pasternak's *Doctor Zhivago* for the number-one spot on the *New York Times* bestsellers list. Szeftel personally saw Nabokov checking the list weekly in the Periodicals Room of the Cornell Library. It was to Marc Szeftel (and Classicist Harry Caplan, which may explain the use of Latin) that Nabokov, happy with his top ranking for the week, made the statement about defeating Pasternak's novel (which Andrew Field first quoted in his biography)—"Delendam esse [sic] Zhivago!"[23] Around the same time, Véra Nabokov was seen in bookstores around Ithaca "picking up copies of *Lolita* . . . and placing them in front of copies of *Dr. Zhivago*."[24] Even when the book became a bestseller, Nabokov apparently was still apprehensive about its possible repercussions for his job. When Szeftel told Nabokov that he thought "the storm ha[d] blown over," Nabokov suggested this was far from clear: "There still can be protests that a man who wrote such a book about a teenage girl is teaching innocent coeds. Innocent coeds! It's an American myth!" Szeftel further suggested to Nabokov that, given the fabulous sales of his novel, he might finally "feel free to leave teaching" anyway, to which Nabokov allegedly replied: "No, it may still be dangerous. I love Cornell!"[25] Cornell at that point loved him too. The campus was all abuzz about *Lolita*'s success, and one of Cornell's oldest organizations, "Book and Bowl," decided to do something about it.

Book and Bowl, founded in 1907 by Everett Ward Olmstead, a professor in the Department of Romance Languages, was conceived as a forum where students, mostly upperclassmen, could freely mix with their professors in an informal atmosphere and discuss literature and arts.[26] The "Bowl" referred to a punch bowl (or, at times, even a soup bowl), which was a constant companion at these meetings. As one of the speakers during the 1957 fiftieth anniversary banquet explained (in poetic form), both ingredients were deemed to be important: "The Book and The Bowl / They both have a soul; / The soul of good books in the thoughts they awake / The soul of our feasts in the friends who partake."[27] During World War I, Book and Bowl ceased to function, but it was resurrected in 1922 by yet another Romance Languages professor, Morris Bishop.[28] Meetings usually took place at the homes of Book and Bowl members. Until 1961 it was an all-male club, so wives of the members were often expected to prepare the food and then leave the room or even the house. Some—like Kitty Szeftel, at whose house several meetings took place—strongly disliked this policy even though they never challenged it.[29] In the late 1940s and 1950s, when Nabokov and Szeftel were on campus, Book and Bowl provided a vibrant forum, and meetings were often held once or twice a month. Szeftel joined the society in 1946, at which point he paid the invitation fee of ten dollars, followed by five dollars per term in subsequent years.[30] According to Book and Bowl records, Szeftel was actively involved in the organization, and for one year (1954–55) served as its secretary. Nabokov, on the other hand, was never a dues-paying member of the society, and Szeftel, for one, appears to have resented that: "[W]hen he became our colleague at Cornell, the Book & Bowl (of which I was a member) extended to him an invitation to join us. But this meant a fee (a small one), and Nabokov refused. Vera told me in this connection that, if they had to follow up all such invitations, it would wash them out completely. May be they were also protecting their time & social freedom, but, if so, this, too, was exaggerating [i.e., overdoing it] with regard to colleagues, most of them members of the same modern literatures division."[31]

Topics at Book and Bowl could vary from traditional ("Young Joyce," by Robert Scholes, for example) to slightly less so (M. H. Abrams remembers giving a paper on "The Striptease as a Literary Motif").[32] Some were even tongue in cheek—at one session it took the participants a long time to realize that Morris Bishop was pulling their collective leg by showing his slide collection of antique postcards while pretending that the pictures had been taken during his and his wife's recent trip to Europe.[33] One of the all-time hits was a talk by Peter Kahn. It took place at Professor Arthur Sweets's house on May 21, 1958, and was entitled "How to Look at Nudes—with Slides." Nabokov was invited by Kahn to attend, and he reportedly accepted the invitation with much enthusiasm. On the day of the talk, Kahn had to pick Nabokov up because Véra, in a rare case of rebellion, had refused to drive her husband to a meeting that was for men only and presented such a risqué talk.[34]

Lolita was featured at two autumn meetings of Book and Bowl in 1958.[35] The first gathering took place in Marc Szeftel's house on October 23 and featured Richard Fariña, then a Cornell undergraduate, reading from the novel. On November 13, Marc Szeftel gave his talk in M. H. Abrams's home. He called it "*Lolita*: Considerations of a Non-Professional Critic." Abrams remembers Szeftel volunteering to give the talk, but his recollection of the talk itself is virtually nonexistent, possibly because, as other participants have suggested, Abrams was called out of town at the last minute and was not present.[36] James McConkey remembers that Szeftel "was sort of apprehensive that Nabokov might get wind" of his talk and show up. Szeftel was particularly worried, according to McConkey, about Nabokov's reaction to his comparison of the author of *Lolita* to Dostoevsky.[37] Andrew Field writes in his biography that Nabokov was dissuaded from coming to the meeting by Abrams. This version of the events was probably given to him by Szeftel who wrote, in "Lolita at Cornell," that the Nabokovs "learned about the talk, and wanted to come, but Mike Abrams did not encourage them, probably to save me embarrassment." Yet Abrams does not think that was the case at all: "It was much more likely to have been Szeftel who wanted the freedom of speech without the awesome presence of Nabokov himself who didn't take anything but highly favorable criticism lightly."[38] Szeftel's diaries also give a slightly different version of what happened. "I gave a talk on 'Lolita' to the Cornell 'Book and Bowl'," Szeftel reminisced on August 29, 1970, ten years before "Lolita at Cornell" was published. "N. wanted to come, but I thought it may become embarrassing both for him and myself, for the talk, though full of praise, was not a panegyric, while the Nabokovs are very sensitive even to the mildest criticism."[39]

Szeftel's talk started by emphasizing the book's popularity—"Tremendous success, 11 weeks first on the bestseller list. Even the Marine Corps read it and children know about it"—and then proceeded to analyze the book's different "motifs" ("The motif of all-devouring passion," "The motif of evasion from reality," "The motif of the double"). The paper also mentioned Nabokov's affinity with Dostoevsky ("I pronounced the name of a writer, for whom N. does not have much respect . . . and still [they have] something in common"). As McConkey pointed out, Szeftel felt much more comfortable discussing this issue in Nabokov's absence, especially since Szeftel declared in his talk that "Dostoevsky's art is more impressive" when it comes to showing the psychology of his characters. Szeftel's overall appraisal of the novel would not have pleased Nabokov either. He found the novel "not perfect. . . . There is thinness, and prolixity at the same time, in its texture," and suggested that "[i]n spite of all its sparkling brilliancy," it was not "a great book": "It does not contain any meaningful revelation. It does not reveal any depth of human soul, like Dostoevsky, and it does not offer us any vision transfiguring the external world, like Gogol. At most does it have the value of a clinical study of an abnormal sexual case, all along with witticism of charming, but not deep a character [sic]. And I am afraid, Balsac will overlive [i.e., outlive] it."[40]

A month after the talk, James McConkey, who was at the time one of the editors of *Epoch: A Quarterly of Contemporary Literature,* sent Szeftel a letter inquiring whether Szeftel "could be persuaded to write a portion of that excellent Book and Bowl talk on *Lolita* for a review in the next issue of *Epoch. Epoch* has not published any sort of notice about *Lolita* or Nabokov, an omission we would like to remedy; at a recent editorial meeting I mentioned some of the comments which you had made during your talk, and was immediately commissioned by fellow editors to approach you on the possibility of a review."[41] Szeftel declined the offer, since he was still afraid (and probably rightfully so) that his views would anger Nabokov and further complicate their relationship.[42] Véra Nabokov apparently told Szeftel soon after the meeting that "she and Nabokov had heard about my interesting talk and expressed disappointment that its content remained a mystery to them."[43] Within the next three years, both Szeftel and Nabokov left Cornell. In 1959—the same year Szeftel had a heart attack (which Pnin mercifully escaped at the end of the book)—the Nabokovs departed for Switzerland. In 1961, after accepting a job offer from the University of Washington, the Szeftels moved to Seattle.

Once he and Nabokov were no longer colleagues, Szeftel, remembering warmly the praise he had received for his Book and Bowl talk, began to reconsider whether he should not capitalize on his acquaintance with Nabokov and write a full-length literary study. Being a historian and not a literary critic does not seem to have disturbed him. "What do I have on him?" Szeftel mused soon after the Nabokovs' departure: "My paper . . . was praised at the time as unusually 'perceptive' and as the first balanced review given to the book. Another question—should I write an essay on 'Lolita' . . . , or an essay on Nabokov? The latter would require additional readings and much more work, for which time would have to be found. The latter is a problem, for there are other things to be done. But I am tempted. I think the answer may be to write, first, an essay on 'Lolita,' and to see what will be the reaction."[44]

Szeftel remembered that one of the participants at the meeting approached him after the talk and suggested that he should write an article on "Dostoevsky in Nabokov." Unlike Nabokov, Szeftel not only liked Dostoevsky, he also felt much affinity with those of his characters, who, like Makar Devushkin, were faced with lack of respect and even outright humiliation yet managed to retain their dignity.[45] So now Szeftel was seriously contemplating this particular "Nabokov/Dostoevsky" angle:

> N. would be furious, but matter would not lack . . . 1. the motive [i.e., motif] of the double; 2. life as a game . . . ; 3. love for a pubescent girl. . . . Dostoevsky did not polish his prose, Nabokov does it very carefully, but D. had no time, he had to write for living. D. had a message, a deep moral and religious message to communicate, a vision of life based on pity for suffering. N. considers any message as dead wood in literature, but in spite of himself here and there pity for suffering rears his head also in his novels. This is not surprising for both N. and D. derive from the same source, from Gogol. D. directly,

N, through Belyi. . . . [Both] stressed the other side of life, beyond
reality, the reflection of life in '*krivoe zerkalo*' [a crooked mirror] of
imagination. For N. this is only a game, which he plays very ski[ll]fully.
For D. this was a glimpse of higher reality, a reversal of all values
around the Christian concept of suffering. It seems to me that D. went
farther, that he completed . . . what N. only sketched. This is my sketch
of the N.–D. article![46]

Relying heavily on Nina Berberova's 1959 article, "Nabokov i ego 'Lolita' "
("Nabokov and His Lolita"), Szeftel started making preparatory notes for
the essay.[47] It was going to have "six steps": "topic, external content, internal
content, external form, internal form, revelation of the myth." It was also
going to follow closely the themes highlighted in the Book and Bowl talk
and to suggest that *Lolita*'s subject was "not new, either for N. himself,[48] or
generally (Dostoevsky in 'Crime and Punishment' and, especially, 'Stavrogin's Confession')," and that the novel had strong themes of "the double,"
"liberation" or "catharsis" ("passion—love & pity; the rivals merge into one,
one of them destroying the other"), and "destiny" ("style where . . . contrasts
merge into one musical and pictorial unity, dominated by destiny").[49] In
1960, after Nabokov had already left Cornell but while Szeftel was still there,
Szeftel offered his future article to Roman Goul, the editor of the émigré
publication *Novyi zhurnal* (The new journal) where Berberova's article had
appeared a year earlier. Goul politely declined the offer, suggesting that two
long articles on *Lolita* in two years might be rather excessive.[50]

At some point during the preparation for the article, it occurred to Szeftel
that, in order to do *Lolita* full justice, he might need a copy of the then-
unpublished screenplay Nabokov had written for Stanley Kubrick's 1962
movie. Early in 1963 Szeftel wrote to Morris Bishop asking for the Nabokovs'
address. Bishop responded that he and his wife had "not heard from the
Nabokovs for a long time. They seem to have settled down in Montreux . . .
near Dmitri, who alternates singing at La Scala with professional automobile
racing."[51] On July 2, 1963, Szeftel wrote to Nabokov, in care of his publisher,
asking for a favor:

> Dear Vladimir:
> It has been a long time since we have talked to each other orally or
> even by way of letter. I know that everything is well with you and
> yours; I have been getting echo[e]s about you from Morris Bishop.

I have in a rough draft a study about your *Lolita* and would like to complete it. I feel that to do it I need the script of its film version. Would it be too much to ask you to send it to me to Seattle (you probably have known that two years ago I came over here from Cornell).

I have seen the film and have enjoyed it, as I enjoyed the book, very much.

With my very best to you and Vera.

> Sincerely yours,
> Marc M. Szeftel
> Professor of Russian History[52]

It was in Ashland, Oregon, exactly ten years earlier, that Nabokov first wrote and then mailed to *The New Yorker* his story "Pnin" about a literature professor who, knowledgeable as he might be, should never be mistaken for a sophisticated literary critic. Now the person whose life and personality helped to mold the fictional character, was writing to him, from the same Northwest, offering himself as the potential author of a *Lolita* study! Nabokov, it seems, was not amused.

Two weeks later Szeftel got a brief response from Véra Nabokov:

> Dear Marc Yurievich,
>
> V.V. asks me to thank you for your kind letter. He regrets that he cannot send you the screenplay of LOLITA.
>
> We hope you like the Northwest as much as we did when we made a long stay at Ashland, Oregon. We also hope that you and your family are well and happy.
>
> > With kind regards from us both,
> > Sincerely,
> > Véra Nabokov[53]

Szeftel was, no doubt, hurt. It is not known how he explained this abrupt refusal at the time, but in later years he chose to spare himself and attribute it to Nabokov's financial concern about making the screenplay public before it was published. Szeftel did, however, designate the day he got Véra's postcard as the official end of his relationship with the Nabokovs.[54]

Nonetheless, he did not give up on the idea of writing a study of *Lolita*. If anything, Szeftel's interest in Nabokov only increased throughout his Seattle years, bordering on obsession and acute envy. His daughter remembers that she "grew up hearing the name . . . constantly," as if Nabokov were "someone in our household."[55] "N[abokov] became a world literary figure," Szeftel noted in his diary in 1970. "Books have been written about him, an already considerable number of books. He is 71, and apparently in excellent health, busy as ever writing books and chasing butterflies. A peaceful, rich in every way, creative old age. All this is due to 'Lolita.' "[56] A year later, complaining about his own old age with its infirmities and depressions, Szeftel exclaims: "But I was told, on the other hand, that Nabokov, this 'favorite of gods' (*liubimets bogov*), at 72 is quite a young man (*sovsem molodoi chelovek*)! Not everyone is as lucky as this fortunate one (*Ne vsem tak vezet, kak etomu schastlivchiku*)."[57]

Throughout the 1960s and 1970s Szeftel's own luck appeared to have been changing for the better. He was gradually becoming known as a historian. In 1963 Éditions de la Librairie Encyclopédique in Brussels published *Documents De Droit Public Relatifs A La Russie Médiévale*, a collection of Russian medieval public and legal documents which Szeftel translated into French, and for which he provided the introduction and commentary. The volume grew out of Szeftel's pre-war graduate work, which had been initiated and directed by Alexander Eck.[58] The book was generally well received. In *Slavic Review*, George Vernadsky praised it as "valuable . . . to American scholars who are able to read French" and "an important contribution to the field of medieval Russian studies,[59] while Oswald P. Backus suggested in *The American Historical Review* that the "volume ought to enjoy an excellent reputation." "[O]ne may hope," Backus continued, "that it will be followed by additional collections edited by the same scholar."[60] Favorable reviews also appeared in *Speculum*[61] and even in *Voprosy istorii* (*Issues of history*), the major Soviet historical journal.[62] In the mid-1970s, after Szeftel had retired, he completed and published, also abroad but this time in English, two more books: *Russian Institutions and Culture up to Peter the Great* (London, 1975 and *The Russian Constitution of April 23, 1906: Political Institutions of the Duma Monarchy* (Brussels, 1976).[63]

Szeftel was not satisfied, however. He felt that "real" fame, appreciation, and material success were as elusive as ever, and that less and less time remained to do something about it. He would not give up the idea of writing a study on Nabokov, which alone, he believed, could finally make him better known, even illustrious, as if, by attaching himself to Nabokov's success through a study of *Lolita,* some of Nabokov's stardust and good fortune might rub off on him.

He followed the published news of Nabokov's life and activities with both zeal and resentment: "Nabokov becomes even younger! The great commercial success which was 'Lolita' make him sell all he wrote before it, whether in English or in Russian, and the Russian novels have been appearing in translation one after another, even those written more than 40 years ago. . . . [There is] a new interview of Nabokov by the 'New York Times Book Review' . . . the interview has not been pleasant to read. N., obviously, has lost the ability to talk like a simple, though exalted, human being. . . . The interview became a smart-alecky performance, a naughty boy performance, which is beneath Nabokov's talent. And age! At 72, after so much success, it is time to grow up, finally, and to lay off the 'enfant terrible' silly game."[64]

In 1973 Szeftel was deeply hurt when a former student, Robert C. Howes, published a new translation of *Slovo* (*The Tale of the Campaign of Igor: A Russian Epic Poem of the Twelfth Century*), and, without mentioning Szeftel, glowingly acknowledged Nabokov: "I owe a special debt of gratitude to Vladimir Nabokov, several of whose courses on Russian literature I attended at Cornell University from 1948 to 1950. His brilliance as a teacher and his personal kindness to me will always be cherished."[65] This was very unlike Howes's acknowledgment in a previous published translation, *The Testaments of the Grand Princes of Moscow* (1966), in which he thanked Szeftel profusely for his assistance: "I undertook the translation of these documents at Cornell University in 1959, at the suggestion of Professor Marc Szeftel. During much of my work on the documents, Professor Szeftel aided me immeasurably. . . . His high standards of scholarship and profound understanding of Russian history encouraged me. . . . If there is any value in this book, much credit should go to Marc Szeftel."[66] Now, almost ten years later, Szeftel felt betrayed and unappreciated, fearing that his position in the heart and mind of a former student had been irrevocably usurped by Nabokov: "My own historical commentary to the *Slovo* has not been mentioned by Howes (who got his Ph.D. at Cornell from me in 1961!), and, when I have asked him for a copy of his translation . . . no answer came to this request."[67]

Szeftel generally viewed his failures and Nabokov's successes as somehow connected. In his diaries during these years he often appears unable to think of his sicknesses and misfortunes without evoking the image of Nabokov: "With age my patience has been getting thinner. . . . It is, probably, based on the diminished physical endurance. . . . it is late in the day, and dusk is closing in! . . . Dusk outside, dusk inside . . . Does ever Nabokov, the eternally young Nabokov, have this feeling of pervasive greyness?"[68]

Szeftel's records of books and materials read or looked at during the 1960s and 1970s are full of entries not only for Nabokov, but also for Nabokov's father and even his cousin (Szeftel apparently read Nicolas Nabokov's 1951 book, *Old Friends and New Music*). Among books by or on Nabokov that he studied or perused in these years are *Pale Fire* (1962), *Nabokov's Congeries* (1968), *Ada* (1969), *Annotated Lolita* (1970), *Strong Opinions* (1973), and Carl Proffer's *Keys to "Lolita"* (1972). Szeftel also looked at numerous contemporaneous reviews, including those on *Eugene Onegin,* and listened to a twenty-minute "phonotape," entitled "Nabokov: Self Portrait" and produced in 1974, which he found at the University of Washington Media Center.[69] He gave his projected study the preliminary title of "Vladimir Nabokov: A Point of View."[70]

In further preparation for the study, Szeftel decided to develop a talk on Nabokov which he could give at different colleges and universities. Thus when in 1974 the Russian Department of the University of Durham in England invited him to speak either on Ivan the Terrible or the Duma period, Szeftel offered, instead, a lecture on Nabokov. Since the University of Durham was primarily interested in Szeftel as a historian, they ended up by compromising: Szeftel agreed to give two talks, one on the Duma and one on Nabokov.[71] Szeftel's notes on the Durham talk suggest that it was largely a biographical affair. He detailed Nabokov's life prior to Cornell, his interests and hobbies besides writing novels, his "Russian" period as Sirin, his Cornell years, and his "American" period climaxing in *Lolita*, which Szeftel, in a rather contradictory fashion, describes in these notes as "a mediocre novel but an excellent book" (echoing the equally contradictory description, quoted in an epigraph to this chapter and found in his diaries, of *Lolita* as "a weak novel, but an excellently written book"). He also calls the novel an "inflated novelette," and poses a question for himself and his listeners: "[I]f 'Lolita' had an unobjectionable topic, what would have been N.'s success as a writer in U.S.A. and West[ern] Europe?" We do not know whether he attempted to answer this question in his talk, but in his notes he left it unanswered.[72]

In subsequent years Szeftel attempted to offer the same lecture on Nabokov (an advance copy of which he always sent with his proposal) to different universities in the vicinity of Seattle. Neither the University of British Columbia, nor Seattle University, nor even his very own University of Washington were interested, however, and Szeftel had to be content with giving his lecture, gratis, for his daughter's book-discussion group.[73] She remembers the talk well: "He read a paper that he wrote for about an hour and a half. He spoke of Nabokov's writing, his genius, and his work in a more admiring way than he had spoken in private. The paper presented a great deal of respect; in private there were sometimes . . . complaints and he sounded a little envious."[74]

In the middle of all this activity, Szeftel heard the news of Nabokov's death, which truly stunned him. That Nabokov, this "eternally young" gods' favorite, should be dead defied all logic as far as Szeftel was concerned. "It is surprising to me, for I have always considered Nabokov as physically indestructible," Szeftel recorded in his diary on July 15, 1977.[75] "Nabokov's sudden death on July 2 in Switzerland," he wrote in a different entry. "How did it happen? . . . . We have drifted apart completely since N. left Ithaca, but we were pretty closely connected before . . . Thus, people of my generation disappear . . . he was 78 . . . I wonder when my turn will come: 75 and 78 are close numbers."[76] Several days later he sent Véra Nabokov a letter of condolence and received a formal acknowledgment: "Mrs. Vladimir Nabokov and Dmitri Nabokov are deeply touched by the expression of your sympathy on the occasion of the death of Vladimir Nabokov. Montreux, July 1977."[77]

5 / Life After Nabokov

> Strange: I am constantly haunted by the realization of a threefold
> deficiency—love of women, ... material success, ... significant
> scholarly achievement.... Only three more years left until I
> retire, and how many more years to live, I don't know.... One
> thing is clear: I am totally alone. No one cares how I feel.
>
> Marc Szeftel

Nabokov ended *Pnin* with a picture of the protagonist's little sedan
"spurt[ing] up the shining road, which one could make out narrowing to a
thread of gold in the soft mist where hill after hill made beauty of distance,
and where there was simply no saying what miracle might happen" (*Pnin*,
191). Here the roads of Pnin and Szeftel definitely diverged, for when Szeftel
moved to Seattle, where he would live out the rest of his life, he found mists
and hills aplenty, but very little of gold and miracles.

As with his 1945 offer from Cornell, Szeftel in 1961 was not the University
of Washington's first choice among top Russian historians. One member of
the history department, Donald W. Treadgold, a prominent Russian historian and, at the time, editor of the *Slavic Review*, originally wanted the
search committee to offer the position to Gustave Alef, Szeftel's one-time
student, who was teaching in neighboring Oregon.[1] At least one of Treadgold's colleagues, Scott Lytle, was for one reason or another, opposed to
Alef's candidacy, and, as a compromise, the department decided to go with
Oswald Prentiss Backus of the University of Kansas. After a long delibera-
tion, however, Backus declined the offer, so the department found itself
having to act lest it be forced to postpone the hiring till the following year.[2]
On March 29, 1961, Treadgold wrote to George Vernadsky, the medievalist
at Yale who had worked with Szeftel on *La Geste Du Prince Igor'*, explaining
the situation to him: "Unhappily, as I am sure you know, Backus finally
decided to refuse our offer. ... We are still, naturally, seeking to fill the post.
Rather unexpectedly the name of Marc Szeftel has entered the picture. He is
59, which would give him ten or eleven years with us, if his health holds out,
before retirement. I ask if we may ... impose on you to write us a brief
evaluation of his scholarly competence and character."[3]

On April 9, W. Stull Holt, Acting Executive Officer of the Department of History at the University of Washington, got an informal letter from classics professor Harry Caplan, Szeftel's colleague at Cornell, with a warm recommendation. "1. Good men in the field of early Russian history are extremely rare in this country. 2. I have read some of his work, which to me seems sound and solid. 3. He knows thoroughly the Slavic languages and French, as well as other languages of Europe. 4. He is pleasant, mentally alive, good company, comes in occasionally for a visit. 5. Enjoys a good reputation as a cooperative colleague. . . . Gates and Marcham praise him highly to me. 6. He is serious, learned, he prizes his dignity, and expects considerate treatment. 7. As a teacher, he is hard-working, competent, expects his students to master thoroughly the basic facts."[4]

Szeftel came for a campus visit during the last week of April. On May 9, 1961, he got a letter, signed by Holt and George E. Taylor, Director of the Far Eastern and Russian Institute, officially offering him the job. According to Kitty Szeftel and Gardner Clark, Szeftel merely intended to use the offer to get a substantial raise from Cornell. With that in mind, he went to see Knight Biggerstaff, who was his chair at the time. Much to Szeftel's astonishment, Biggerstaff congratulated him, shook his hand, and wished him the best of luck at the new place.[5] Having his "bluff" backfire on him, Szeftel had little choice but to accept the offer from the University of Washington, which he did on May 30[6] (only one day before Backus called Treadgold at seven in the morning to say that he had reconsidered his decision and was ready to accept the offer).[7] More than thirty years later, Biggerstaff still thinks it was the right decision and is rather blunt about why the department at Cornell decided to let Szeftel go: "We thought we could do better." Biggerstaff also remembers that George Taylor "chided" him in later years "for selling Szeftel to them."[8]

"You will have much in Seattle to be grateful for," a former colleague wrote to Szeftel in October of 1961, "including the absence of Ithaca winters, the long growing season, and the marvelous scenery at your backdoor."[9] But soon after his arrival in the Northwest, Szeftel began to regret leaving both Cornell and the East Coast. The "marvelous scenery," which included majestic snow-capped mountains and deep blue lakes, left him indifferent. He pined for good bookstores, good museums, and even good coffee and cafés, for, back in the sixties, Seattle was yet to develop the kind of gastronomic and cultural sophistication which it now boasts. And while Szeftel was still angry with Cornell,[10] the University of Washington was not exactly proving to be what he had hoped for. (In this respect, the fictional Pnin was much luckier with his new place of employment.)

In the spring of 1961 when the Department of History wooed him, Szeftel had been rendered almost unrecognizable by the heaps of praise bestowed on him in the search committee's letter to the dean. Szeftel was, the dean was assured, "one of the foremost historians of Russia presently active in any country. . . . profoundly cultured and broadly informed, with an active wit, a penetrating sense of humor, and good judgment."[11] Perhaps they believed what they said (thus setting themselves up for a huge disappointment, which developed almost immediately upon Szeftel's arrival on campus), or were afraid they would not be able to hire anyone that year. In any case, as an incentive for Szeftel to join their faculty, the department, while not offering him a significantly higher salary than Cornell's, showered him with substantial "extras": "a research grant of at least $2,500 for the summer months and also some assistance in travel and probably an occasional quarter off for research." It was further stated that "The summer salary . . . will continue until your retirement" and that the university was "willing to guarantee up to an additional $400 per annum . . . to cover additional medical expenses that are incurred in your leaving Cornell."[12]

Several days after Szeftel accepted the offer, George Taylor, who had been responsible for finalizing Szeftel's appointment, got an angry letter from Philip W. Cartwright, the associate dean of Social Sciences, who complained that Szeftel had been promised much too much. The University, Cartwright asserted, had no business guaranteeing Marc Szeftel an annual summer salary or paying for his additional medical expenses.[13] Taylor readily repented: "[H]ow do I get off the spot? I accept your rap on the knuckles, but do we need another letter to Szeftel? Or what?"[14] Without much explanation or any apology, Szeftel's summer support was discontinued soon after he arrived in Seattle, and thus began the long and tortuous history of Szeftel's salary disputes and grievances at the University of Washington.

As Szeftel quickly found out, his salary was the lowest among the full professors in the department, with top salaries exceeding his by more than one third.[15] Being in age the most senior professor on the faculty, he felt even more upset over the discrepancy. As at Cornell, Szeftel's promotion in subsequent years was painfully slow. In 1964, after his *Documents De Droit Public Relatifs A La Russie Médiévale* was published, Szeftel, astonishingly enough, received no recommendation for a merit increase and thus no increment to his salary. According to at least one source, Szeftel's chairman stated at the time that, since he did not read French, he could not assess the value of Szeftel's study.[16] This situation was somewhat corrected in the 1965–66 academic year, for which he received a respectable raise, yet Szeftel's salary still remained at the bottom, and even some associate professors were beginning to outstrip him in their earning power. Then, in the 1966–67 academic year, Szeftel again received no merit increase. That was the last straw. "I write to you for two reasons," he declared to Don Treadgold in a letter of February 1967:

> First, I came here in 1961 as a result of your initiative. Second, you have been the colleague with whom I have been closest associated here since then. . . . In 1961 I have hesitated whether to accept the University of Washington offer. It was a low nine month salary offer, due undoubtedly to my candor regarding my salary figure at Cornell during the interview. Still, I accepted it, for I was told by those who knew this University that three principles were honored by it which would gradually compensate for this initial deficiency. First, that this University does not know any discrimination of age in its salary policy. Second, that no discrepancy is allowed to stand between salaries of scholars of comparable seniority and achievement. Third, that yearly increments of salary honor, *above* all other services to this University, the faculty member's yearly activity adding to the University's *scholarly* record and prestige. I am sorry to say that in my case these three principles were not honored at all during the elapsed four year period. . . . I would hate to conclude on that basis that I have committed a mistake of judgment in 1961.[17]

To some of his colleagues, Szeftel's complaints sounded both excessive and unjustified. Thus, Peter Sugar, a specialist in Central European history who joined the department as an assistant professor in 1959, believes that Szeftel simply "didn't understand how our system worked here. He did not publish enough to be promoted. He did not attract enough graduate students, and he also often refused to serve on our committees." Nor did Sugar think much of Szeftel as a colleague: "I sat with him on several Ph.D. orals. I didn't enjoy it. If it was his student, every question was a leading question. If it was somebody else's—like Treadgold's or mine—it was a question to show that the student wasn't well trained." Sugar is also of the opinion that Szeftel "had very little interest in undergraduates, and whatever level was appropriate [for them] didn't concern him."[18] Many undergraduates, apparently, showed, in turn, little interest in him as a lecturer. Thus Szeftel's daughter, who visited several of her father' undergraduate lectures in the sixties, remembers that while she enjoyed them, she found herself in a definite minority: "Lots of people in the class were restless, and they were there only because they had to be. My father really resented it."[19]

The late Imre Boba, who was first a student of Marc Szeftel and then became his colleague and closest friend on campus, readily acknowledged in our 1993 interview that Szeftel was probably too "rigid" and "monotonous" to keep undergraduate students interested in his subject matter, but he also maintained that his friend and one-time advisor "was very good for graduate students," and, in general, had good reason to feel underappreciated: "They did not treat him as a senior professor. . . . His salary was below the level of full professor. . . . He was demanding equal treatment." Boba, who was himself an immigrant from Eastern Europe, strongly suspected that Szeftel's "foreignness" had something to do with the lack of proper respect and recognition. Many Americans on the faculty, he believed, felt that refugees like himself and Szeftel were already lucky to get a university job and should not be too demanding.[20] Peter Sugar, also born and raised in Eastern Europe, vehemently opposes this view: "Nonsense! I never felt that. . . . I have no complaints. There were chairmen with whom I disagreed and often, but it was not because of my nationality." Sugar says he always felt that Szeftel's "exile" from the rest of the department was actually self-imposed: "I remember towards the end of his active work here, I was amazed at a department meeting when something was being discussed and he said 'we.' He was suddenly one of us! It was a sensation to me! Finally he felt part of us and not somebody in exile, which was the impression he always gave."[21]

Whether because Don Treadgold felt responsible for having brought Szeftel to Seattle, or because he genuinely believed that his colleague was treated unfairly, he, more than anyone else, took Szeftel's complaints to heart and on a number of occasions went to bat for him.[22] "It was hazardous, perhaps," he wrote to his colleagues and Dean Cartwright several days after he received Szeftel's letter, "to bring a man of sixty, already transplanted by several thousand miles, across this country. I have done my best to maximize the usefulness of so doing. However, I must confess that his preoccupation with what he feels, with more than a simple prima facie justification, to have been discriminatory treatment in salary has impeded such efforts by me and others."[23] "I . . . know," Treadgold stated in a letter to the chairman of the History Department a year later,

> that some have expressed the view that Marc does not do many other things in addition to his scholarly work. The fact is, I think, that he does do a number of things; he is devoted to the welfare of his graduate students and to his undergraduates to the extent he thinks they show the requisite amount of seriousness; he does whatever committee jobs he is asked to perform willingly and conscientiously; if he has not been asked to do more than he has perhaps that is not entirely his fault. . . . My belief is that if Marc can be given the proper raise now, his remaining years here can be spent profitably and fruitfully; it will remove the feeling of injustice which weighs on him now and prevents his spending his energies in the best possible manner. . . . My position all along is that it makes no sense to have the old gentleman spend his remaining two or three years writing memos about his salary instead of writing in his field. This may not be a very principled position, but it is closely related to the realities of the case.[24]

Treadgold's efforts were to little avail, however, and Szeftel spent the last years of his tenure at the university still complaining about the lack of proper acknowledgment for his achievements and about inequities in salaries. He firmly believed that in this situation he was a victim of not only his foreign origin but also of his "obscure" field: "Much younger people, hardly known as scholars and little productive, are given higher salaries simply because the Chairman's system of values does not place considerable weight either on my field, or on the type of research (too intensive). . . . What should be the criterion of a value for a teacher and a scholar? His scholarly distinction, or his administrative usefulness for the Chairman? The *level* of his teaching or its appeal to crowds of freshmen and sophomores?"[25]

While Szeftel may have shown bravado (some called it arrogance) when defending his record to colleagues and the administration, privately he continued to be as ineffective in convincing himself of his "scholarly distinction" as he was in convincing others.[26] Thus he confessed to his diary in 1969 that it was "solely through my own fault [that] I missed out on a *major* scholarly contribution. I obviously have accomplished something but I could have accomplished *five* times as much."[27] He was well into his sixties now, and he felt he could no longer fool himself with an idle hope that one of these days he might still make a bold leap toward the realms of scholarly immortality.

He was also finding it harder to work. In his diary entries he lamented again and again that his memory and powers of concentration were rapidly diminishing, that he suffered from insomnia at night and then often fell asleep while reading a book in the library, that his poor hearing was giving him problems in teaching and communicating with colleagues. He wondered whether he was developing *hystérie sénile,* a condition described by Maurice de Fleury, a turn-of-the-century French physician, whose book Szeftel owned.[28] At home, too, things were very difficult. Szeftel's relationship with his son, Marc Watson, was often tumultuous and was deeply dissatisfying to both sides. Szeftel expected Marc Watson to follow in his footsteps, to show a craving for serious learning, to be less American and more European in his upbringing and tastes. Marc Watson, like many American youths at the time, followed strong ideas of his own, including conversion to Buddhism, which upset his father.

Szeftel's relationship with Kitty Szeftel was also not without its share of problems. Reading Szeftel's diaries, it becomes obvious that he respected and admired his wife. With their different personalities and backgrounds, however, Marc and Kitty's emotional relationship appears to have been rather distant, and, according to their daughter, each often felt the lack of true affection and warmth on the part of the other.[29] In the Seattle years of his life, Szeftel seems to have actively craved female attention, and, unlike Timofey Pnin, who successfully resisted similar impulses of his "aging flesh" (*Pnin,* 42), he was oddly aggressive in trying to get it. Soon after his arrival at the University of Washington, women faculty, staff, and students knew better than to ride elevators alone with him. He was, according to Don Treadgold, "a pincher, and a hugger, and a kisser."[30] Peter Sugar is more emphatic: "Oh, God! He was horrible with women! Absolutely horrible. All you had to do was to be a member of the History Department to whom the secretaries were willing to talk and you would hear constant complaints!"[31] One female member of the Slavic Department can still envision a sixty-five-year-old Szeftel chasing her around the table, trying to steal a kiss. He looked, she thought, like "an excited little boy."[32] It appears to be a general consensus that such behavior, while extremely annoying, never amounted to "anything serious." Many were puzzled, however, since these actions seemed somewhat out of character for serious, solemn, and "straight-laced" Szeftel.[33] Don Treadgold was not particularly surprised, though, since he believed that, emotionally, Szeftel was, indeed, "a little boy": "In some ways, he never grew up. He had a limited range of experience even though he'd been in many countries."[34]

Szeftel's "juvenile" exploits are sometimes featured in his diary as well. Once, for example, he recorded flirting with a young woman on a bus: "She had regular features and wore large dark glasses. All of a sudden, I found myself wanting to say something nice to her. I turned to her and said: "You, probably, have very beautiful eyes, but you covered them completely.' She smiled, took off her glasses, and revealed smallish eyes, without much beauty. I did not, however, take my words back and said: 'They are, indeed, beautiful.' My glasses were clear, and did not cover my eyes but I took them off: 'And now I will show you my eyes!' I was rewarded with a compliment: 'Blue eyes! Very beautiful.' 'Yes,' I said, 'they used to be beautiful.' When I was getting off the bus, I received one more smile. Innocent pleasures of the daring old age! I had less daring when I was a young man, and when this daring made more sense. But it's still nice to know that there is at least a small glimmer of life in me! ('sokhranilas' iskorka zhizni!')."[35] The last three sentences, with their refreshing self-irony, may carry some clues to Szeftel's impulsive behavior at the time. Burdened by intimations of mortality and poor health, Szeftel may have been seeking, if not some reassurances of virility—that, he believed, he had irrevocably lost in 1959 as a result of his prostate operation—then at least some confirmation that women could still find him physically attractive. Not able to compete successfully with his fellow men in the questions of "distinction," he was instead trying, at times too desperately, to feel appreciated by at least one of the two genders. "I always liked the female company better than male," Szeftel wrote in 1970, "and that has not changed—on the contrary! . . . But I cannot forget, that my former physical powers are no longer there . . . and I keep thinking that it's all futile: my impulses don't go beyond tenderness."[36] Whatever Szeftel's reasons were, his unwanted, and, to many, rather pathetic, passes at women did not do much to improve his stature on campus. "A lot of people thought that he was a figure of fun," according to Treadgold, and in that, it was not very different from his past image at Cornell.[37]

But it was, obviously, the very opposite of how he wanted to be perceived. Sophie Tatiana Keller remembers that her father "hated to be laughed at, as anyone does who is insecure, and he was easily offended, very sensitive. He thought it was terrible that people would make fun of other people!"[38] Keller believes her father "really resented the fact that he didn't have students who would—almost like for an Asian guru—sweep the floor to be spoken to by him, and carry his shoes. He really wanted to be worshipped."[39] Imre Boba, who felt that, in many ways, his one-time advisor never had stopped viewing him as a former student, was among the very few who treated Szeftel with utmost respect. He addressed Szeftel in a traditional Polish way, "Pan Professor," brought his coffee to the table where they were eating lunch, and, in general, showed him the kind of attention and reverence that "a big European Professor" would consider his due.[40] (In his diary, Szeftel liked to quote a friend who told him once: "In Europe, you are a Professor; here, you are just a teacher.")[41]

At some point in his career, Szeftel appears to have assumed that seniority in age might make people appreciate him as a "sage." There were, to be sure occasional moments of honor. In 1976 the American Association for the Advancement of Slavic Studies (AAASS) conferred on him the award for "Distinguished Contributions to Slavic Studies." With the award, Szeftel received a certificate praising him for his "mastery of sources and disciplined critical judgment . . . that have aroused the admiration and emulation of your colleagues."[42] Yet throughout the 1960s and 1970s Szeftel's share of professional slights far outweighed his share of professional honors, and not all of these slights were from the University of Washington. He was particularly hurt and offended by his exclusion from the 1967 Festschrift for Roman Jakobson (to commemorate his 70th birthday) published by Mouton: "three vols, of about 2500 pages . . . , written by many scholars of different nations (as many as 200). . . . I am obviously considered . . . a marginal figure. The fact that no Festschrift has appeared to honor me is different, but not to be asked to participate in honoring [a] fellow-scholar with whom I have been connected for so many years . . . and published jointly two major works and have been preparing a third one! Forgetfulness, oversight? This in itself is an index of [the] importance attached to my cooperation." He similarly bemoaned not being invited to contribute to two festschrifts for B. O. Unbegaun, whom he had known for thirty-three years and with whom he occasionally worked.[43]

In the late 1970s, soon after Nabokov's death, there were further slights on the Nabokov front. In the summer of 1978, already well into his retirement, Szeftel wrote in his diary that "[a] Vladimir Nabokov Society ha[d] been formed at Kansas, with a newsletter to be published twice a year." "I have quite a bit to contribute," he continued, "and have joined it ($2 a year)."[44] Stephen Jan Parker, who was (and still is) the editor of the *Vladimir Nabokov*

Research Newsletter (later renamed *The Nabokovian*), alerted Charles Nicol, who, with J. E. Rivers, was editing *Nabokov's Fifth Arc: Nabokov and Others on His Life's Work,* that Marc Szeftel could be a potential contributor of reminiscences. Nicol wrote to Szeftel in January of 1979, asking him if he would be interested in submitting his personal reminiscences for consideration: "Our project has already collected most of the essays we need, and our final deadline is March 1. We are, however, notably lacking in personal materials, and would welcome a contribution such as yours, on the man rather than on his literature."[45]

Szeftel was indeed interested. He immediately responded and promised an essay of 3,000–4,000 words, to be titled "Around Lolita."[46] Nicol was "delighted" but a bit guarded: "The title suggested, 'Around Lolita,' gives me some problem, since it sounds like an essay on *Lolita*—and we already have two of those! But reminiscences of that time, whether connected with *Lolita* or not, are certainly of immense interest to us."[47] Szeftel spent most of February writing the essay. Despite Nicol's concern, he was apparently not about to cut the "literature" part totally out of his piece. "I have started my work on 'Lolita' from looking over the two Field books on Nabokov [i.e., *Nabokov: His Life in Art* and *Nabokov: His Life in Part*]," he wrote on February 1, "and found quite a bit on *Lolita*'s ancestor, the novella *Volshebnik* [i.e., *The Enchanter*]."[48] Several weeks later Szeftel's essay was ready, and on February 21 he mailed it to Nicol. Failing to get an acknowledgment that the paper had been received, Szeftel wrote to Nicol in the middle of March to ascertain whether "Around Lolita" or "Lolita at Cornell," as it was now called, had safely made it into Nicol's editorial hands. Nicol wrote back on March 21, apologized for "incorrectly assum[ing] that the certified mail would assure you of the paper's safe arrival," and proceeded to detail some of his further concerns: "I am somewhat worried about certain aspects of the accuracy of the paper. The chronology seems occasionally shaky, and your manuscript contains anomalies. . . . Memoirs depend on the reliability of their narrator."[49] It was not till July 8 that Szeftel got the ultimate rejection from Nicol: "I am returning your interesting reminiscences, 'Lolita at Cornell.' Unfortunately, it did not fit in with our other essays as well as we had hoped. Your essay has some valuable information, and should be able to find a publisher. I do suggest, however, that you be more careful of the small details which, when in error, cast doubt on the whole."[50]

Szeftel had sensed the possibility of the rejection already in March, and therefore had written to Stephen Jan Parker asking him whether the *Newslet-*

ter intended to publish personal reminiscences about Nabokov. On April 2, Parker responded that they "will indeed now accept such items for publication"[51] and on April 27, he assured Szeftel that his "proposed title, 'V. V. Nabokov, My colleague at Cornell,' is just fine and the proposed length of 3,000–4,000 words is perfectly acceptable."[52] On July 24, two weeks after getting the rejection from Nicol, Szeftel sent "Around Lolita," a.k.a "Lolita at Cornell," a.k.a "V. V. Nabokov, My Colleague at Cornell," to Parker. Parker's rejection arrived in September: "After very careful consideration, I regret to say that the *Newsletter* will not be able to publish your piece . . . We find it unsuitable in regard to both style and content, and do not feel it should appear in the *Newsletter* in its present form."[53] More than fifteen years later, Parker still remembers Szeftel's essay well:

> It is a poor piece in which Szeftel, in direct quotation marks (!), gives a few snitches of dialog he presumably had with VN in the halls and elevator of the Cornell library more than 25 years earlier (!). That Szeftel's general memory is very poor is quite clear. He remarks that when he returned from sabbatical in 1960 he learned of VN's resignation from Cornell—Nabokov resigned in fall 1958, and left in January of 1959—so, unless Szeftel was on sabbatical for two years (unlikely) he doesn't even have a fix on some basic dates. How good, then, could his memory of direct quotations be? It is really an insubstantial piece. It is a piece about Marc Szeftel, not Vladimir Nabokov. I suppose he was seeking reflected glory—at least that was the shared opinion of Nicol and myself.[54]

Szeftel was stunned by the curt rejection, yet was not quite ready to give up.[55]

He decided that his next attempt at publication should take place where it all had started—at Cornell. With that in mind, Szeftel spent the following several months enlisting help and assistance in the publication of his essay from his former colleagues and well-wishers—Felix Reichmann, M. H. Abrams, Harry Caplan, and James McConkey. The latter, it seems, was finally getting the manuscript he had solicited from Szeftel after the Book and Bowl meeting, more than twenty years earlier.[56] McConkey forwarded the essay, now firmly entitled "Lolita at Cornell," to John Marcham, the elder son of Szeftel's former colleague F. G. Marcham, and, at the time, the editor of *Cornell Alumni News,* where the piece finally appeared in the November

Uriel and Anna Szeftel, Marc Szeftel's parents, circa 1902, the year that Marc was born. This picture was taken at Uriel Szeftel's photography studio in Starokonstantinov. (*Courtesy of Division of Manuscripts and University Archives at Suzzallo and Allen Libraries, University of Washington*)

The cheerful toddler: Marc Szeftel as a very young boy in Starokonstantinov, circa 1904–5. (*Courtesy of Kitty Szeftel*)

Top: Marc Szeftel (bottom), aged seven or eight, during his gymnasium years. (*Courtesy of Kitty Szeftel*)

Center: Marc Szeftel with his mother, Anna, her niece, Martha Frenette, and Martha's husband, Robert Frenette. Antwerp, 1936. (*Courtesy of Flora Sheffield*)

Bottom: A war refugee: Marc Szeftel shortly after his 1942 arrival in the United States. (*Courtesy of Kitty Szeftel*)

Kitty and Marc at their wedding on June 18, 1949. To their left are Marc's colleague, Ed Bassett, and Kitty's cousin, Susan Orr, who served as the Szeftels' witnesses. (*Courtesy of Kitty Szeftel*)

Marc Szeftel in Ithaca in the 1950s. (*Courtesy of Kitty Szeftel*)

Roman Jakobson, 1949 (*Courtesy of The Roman Jakobson and Krystina Pomorska Jakobson Foundation, Inc.*)

Véra and Vladimir Nabokov in Ithaca in the early 1950s. (*Courtesy of Dmitri Nabokov*)

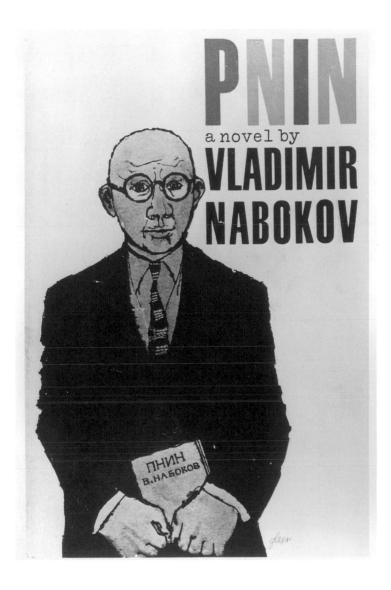

The cover of the first edition of Pnin (1957), with Timofey Pnin holding a then-non-existent Russian copy of Nabokov's novel. "The jacket is absolutely splendid. . . . I never imagined that an illustrator could render an author's vision so accurately" (Nabokov to Jason Epstein, November 13, 1956; in *Selected Letters*, p. 192). The drawing is by Milton Glaser. (*Courtesy of Doubleday, a division of Bantam Doubleday Dell Publishing Group, Inc.*)

Nabokov in Ithaca, 1957, with his novel *Pnin,* for which he had just received a
National Book Award nomination. (*Courtesy of the Department of Rare and
Manuscript Collections, Cornell University Library*)

Morris Bishop (*Courtesy of the Department of Rare and Manuscript Collections,
Cornell University Library*)

Marc Szeftel talking with a student. University of Washington, 1970s (*Courtesy of Division of Manuscripts and University Archives at Suzzallo and Allen Libraries, University of Washington*)

Marc Szeftel in his post-retirement office at the University of Washington. (*Courtesy of Kitty Szeftel*)

Celebrating his eightieth birthday: Marc and Kitty Szeftel on February 10, 1982.
(*Courtesy of Kitty Szeftel*)

Marc Szeftel's grave in Lake View Cemetery, Seattle.

1980 issue. Szeftel got a modest honorarium[57] as well as John Marcham's assurances that he and his staff "very much appreciate[d] being able to publish" the article.[58] Among Szeftel's papers one can find a memo in his hand detailing how the offprints of "Lolita at Cornell" should be distributed. First on the list, right above "myself" (i.e., a copy of Szeftel wanted to keep) and Yuri Ivask, is Charles Nicol. . . . [59]

"Lolita at Cornell" combined most of the episodes Szeftel had previously recorded in his diaries and written up in his talks. He recounted such matters as Nabokov's telling him that he was "in the process of writing the American version of 'The Magician' (*Volshebnik*) [i.e., *The Enchanter*]"; Bishop's apprehension about having to defend Nabokov because of *Lolita's* controversial subject matter; the competition between *Lolita* and *Dr. Zhivago* on the *New York Times* Bestsellers List and Nabokov's quasi Latin jape about the rivalry to Szeftel and Harry Caplan; and Véra Nabokov's unease about all the criticism *Lolita* was receiving as a "scabrous" book. The second part of the essay he devoted to things "literary," mostly the "motif of the double," and the theme of "the obsession." He also mentioned the homosexual who had been allegedly "cured . . . of his condition" by reading *Lolita*, and suggested that Nabokov had felt that in this way the novel's impact was quite "moral." After quoting his peers' reactions to the novel at the time— "the artistically beautiful description of the American scene" (Arthur Mizener); "an inflated novelette" (Gunther Thaer); "a . . . sprawled novel" (M. H. Abrams); "A la maniere de Nabokov" (Jean-Jacques Demorest)— Szeftel ended the article by revisiting the episode of Nabokov's, through Véra, denying him a copy of *Lolita's* script. He rationalized that Nabokov wanted to publish the script as a separate volume. He also linked Nabokov's refusal to the fact that his own study had never been written, and hinted that this whole episode had become at least one of the reasons why this was his and Nabokov's "last contact before Nabokov's death in 1977."[60] Szeftel's single regret after the article came out was that he had forgotten to mention M. H. Abrams's comment at the end of Szeftel's talk for Book and Bowl: "I have known that N. is a talented writer, now I think he is a genius!" "I wish I had said it," he lamented in his diary, "thinking of Vera Nabokov's feelings (my paper was *mostly* high praise!)."[61]

Encouraged and emboldened by the fact that someone found his article worth publishing, Szeftel once again seriously contemplated writing a study of *Lolita,* or of Nabokov in general. "I have been thinking about a Nabokov topic," he wrote in April of 1980. "McConkey mentioned in his letter that he very much liked my Cornell talk on N., and especially my reflections on N. and Dostoevsky, and I have noted 'N. and D.' as a topic to study. But when?"[62] He began reading materials related to Nabokov, among them *The Nabokov-Wilson Letters,* which came out a year earlier, and where he found a reference to himself as one of the "brilliant" contributors to *La Geste Du Prince Igor',* which Nabokov was so highly recommending to Wilson. Nabokov's published remark (as well as, probably, his death) appears to have softened Szeftel's general disposition towards his one-time colleague, for now he defended Nabokov from the criticisms of friends such as Yuri Ivask. Thus in May of 1980 he wrote in his diary: "From my letter to Ivask: Nabokov was primarily an aesthete and an acrobat, this is true, but underneath he harbored much humanity, which is visible in 'Lolita,' 'The Defense,' and elsewhere although he might have tried to repress it. He also has shown spirituality in his poems, and V. E. [i.e., Véra Evseevna Nabokov] may be right in saying that N.'s main theme was other-sidedness (*potustoronnost'*) [i.e., the otherworld]. If I do write an article on 'Nabokov and Dostoevsky' I will bring these two things out."[63] Szeftel also now believed that Nabokov would not be soon forgotten: "[W]ill Nabokov's glory survive? All I can say at present is that it *may* survive, both in Russian and American literature, permanently. I have *almost* said: it *will* survive!"[64]

Szeftel sent one of the offprints of "Lolita at Cornell" to Gleb Struve, who had known both Nabokov and his father quite well from their days in Berlin. In return, Struve treated him to a piquant anecdote about Nabokov's early years: "Struve tells about a private evening devoted to Nabokov's erotical (or even pornographical) poetry, read by him. Of these poems only 'Lilith' has been published in N.'s 'Poems and Problems' (and later in 'Stikhi'). This reading happened when N. was not yet married, and Struve assumes that Vera did not know these poems. Certainly not at that time, but as all N.'s papers found themselves in her hands, she might have read them, if N. himself did not destroy them. . . . What was on young Nabokov's mind before he married Vera, I do not know. Probably, quite a few frivolous things, to expect from a very handsome, young Russian. The only thing he told me about this period was his affair with the actress Gzovskaia (which did not last, for she went into N.'s arms only to make her friend, Gaidarov, jealous). But in his Cornell period, his language was prim (and still more so, that of Vera)."[65]

After 1980, Szeftel's diary entries become scarce. In 1981, he mentions that *Who's Who* has "unlisted" him after twenty years of his presence on its pages, and that Cornell University Library does not have his 1976 book (*The Russian Constitution of April 23, 1906*). He mentions a visit to a lawyer to update his and Kitty's will and complains that, while he knows that it is "an innocuous performance," he "cannot shed some idea of discomfort about it. I believe it is caused by *concretization* of the idea of death, my own, but especially that of Kitty." He also asks Don Treadgold to become his "literary executive."[66] Szeftel's interest in Nabokov, however, does not seem to have diminished during these last years. In December of 1981, he read Joseph Frank's review of Nabokov's *Lectures on Russian Literature* and was both glad and somewhat sad that someone else made public Nabokov's link to Dostoevsky: "Especially good are the three paragraphs *re* Dostoevsky, showing a certain parallelism between N. and D. This parallelism is an old idea of mine, and I wrote to Frank to tell him about it (I have also sent him a reprint of my article on 'Lolita')."[67] Frank responded, and suggested that Szeftel should republish the article in a more conspicuous manner.[68]

In retirement, when he no longer needed them for his academic advancement, Szeftel published two books in a rapid succession, yet the feeling of failure never left him. In 1983, he saw a detailed bibliography of another Russian historian (and another Marc), Marc Raeff, in *The Russian Review*. This occasioned what Szeftel himself termed "an unflattering comparison": "He has many reviews, and quite a few books. More than I have, even though he is twenty years younger. . . . He has worked more than I have, and in a more systematic fashion. What I could have contributed, I did not contribute fully (*Ia togo, chto dat' mog, ne dal polnost'iu.*) I spread myself too thin and wasted too much time in vain (*Slishkom razbrasyvalsia, i mnogo vremeni tratil v pustuiu*). And now it is too late. Pangs of guilt are tormenting me! (*Muchaiut ugryzeniia sovesti!*)."[69] Sophie Tatiana Keller remembers feeling particularly sorry for her father during these last four years of his life: "He was bitterly disappointed. He was greatly wounded that his life had been to him one long injustice. . . . All he wanted now was peace and quiet. . . . He had a great fear that after his death no one would care any more. He had no sense that his life had some enduring purpose."[70]

In his diaries, he now speaks more and more frequently of his desire to die: "I am terribly tired. . . . Everything is difficult in this old age: it's difficult to live. Live for what? Where can I get the strength? (*Sprashivaetsia, chem to zhit'? Kakimi silami?*)."[71] Living in relative isolation in the rainy Pacific Northwest did not help either: "Th[e] disappointment continues to depress me. With my health problems becoming ever more damaging, will I ever be able to fill this enormous gap, and when? The grey Seattle routine can hardly be a compensation: spiritually and intellectually I do belong elsewhere, above all to the French-speaking Europe, and I am so far from it!"[72] His health was rapidly deteriorating. Upon hearing of the suicide of his friend, historian Sergei Pushkarev, at the age of ninety-five, Szeftel wondered whether he himself should follow suit.[73]

In December of 1984, Szeftel fell down the stairs and hit his head. He experienced a series of strokes and spent several months in a hospital. He was seemingly getting better when he suffered a severe heart attack. Kitty Szeftel did not want him to die in the hospital and fought with his doctors to allow him to be taken off the respirator to be moved back to his house. She finally prevailed. Sophie Tatiana Keller, who is a nurse, moved in with her parents to take care of her father. She says she spoke French to him during these last days, and it appeared to have a soothing effect. Kitty also spoke French to him. At times she was not sure whether he was listening, but then she "would make a grammatical mistake, and his eyes would open, and he would correct it." Both Keller and Kitty asked him whether he wanted to be buried according to Jewish ritual. He said he did not. Keller felt, however, that deep inside he really wanted to, so she kept asking, and he kept saying "No."[74] Even deeper inside, he may not have been able to forgive the rabbis in Warsaw for having taken almost every franc he earned in Belgium to grant him an annulment.

Marc Szeftel died on May 31, 1985. A simple ceremony was held in Kitty Szeftel's Episcopal church, even though he never officially belonged to it. He is buried near Seattle's Volunteer Park, which overlooks the dark blue expanses of the Puget Sound and the snowy rugged caps of the Olympic Mountains—in short, the same "marvelous scenery" that had failed to impress him during his lifetime. The plaque on his grave reads, simply: Marc Moïse Szeftel. Dedicated Scholar. 1902–1985. His family thought he would have been pleased with such an inscription, because, they felt, it "summed up his life."[75] An obituary in the Seattle Times called him "the preeminent figure in medieval Russian history outside the Soviet Union."[76] Donald Treadgold, writing Szeftel's obituary for Slavic Review, described him as "first and foremost a scholar" as well as "a cultivated and civilized man." But, in another manifestation of Szeftel's poor luck, this description, the most complimentary of the whole piece, was for some reason excised by the editors.[77] By then, however, it may all have been "indifferent to the insensible body," as Timofey Pnin would say, intimately Pninizing Pushkin (Pnin, 68).

Conclusion

The history of man is the history of pain!

—Timofey Pnin

If Nabokov and Szeftel had stayed in Russia, and if the Russia of their childhood had stayed the same, their paths would probably never have crossed. At best, Szeftel could have followed in the footsteps of some of his more successful relatives and become a provincial lawyer. Nabokov's sights would have obviously been much higher: his more successful relatives habitually became not just lawyers but Ministers of Justice who hobnobbed with Russian tsars. It is a revealing comment on the history of the twentieth century that the two men found themselves in virtually identical situations when they met at Cornell in the 1940s. That their paths crossed may have turned out to be fortunate for one man and his readers, but rather tragic for the other. In Russia, Nabokov would never have become a realistic measuring stick for Marc Szeftel's sense of what his own self-fulfillment and success might have been. At Cornell, he did.

No one will ever confuse Marc Szeftel with Vladimir Nabokov. Like Cincinnatus in *Invitation to a Beheading*, Nabokov discovered that his gift and spirit might soar high enough to conquer not only the new circumstances of his existence but also his physical mortality. He never doubted that he had a higher purpose in life, that no revolution could deprive him of his true riches, and that he was free to live his life as fully and meaningfully as he wished. Marc Szeftel's personal history appears to have been, indeed, "the history of pain": his tragic losses, constant wanderings from place to place, as well as his lack of clearly visible talents, recognition, and material success caused serious doubts as to the larger meaning of his presence on earth, and this weighed heavily upon him throughout his life.

In the long run, Nabokov's and Szeftel's relationship was much like that of VN and Pnin in the novel. Szeftel did eventually turn Nabokov into a larger-than-life, almost superhuman being, and while he was in awe of Nabokov's success and vitality, he also resented and painfully envied him. Like Pnin, Szeftel had integrity, moral convictions, and a devout commitment to scholarly pursuits. Like Pnin, he was also, undoubtedly, vastly superior in those qualities to many who made him into a figure of fun. Unlike Pnin, however, he never possessed enough self-confidence to rise above his tormentors and drive off into the misty sunshine where miracles could still happen. Pnin found his niche, his "comfort zone," in a place far away from both Waindell and VN. Szeftel tried but did not succeed.

While writing this book I often found myself wishing I could do with Szeftel's life what Nabokov had done with Pnin's—to balance the "sacred" and the "profane," to give it its share not only of tribulations but also triumphs. But fate dealt much more cruelly with Szeftel than did Nabokov with Pnin. Despite VN's protestations to the contrary ("Some people—and I am one of them—hate happy ends"), Nabokov, after all, liked happy endings, especially for those of his creations about whom he had learned to care. Thus, he made Cincinnatus overcome death, spared Krug the agony of loss and defeat by dissolving his mind into blissful madness, and caused Pnin to triumph over those who used him as fodder for their own ego-boosting.

Herein lies the difference between the writers of fiction and the rest of us. *Pniniad* is in many ways my tribute to this special power of fiction which takes control over the ordinary and transforms it into the extraordinary. It is also my tribute to Nabokov, who was one of the best practitioners of this kind of fiction in the twentieth century. Yet, even more, I like to think of this book as my tribute to Marc Szeftel and the human pain that his life embodied but could never transcend—much of it being the collective pain of his whole generation and probably his whole age.

APPENDIXES

From Marc Szeftel's Archive and Writings

Appendix 1
Szeftel's "Intellectual Autobiography"

Szeftel's "intellectual autobiography," which he wrote in the 1970s and 1980s, is not in the archive but was given to me by his son, Marc Watson Szeftel, who had partially edited it. Szeftel's own original of the autobiography has been, apparently, lost. The document we now have breaks abruptly around 1916. The original autobiography was probably much longer, for Szeftel noted in his diary on October 22, 1977, that he had "completed the story of my intellectual development up to 1945, when I started teaching at Cornell." Since the autobiography as I received it had already been "tampered" with, I had no choice but to edit it further, mostly eliminating obvious inaccuracies of the kind that are impossible to imagine as having existed in the lost original. It is also published here in an abridged version.

In his diary entry of September 9, 1976, Szeftel explains why he chose to write an "intellectual autobiography" rather than a more personal one: "I should, finally, start writing my autobiography, but only an intellectual one. The rest I don't want to recall, even a few pleasant events. The unpleasant is too painful to recall, and I had much of that, as I also had much of what retroactively I would want to change." In another diary entry, the same year, he wrote: "I have time left . . . to record *the most essential* of what I have experienced on an intellectual plane. I am reluctant to revisit what I have lived through non-intellectually. Why dig out things from the past? If I had talent (like Nabokov, for example) than it would have been different. As it is, I am afraid I would tell my story awkwardly."[1]

INTELLECTUAL AUTOBIOGRAPHY

There is no pedigree in my case. My father was a photographer, first in a small Ukrainian town, Starokonstantinov (where I was born), then in Lublin, Poland, and finally in Antwerp, Belgium. The name Sheftell (not so rare among the Lithuanian Jews) seems to be a diminutive of Sabbatai (Shabsai in Hebrew). There were other lines of the same name (not consanguinal, as it seems): the Sheftells of Shklov and those of Slutsk. Those of Shklov descended from the famous XVIth century cabalist Shelo (from the initials of his book Shnei Lukhoth Habrith, i.e., the Two Tables of Covenant, revered among the Hassidim). No kinship is possible in this case, however desirable: we belonged to the Israelis, i.e., the lay descendants of Israel, while Shelo was a Levite; his progeny carried the name of Horwitz. Also the Slutsk Sheftells had distinction, but a modern one: Mikhail Isakovich Sheftell, a prominent civil lawyer in St. Petersburg and a deputy to the First Duma was one of them.

My father did not have the benefit of formal schooling, but his Russian was flawless in speech and writing. He must have been self-taught, for they spoke Yiddish at home, and obviously he put considerable effort into it. He spoke Russian without any Jewish accent, and as he had not typically Jewish looks he was taken for a Russian intellectual most of the time. There were books at home and cultured conversation. My mother had to leave school at 16, but her Russian was also fluent and literary, although she had a very slight Jewish accent. Her features were regular and rather Jewish. Her correspondents praised her letters for their literary polish, but on the whole, my sense is that my father was more cultured and erudite than my mother. She did not know Hebrew, which my father wrote and even spoke well.

I do not know very much about my paternal lineage. My father was born in Kiev in 1874, where my grandfather was an accountant in a sugar mill, and at some time the keeper of a small inn. My paternal grandfather visited Starokonstantinov when I was a child, and I vaguely remember his going away. I must have been very young at that time, a small child, for nothing else stuck in my mind. But his portrait hung in our living room and I looked at it many times: everyone noticed my very close resemblance to him (also to my father, who, however, was much better looking than either of us: he greatly resembled Leonid Andreev). I heard, however, certain things about my grandfather which impressed me.

He was a very religious man, and, as my father was saying, faith gave him great enjoyment and impressive patriarchal features in the Old Testament sense. Two instances of the depth of this faith were quoted by my father. My grandfather's employer, a big Jewish businessman, owner of a sugar mill, was accused of an illegal financial action. The investigative judge called my grandfather as a witness, but in all conscience he could not quote anything to his employer's benefit. The judge insisted, and even pointed out that out of loyalty to his employer my grandfather should testify favorably for him. He could not, however, sway his testimony, in spite of the obvious threat to his livelihood. Another instance was grandfather's behavior during a Jewish pogrom (one of the several Kiev pogroms, I do not know which—it might have been that of 1881). My grandfather was liked by his Christian neighbors, who, to protect him and his family, put out icons in front of his house to show that the house was Christian. It was obviously not true, while my grandfather's Jewish religion would not admit any travesty. He was not at home when the icons were placed. When he returned and saw them, his first gesture was to remove them ("I do not want any help from him [sc., Christ]," he said) and to start praying, an extremely dangerous challenge! Fortunately the house was, for some reason, spared by the hooligans. My great-grandmother, however, became stone deaf in this pogrom: she had hidden in a barrel, and hammer blows on the barrel completely ruptured both eardrums. What was the extent of my grandfather's religious erudition I cannot say, but he must have had some. After his death, an almost complete Mendelssohn's translation (with a commentary) of the Bible, book by book, was brought from Berdichev (to Lublin, I believe), many volumes. The commentary is quite enlightened, written in a beautiful Hebrew. It is surprising that such a pious man had in his library such an "heretical" work.

I also knew my paternal grandmother, who visited us in Lublin sometime before World War I, coming from Berdichev where my grandparents moved from Kiev, but I cannot locate in my memory any closer contact with her. She was a very pious woman, I remember, while our household was almost completely free of religion; how my mother dealt with this situation I do not know, but it was probably difficult for both of them.

My father had four sisters, and an older brother who lived in Kiev. I visited my uncle in Kiev when I was eight or nine—1910 or 1911. He had no children; this was the only time I saw either Kiev or my uncle. I remember quite vividly what I saw of Kiev during this three-day visit, especially the monuments, seen from afar. I was keenly conscious of my status as a Jewish child in the city. My father spent the first 21 years of his life in Kiev, but as a Jew, he was not allowed to live there once he had left, or even to appear there without permission, which was difficult to obtain. This is why we did not dare stay more than three days in my father's native town! My uncle's haberdashery was in the center of the city, on Bol'shaia Vasil'kovskaia, not far away from St. Sophia, and I once yielded to the temptation of taking a walk there, which is how I was able to catch a glimpse of the church. There was considerable panic when my absence was noticed, and I was severely admonished for exposing myself to arrest for being in Kiev illegally.

Although, as a historian of the Duma period, I try to be as objective as possible, probably bending over backwards to see positive features in the Russian pre-revolutionary development, even in the monarchy itself, it is difficult for me to discount these memories. The Soviet state that has replaced the Russian monarchy has certainly been bad in many ways, and in some respects much worse than the monarchy (especially during its brief constitutional period). Nonetheless, one cannot whitewash the horrible system of persecution to which the Jewish people were subjected under the Empire! So many unjust sufferings, and so much energy wasted: both the Government's energies and those of the Jews were stifled and frustrated.

My uncle was killed on the streets of Kiev when Denikin's forces entered the city in 1919. I remember my father, who was visiting me in Warsaw, suddenly crying over the Jewish paper where the victims were listed by name. My uncle was killed by those brutes as a Jew in their moment of triumph over the Communists. The Jews themselves were victimized by the Communist regime, since the majority of them operated small businesses, and were persecuted as capitalists. Hatred of Jews was latent in Russia, however, especially in Kiev, and the anti-Communist propaganda blamed the non-Christian Jews for the rise of Communism. The triumph of the White Army meant destruction for my uncle, after he had been financially obliterated by the Communist decrees.

On my mother's side (she was a Kovner) there was much more distinction. She was born in Wilno (in Lithuania, at that time a part of the Russian Empire), also in 1874. Her father was a solicitor later in Vitebsk. There was a considerable knowledge of Hebrew in the family (my maternal great-grandfather was a "melamed," a teacher of religion; his mother's name was Boiarin), and my grandfather published articles and poetry in Hebrew. There was a poem written by him celebrating, in Hebrew verse, the advent of Emperor Alexander III. My grandfather's loyal poem drew the Government's attention, and one day an official appeared in his modest office asking him what award he would desire for it. My grandfather asked for a free subscription to the *Gubernskie vedomosti* (an official paper)! My mother commented that he was obviously not aware of realities: he could have asked for free education for his children. I do not have his picture now, but he bore a striking resemblance to Freud.

I never met my maternal grandfather (he died before I was born), but my mother told me much about him. He had the reputation of a very good lawyer, but had little practice, for people were afraid to contact him. If the case was not to his liking, he used to send the client away with a sermon on what is right or wrong. So there was poverty and no possibility of giving secondary education to all the children. The son (the only son) became an attorney, but not all the daughters could finish school. My mother's older sister Hinda (Henriette) completed her secondary education and went to Paris to study medicine (no such possibility existed at that time in Russia for a woman, especially a Jewish woman). She lived there in misery, but became a practicing doctor, having married a Frenchman, Louis Delaruelle. My mother told me that they got acquainted on a bridge in Paris, when he saw her about to commit suicide. They had four children, two girls and two boys. My mother's younger sister Rachel (Aunt Ona) also finished the gymnasium, but in her university years she married a Russian engineer, son of a baptized Jew who kept the name of Rosenberg. We visited them and their two school-age children in Smolensk in the fall of 1914. As for my mother, she had to leave school at the age of 16 and learned photography as a profession. She took a job with a Smolensk photographer, where she met my father.

Of the three brothers representing his generation of the Kovners, my grandfather was the least distinguished one. His brother Savielli achieved distinction as a historian of medicine. We had in our library at home several volumes of a history of medicine by him, published by the Kiev University Press. He also obtained a prize for his book on Spinoza. The other brother, Albert, had a stormier existence, described by himself in a published autobiography. I don't remember its exact title, but I think it was *Vokrug zolotogo tel'tsa* (Around the golden calf). He started as a Hebrew publicist with positivist views and made enemies by his criticism of the Jewish intellectual authorities of the 1870s. Then, when he had a modest position in a St. Petersburg bank, he was driven by pity for a young woman sick with tuberculosis and without money. Under the influence of Dostoevsky's *Crime and Punishment*, he took the bank's money for her and was arrested on his way abroad. He received a sentence of several years, with deportation to Siberia afterwards. Liberated from jail, he applied for permission to return to European Russia, but the Jewish community of Wilno gave a negative opinion concerning him. Then he remembered the prosecuting attorney (N. Muraviev, later Minister of Justice) had told him after his trial that if he needed help after having completed his sentence, to contact him. So he wrote to him, and was told to embrace Orthodoxy as a prerequisite for this help. By that time, in the Siberian town where he lived, he had developed an attachment to a Russian woman who was Orthodox. To marry her and to get out of Siberia, he accepted Muraviev's advice. Not only was he then able to leave Siberia, but he was appointed Internal Revenue Director in one of the Polish provinces (in Lomza), and this office he performed until his death. He is buried there, in the Orthodox part of the cemetery. There are plays by him, written in Russian under the pseudonym of Korner. When in prison in Moscow and waiting for trial, he wrote a series of letters to Dostoevsky, published by the latter in his "Dnevnik pisatelia." Salo Baron wrote about him in his *The Russian Jew* as one of the "Famous Converts."[2]

Starokonstantinov was a predominantly Jewish town, but its main cultural influence was Russian. There was a Russian-Orthodox church not far away from the place where we lived, on the same Aleksandrovskaia street, with a small garden, which probably accounted for the name "Green Church" (*Zelenaia tserkov'*). Its modest inside made upon me the impression of darkness and disorder and it did not appeal to my childish mind. But we children used to run up and down the wooden belfry next to the church. Once I even ventured to stir the great bell of the belfry to see how it worked. I then ran down the stairs, but was noticed by the priest, who had come out to see what was going on. Later he asked my father in jest whether his son was contemplating a career as a sexton (*ponomar'*). This was the closest I came to participating in the activities of the Orthodox church in my home town!

The city was small 25,000 inhabitants, and hardly touched by modern technological development. It was not in my time located on a railroad line, and to get to the train, one had to travel via horse-drawn coach in one of three directions, each about 35 miles (50 *versts*) away: Polonnoe, Shepetovka, or Proskurov. It could be slow; once, I remember it took 10 hours for us to reach Shepetovka. The trip in winter (or in fall, with its mud) could be quite uncomfortable, and I remember once or twice the coachman trying desperately to get the coach out of the snow, with the help of some of the huskier passengers. On some occasions horses had to be changed, and this meant stopping in modest, ill-kept inns (*Korchma*) on the way, usually Jewish-owned. Woods had to be crossed, silent and forbidding with the approach of night, and I thought of bandits who might lurk in the shadows. It was easy to miss the train and, as there were no more than two trains a day, this meant long hours of waiting in the station, sometimes at night, sleeping on the benches.

Trains appeared to me at that time as symbols of brightness and light, as did streetcars, which I saw later on in Kiev, Smolensk, and Vitebsk. Neither streetcars nor electric lights existed for the public in our isolated city. Streets were lighted by kerosene lamps, and there was real excitement when tall lamps with incandescent bulbs were erected, symbol of higher civilization, shortly before we left Starokonstantinov forever. Gas had not yet come to the city, but there was already a movie theater where I remember seeing comedies by Max Linder (French) and Glupyshkin (Russian). The town was slowly moving toward progress, however, and the boarded sidewalks (holes, dangerous ones, in them) on our street, one of the two main streets, were being replaced by flagstones, another symbol of higher civilization.

There were, however, bookstores and libraries, good lending libraries, in that town, and books were being read as well as good Russian liberal newspapers, coming from Kiev, Moscow, or St. Petersburg. I became an avid reader early in life, and browsing in those libraries gave me great enjoyment. What did I read? All manner of books—those for children and those for adults. *Little Lord Fauntleroy,* Henri Malot's *Sans Famille* (translated into Russian as *Rene Malagan,* it made a tremendous impression on me), Mark Twain's *The Prince and the Pauper,* in Russian translation of course. Also the history of Poland (translated into Russian) by W. Smolenski; my father saw me with this book and made me discuss it with a Polish landowner who visited my father on business and who was, it seems, impressed by a Jewish boy reading a Russian book on Polish history. Something more refined than the simple features of the Russian language struck me in those pages, and I found it very attractive. I had a similar impression, when once I found myself in a Polish church with its statues and baroque architecture, more ornate than other structures. I must have been very young at that time, and probably was led to the church by a Roman Catholic nanny, but the memory of this impression is still with me as my first contact with Western culture, however remote.

Our contact with the Jewish culture, particularly mine, was only superficial. The family language was Russian, and I learned Yiddish much later in Poland. Russian books were read, as well as Russian newspapers. Most of our acquaintances were Jewish (there were also Russian acquaintances among the teachers of the gymnasium), but there were only a few people among them with strong Jewish cultural interests. I attended synagogue with my father on the three great holidays of the year. We never missed the celebration of Passover at home, and occasionally we observed the Purim customs or the Hanukkah customs, but my father kept his business open on Saturday and rarely attended synagogue on the Sabbath; and our cooking at home was not according to ritual.

My family's overall lifestyle differed markedly from that of the typical Russian or Polish lower middle class. My parents did not drink, except for wine on the eve of the Sabbath and at festivals; hard liquor was avoided altogether. Neither Mother nor Father smoked. My parents' language was spotlessly clean; I never heard them utter a profanity, even in great anger. Nor did I hear an off-color joke in my home. I am firmly convinced that neither of my parents were unfaithful to their marriage, although my father probably had the opportunity, being an exceptionally handsome man.

I had one brother, three years my junior, and one sister, seven years younger than myself. My sister Tatiana, who resembled me greatly, died at the age of eight from tubercular encephalitis, an incurable disease at that time. There was no tuberculosis in the family, and the disease was explained by my sister's great consumption of milk, which was not pasteurized in Poland in 1917. The loss of this only daughter, a beautiful and bright child, affected our family and friends tremendously. An immense crowd followed her casket at the funeral.

My friends were mostly Russian-speaking Jewish boys, but there were also Christian boys and girls among them. One thing, however, preserved the cultural tie with Judaism: there were Hebrew lessons at home, once or twice a week, which continued until I began attending Polish school in Lublin at the age of 14. My father cared a great deal about this aspect of my education and bought Hebrew books for me. Once, on returning from Kiev, he brought me two presents: Kahane's big Russian-Hebrew dictionary (Kahane, later City Librarian of Tel Aviv, was a distant relative), and Berkovich's short stories in Hebrew. I don't remember whether these stories were Berkovich's own tales or translations into Hebrew of his father's stories. (His father was Sholom-Aleichem.) I was only moderately interested in Hebrew, enough to keep it up, but not to extend it much, and most of this early teaching receded from memory. However, after 60 years, I am still able to read the Old Testament, albeit with frequent reference to a dictionary. In 1926, ten years after giving up the study, I was able to speak Hebrew, when in Antwerp (by now I have lost this ability).

I felt more at home with Jewish history than I did with Hebrew literature, both prose and poetry (a little later). Above all I knew one thing, having felt it very acutely: for no valid reason at all, I did not have the same rights as my Christian playmates and schoolmates, although they were the same human beings—no right to live in Kiev, *numerus clausus* restricting my school possibilities; no right to a position of public service; no right to own land; etc., and much less physical security than that of my Christian friends, for there were in the recent past organized pogroms of Jews. When I ask myself what I owe to my Jewish background, two things come immediately to my mind. On the positive side, the intense appeal of things intellectual ; on the negative side, the permanent feeling at that time that, as a Jew, I would not be given the normal chance of a human being to be free and secure, to assert one's potentialities. Negative side? There was also a positive aspect in this predicament: it developed my sensitivity to all human injustice—social, political and racial.

In August 1914, I found myself with my parents in Smolensk. Our stay lasted only two weeks. This city was beyond the Pale of Jewish settlement, and my father received permission to stay there only for that period. There was a very small Jewish community in Smolensk, which included my uncle, who was a lawyer by training but was barred from practicing law because he was a Jew, and who made his living as a director of an insurance agency. My father did not see much opportunity here for his photography business. So we moved to nearby Vitebsk, in the Belorussian territory within the Pale, and stayed there until the danger subsided. It was different from Poland and the Ukraine, although the Jewish milieu was similar. My acquaintance with "genuine" Russia did not amount to much in this way, and I never got to know the core of the Russian village.

These three months in the Vitebsk gymnasium did not affect my education significantly. There were minor details, such as different textbooks. The Russians were tightening the school rules among non-Russian populations, and the discipline was not as strict. The one meaningful novelty was the good Russian spoken by my Jewish schoolmates in Vitebsk. In Lublin my friends spoke Polish or Yiddish among themselves; at the time I spoke neither, and because of my Russian language, I associated mainly with Orthodox boys. By contrast, in Vitebsk, I was among Jewish boys almost exclusively. I found this natural, and at that point, if asked whether I was Jewish, I would reply "yes" without hesitation—my legal status, especially, made it obvious. However, I would also have answered "yes" when asked if I was Russian, because of language and schooling. There was no conflict in loyalties in my mind between the Jewish and the Russian.

We were in a difficult position, since the war fanned the flames of anti-Semitism in Russia. In school, the new inspector (vice-principal) Iarema, a distinguished Latinist but an excessively harsh disciplinarian, would not miss an opportunity to show his anti-Jewish feelings. When a Jewish boy committed a minor infraction of the regulations, Iarema remarked, before the entire class: "It is amazing that if anything wrong is done, it is either a -man or a -berg." (The boy's name was Fishman or Rosenberg, while many Jewish names had a German sound.) This was a new motif: I had never heard Iarema's predecessor, the physicist Kurbas, say anything similar.

I was surrounded by Russian boys, some of them close friends, who were understandably carried away by patriotic feelings, and I was on their side, with considerably less intensity. When I was asked as usual what books I would like as an award for my good studies in the previous year (I was primus), I offered the money of this award to be used for a military hospital bed. This initiative of mine became a rule for other primuses—it is possible that they cursed me for setting this example—and Iarema came to my class to congratulate me, saying, "We hope that in the future you will deserve still more of the fatherland!" This remark, addressed to someone whose rights as a citizen were severely curtailed on account of his birth, was quite ironic; my mother commented on that when I told her about it. Some of my teachers believed, however, that the cause of Russian political freedom depended upon military victory, and part of this freedom was Jewish equality.

This view was held by my history teacher, a charming person by the name of Firsov, who certainly was not anti-Semitic. This was our first year of Russian history, using S[ergei] Platonov's textbook. (This was a superior work, which I later used extensively in the preparation of my lectures for sophomores at Cornell.) We had just finished the study of the heresies under Ivan II, the most of whom were the "Judanizers." Firsov asked a student named Glinsky to explain this term. Glinsky replied: "Their leader was a *zhid*." (Zhid was an ethnic slur referring to Jews.) Firsov blushed and said, "*Zhid* is a swear-word. This nation is called *evrei*." (*Evrei* was the official Russian name for Jews.) Firsov definitely had decent feelings toward my co-religionaries.

The study of Hebrew influenced me in several ways. I was certainly taken by the great beauty of the language, as I came to know it through Biblical prose and in modern Hebrew poetry and literature. I have not read the entire Old Testament, however; we went as far as Amos, first of the minor prophets. I also read some of the Mishna, probably at my own request; I had been told it was written in beautiful Hebrew. We went no further than this into the Jewish religious legacy: the Talmud, the Midrashim, the Tosephtas and all treatises remained unknown to me, with the exception of the Hagadah, the legendary part of the Talmud, which I greatly enjoyed, and the "Wisdom of the Fathers," a collection of Talmudic ethical maxims. Under the influence of this study of Hebrew I probably became open to Zionist ideas, like so many Jewish boys, by the time the problem of loyalty became acute following the departure of the Russians from Lublin.

The Yiddish milieu affected me in a different manner. The Polish Jews used Hebrew for prayer, but their spoken language was Yiddish. My study brought me closer to the Jews whose daily life was reflected in the literature I was reading. Although I had the same origins as these people, I could not identify with them in any way. I felt myself to be different: if not Russian, then at least European, and certainly cosmopolitan. Jewish life did not appeal to me at all, although it called for all my sympathy, and I did not become a part of it. One aspect of the Yiddish milieu did affect me, however. Yiddish was a vehicle for socialist ideas, and these were strong in the Kulturverein. By this time I was becoming averse to all exclusive nationalist ideologies, and there was much social injustice in my surroundings. A system of thought that stressed internationalism and justice appealed to me, while its "scientific" logic proffered explanations for several complex problems. I wanted to know more, and so, along with a few classmates, I read socialist brochures, trying to penetrate the arid economic theory and Marxist dogma—not an easy task!

The October Revolution, with all its violence, opened my eyes, and my illusions gradually evaporated. When World War I ended and Polish independence was proclaimed, I was firmly on the side of the Poles and against Marxist internationalism in its Bolshevik guise. Shortly afterward, I relinquished all Marxist ideas, even the more moderate ones. An intellectual flirtation was soon ended; while it lasted, I stayed away from all political entanglements. Political activity has never held much attraction for me; its unavoidable parti-pris, intrigues and bad faith repelled me, and above all, I was put off by the internecine squabbles and infighting that are an inescapable part of politics.

Appendix 2

Correspondence with Vladimir Nabokov and Roman Jakobson

Included here are letters between Vladimir Nabokov and Szeftel, as well as notes from Véra and Dmitri Nabokov, and Morris Bishop's initial contact with Szeftel regarding the search that eventually brought Nabokov to Cornell. Also included are letters exchanged between Szeftel and Roman Jakobson concerning Nabokov and the collaboration of the three men on *The Lay*. Throughout Appendix 2, translations from the Russian are mine. Emphases throughout are Szeftel's.

THE CORRESPONDENCE OF MARC SZEFTEL AND VLADIMIR NABOKOV

1. Morris Bishop to Marc Szeftel
   On Cornell University stationery, typed. Morris Bishop was at the time in charge of the search for a specialist in Russian Literature.

28 Aug. 1947

Dear Marc:
   When you have a chance, will you call me up? We are on a Committee to do something about a Professor of Russian Literature. . . .

Yours,
Morris Bishop

2. Marc Szeftel to Vladimir Nabokov
   On Cornell University stationery, handwritten in Russian with occasional English words, such as Russian Area Study, *and* Introduction to Literature. *All English names—Morris Bishop, Bergin, and Fairbanks—are likewise spelled in English.*

103

2–26–1948

Dear Vladimir Vladimirovich,

I am writing to you in Russian instead of English (as would befit the official theme of this letter) simply because it seems to me more natural.

A question has arisen—in connection with the *Russian Area Study*—concerning a course in Russian literature *in English* which should be appropriate not only for those who specialize in language or literature but for all students who are interested in such a popular topic as Russian literature.

I had a talk with Morris Bishop and with Bergin and we came to a conclusion that the most convenient way to resolve this problem would be to offer; during next academic year, not *two* but only *one* course in Russian so that the second course on Russian literature would be of a more general nature and could be taught in English for a wider audience.[1] As to your participation in *Introduction to Literature,* it would remain the same next year (in the future it would be up to you).

As to the course in Russian, for those who are studying it or who already know Russian, Mr. Fairbanks suggested that a more general topic (among the two you had offered) would be preferable for pedagogical reasons.

Now only a technical question remains as to the title of your courses for the catalogue.

That is all. You would oblige all of us, dear Vladimir Vladimirovich, if you agree and specify the titles of the courses.

Cordially,

Yours,

M. Szeftel.

3. *Vladimir Nabokov to Marc Szeftel*
   Typed, in Russian, with the titles of courses and some comments at the very end given in English.

March 2, 1948

Dear Mark Iur'evich,

Thank you for your nice letter. I will give a Russian literature course in English with great pleasure. I will say, however, with all honesty, that I would very much prefer it if that course were to replace not one of the proposed Russian courses but precisely the "Introduction to Literature" course. Russian literature is my specialty, and I teach it with great pleasure, while an incidental course in general literature, and such an elementary one to boot, appeals to me very little, if truth is to be known.

At the very outset of my letter exchange with Bishop, that is how it was supposed to be: he spoke of one course on Russian literature in English, and the other two in Russian. Later, when it had been decided to cancel the English course, I was asked to teach a General Survey course in its stead. I agreed to this reluctantly, only because it seemed to me that since the course "in translation" had been cancelled, I could be most useful in teaching that one. But now, when the course "in translation" has been restored, I would really like to go back to our original plan. Perhaps you could succeed in talking Bishop and Bergin into it. Assure them that with such offerings, I could give my audience much more. I do hope you will manage to convince them.

As to my days and hours, the only thing of importance to me is that my lectures should not start before eleven, and that they should go one after another, with a break of one hour between the second and the third (or, in the worst-case scenario, between the first and the second). If, however, for some reason, someone finds it more convenient that I should give my lectures not on Mondays, Wednesdays, and Fridays, but on Tuesdays, Thursdays, and Fridays, for example, or some other way; or that I should start, for example, at twelve rather than eleven, I have nothing against that either.

If my plan is accepted, then I would then offer:

101, 102. Survey of Russian Literature, etc. (as suggested in my letter to Bishop).

201, 202. Renaissance of Russian Poetry, etc. (as suggested in the same letter).

————.General Survey of Russian Literature with emphasis on the XIX century. Throughout the year. Credit————. Course given in English. Mr. Nabokov. Hours————.

Cordially,
V. Nabokov

4. Vladimir Nabokov to Marc Szeftel
    Typed in English, and handwritten in Russian.

21 March 1948

Dear Marc Yuryevich,

My Russian typewriter having broken down again, I shall write this time in English.

I am delighted that Professor Bishop does not insist on my participation in the General Survey course. Of course, I realize that, had my activity been limited to the courses given in Russian, it would have been essential for me to give one

Vladimir Nabokov
8 Craigie Circle
Cambridge 38, Mass.

21 March 1948

Dear Marc Yuryevich,

My Russian typewriter having broken down again, I shall
write this time in English.

I am delighted that Professor Bishop does not insist on
my participation in the General Survey course. Of course, I
realize that, had my activity been limited to the courses given
in Russian, it would have been essential for me to give one
course in English so as to get better acquainted with the
student body. However, I am sure that with the re-establishment
of the course on Russian Literature in English, there will be
for this ample opportunity anyway.

I have no news as to a dwelling place in Ithaca and
would be very grateful if you and Prof. Bishop could push this
matter. Many thanks for your kindness.

Sincerely,

V. Nabokov

I have had a letter from Dean de Kiewit who also does not
like the idea of the only courses in Russian Literature should
being given in Russian. I hope that the latest arrangement will
meet with his approval.

Я предложил Dean de K. ... то же, что
я писал вам и Бишопу: два курса по русски (общий и
более специальный) и один по английски (общий, с ударением на
19-ом веке). Если бы оказалось, что ... студенты, знающие
русский, ... хватают только на один курс (по-русски), я предпочел
дать, как третий курс, напр. Elem. Russian

A letter from Vladimir Nabokov to Marc Szeftel *(Courtesy of Division of Manuscripts
and University Archives at Suzzallo and Allen Libraries, University of Washington)*

course in English so as to get better acquainted with the student body. However, I am sure that with the re-establishment of the course on Russian Literature in English, there will be for this ample opportunity anyway.

I have no news as to a dwelling place in Ithaca and would be very grateful if you and Prof. Bishop could push this matter. Many thanks for your kindness.

Sincerely,

V. Nabokov

[P.S.] I have had a letter from Dean de Kiewit who also does not like the idea of the only courses in Russian Literature being given in Russian. I hope that the latest arrangement will meet with his approval.

[Handwritten in Russian] I have suggested to Dean de K. the same thing that I suggested to you and Bishop: two courses in Russian (general and more specific) and another one in English (general, with the emphasis on the 19th century). If it turns out that the number of students who know Russian is only enough for one general course (in Russian), then I would prefer to offer as my third course something like Elem[entary] Russian.

5. *Vladimir Nabokov to Marc Szeftel*
    Typed, in English, except for Szeftel's first name and patronymic, which are handwritten in Russian.

15 April 1948

Dear Mark Iur'evich,

I am immensely pleased with the lovely present you made me.[2] I am laid up with a bad cold and your book with its mass of fascinating information is a boon and a blessing.

Bol's[h]oe spasibo [Thanks a lot!]

Sincerely yours,
Vladimir Nabokov

6. *Vladimir Nabokov to Marc Szeftel*
    Typed, in Russian.

January 2, 1950

Dear Mark Iur'evich,

We both are very grateful to you and your kind wife for your cheerful Christmas Card.

As to the "Slovo," I don't have anything against Jakobson mentioning my translation (although it is far from ready yet) in the context you describe.

As you probably know our real estate business is postponed till Spring.[3]

I am looking forward to Vseslav and am very happy that your work is going so well.[4]

Happy New Year!

Sincerely,

V. Nabokov.

7. Marc Szeftel to Vladimir Nabokov
   Typed, in English.

July 2, 1963

Dear Vladimir,

It has been a long time since we have talked to each other orally or even by way of letter. I know that everything is well with you and yours; I have been getting echoes about you from Morris Bishop.

I have in a rough draft a study about your *Lolita* and would like to complete it. I feel that to do it I need the script of its film version. Would it be too much to ask you to send it to me to Seattle (you probably have known that two years ago I came over here from Cornell).

I have seen the film and have enjoyed it, as I enjoyed the book, very much. With my very best regards to you and Vera.

Sincerely yours

Marc M. Szeftel

Professor of Russian History

8. Véra Nabokov to Marc Szeftel
   Typed, in English, on a postcard with the "Hotel Bristol" logo. "Sincerely" is written by hand.

July 16, 1963

Dear Marc Yurievich,

V.V. asks me to thank you for your kind letter. He regrets that he cannot send you the screenplay of LOLITA.

We hope you like the Northwest as much as we did when we made a long stay in Ashland, Oregon. We also hope that you and your family are well and happy.

With kind regards from us both,

Sincerely,

Véra Nabokov

9. Véra and Dmitri Nabokov to Marc Szeftel
    A form printed letter. The stamp on the envelope says "Montreux 1,
    23.–7.77." On the back, the return address is given as "V. Nabokov,
    Montreux-Palace Hotel, 1820 Montreux, Switzerland."

Mrs. Vladimir Nabokov and Dmitri Nabokov are deeply touched by the
expression of your sympathy on the occasion of the death of
Vladimir Nabokov
Montreux,
July 1977

THE CORRESPONDENCE OF MARC SZEFTEL AND
ROMAN JAKOBSON

1. Roman Jakobson to Marc Szeftel
    On Columbia University stationery, handwritten, in Russian and occa-
    sional English.

October 18, 1948

Dear Friend,

I am still at Hunter, and very busy with my literary work. . . . I have just
received [a letter] from Professor A. Irving Hallowell of the University of Penn-
sylvania, [who is] Review Editor of American Anthropologist. He enthusiastically accepts my suggestion that Prof. Nabokov should "be now asked to write a
review of La Geste d'Igor'." "The next deadline for reviews that will be published
in the March-April issue is about December 15th." If Prof. Nabokov agrees, he
wants him to send the review to Dr. Alex Spoehr (The Chicago Museum of
Natural History, Chicago, Ill), to whom Hallowell is transferring the duties of
the Review Editor. Please ask Nabokov whether he is willing to write this review,
and, if he is, by when they can count on it, and I will immediately let the editor
know. Respond immediately to my university address. What's new?
Sincerely yours,
R. Jakobson

2. Roman Jakobson to Marc Szeftel
    On Columbia University stationery, typed, in English; the only Rus-
    sian phrase, bodryi ton *is transliterated and underlined by Jakobson.*

August Byzantine Congress in Brussels. I am invited as
reporter to Paris and I am writing now my paper for them
which must go during the next weeks to their printer.
When will you come to New York? My insistent request to
you xxxkx is to help maximally in the selling of the book
and in publicizing it. Under the given conditions the
book from a technical viewpoint is quite a xxx satisfactory
achievement and the contents is the best that could be
done. I sent some copies to the libraries of Russia /re-
gistered, so that I hope they will receive it/ and to several
xxxkxitxk specialists of the Slavic countries. I chose such
who presumably are not in prison and not in serious danger
of being imprisoned. Vremena!

Devotedly youfs,

Roman Jakobson

Roman Jakobson's letter to Szeftel (March 28, 1948). Handwritten in Russian: "P.S. What is your relationship with Nabokov? Should I send you a copy for forwarding to him? What do you think?" *(Courtesy of Division of Manuscripts and University Archives at Suzzallo and Allen Libraries, University of Washington)*

October 28, 1948.

Dear Friend,

I liked your letter very much for its *bodryi ton* (cheerful tone) and for the excellent news that Nabokov will review our book in the American Anthropologist and that he is translating the Slovo into English. I am sure that it will be the best among the numerous translations of the Slovo and that our common projected edition will be the standard edition. . . .

As ever yours,
Roman Jakobson

3. *Roman Jakobson to Marc Szeftel*
    On Columbia University stationery, typed, in English.

November 22, 1948

Dear Friend,

You have better connections with historians than I, may I then ask you to approach the Catholic historical review for asking F. Dvornik, formerly Professor at the Theological Faculty of Charles University, now at Dumbarton Oaks, to review La Geste. . . . Please write me how it is with Nabokov's review for the American Anthropologist and with his translation of the Slovo.

As ever yours,
Roman Jakobson

4. *Roman Jakobson to Marc Szeftel*
    On Columbia University stationery, typed in English.

Jan. 28, 1949

Dear Friend,

. . . . I think that I found a definite solution for the publication of our volume.[5] The American Folklore Society would like to publish it as the current volume of its memoirs, and so it will appear in a few months. . . .

May Nabokov's prospective translation be mentioned in the preface of the Epic Studies as one of the Igor publications in preparation? Ask him not to forget about the American Anthropologist. . . .

As ever yours,
Roman Jakobson

5. *Roman Jakobson to Marc Szeftel*
   On Harvard University stationery, typed, in English

December 8, 1949

Dear Szeftel,

Why do you not answer my letter? I need immediately your suggestions concerning my tentative list of people to whom our reprint is to be sent.... Answer immediately. You also do not mention how the question stands with Nabokov's article and Nabokov's translation.

As ever,

Roman Jakobson

6. *Roman Jakobson to Marc Szeftel*
   On Harvard University stationery, typed, in English.

January 8, 1952

I was stupified when I heard ... that you complain of having received no letter from me. After you wrote me, not long before summer, asking about your, Nabokov's, and my planned edition of the Slovo I immediately wrote you a detailed letter outlining this common work and informing you of the various news in the literature on the Slovo. When I received no answer to this letter I wrote you twice again. I informed you, among other things, of my two new studies about the Slovo which will come out during this month.... I am happy to learn ... that you, as I, are eager to cooperate and I look forward to hear from you finally and to discuss these questions with Nabokov, as well, as soon as I see him in Cambridge.[6] I have many new observations on the Slovo and its literary environment and I am anxious to discuss them first and foremost with you and Nabokov....

As ever yours,

R. Jakobson

7. *Roman Jakobson to Marc Szeftel*
   On Harvard University stationery, typed, in English.

January 31, 1952

Dear Marc,

Many thanks for your letter of January 15. Now I am definitely returning to

Cambridge and after a discussion with Nabokov I will write you all my questions and suggestions concerning our planned book. . . .

Yours as ever,
Roman Jakobson

8. *Roman Jakobson to Vladimir Nabokov and Marc Szeftel*
   On Harvard University stationery, typed in English.

December 10, 1952

Dear Friends,

I rush to inform both of you that I had a most pleasant and encouraging talk with John D. Barrett, the Vice-President of the Bollingen Foundation. I am sending you a copy of my letter to him where I sum up, according to his request, the results of our conversation. He said that he has no doubt that this volume, which he and Mr. Huntington Cairns are strongly recommending, will be accepted at the next meeting of the Foundation in early January. . . .

Yours sincerely,
Roman Jakobson

9. *Roman Jakobson to Vladimir Nabokov and Marc Szeftel*
   On Harvard University stationery, typed, in English.

January 26, 1953

Dear Friends,

I am happy to send you the letter of the Vice-President of the Bollingen Foundation, informing us that our book is accepted, and a copy of my letter to Mr. Barrett. . . . I think that both for the talking over of all the technicalities to be arranged with the publisher, and for the setting of the whole plan of our common publication, it is necessary for all three of us to meet together. Please suggest to me what will be the best place and the nearest date for such a meeting. I believe that Cambridge would be the most comfortable for such a discussion, since all the necessary material is at hand, either in my private book collection [or] in the Widener Library. Since you, Nabokov, have planned a longer visit here, and since, Szeftel, a modest support for your trip to Cambridge seems to me feasible, I propose to you to discuss this possibility.[7] The other possibility would be for all three of us to meet in New York for our discussion of the whole matter, and for a subsequent common visit to Mr. Barrett. I ask you only not to postpone your decision, and to inform me at your earliest convenience. Superfluous to add that I am most happy to be now in the position to realize with both of you this publication, which promises to be fundamental.

Yours as ever,
Roman Jakobson

10. *Roman Jakobson to Marc Szeftel*
    On Harvard University stationery, typed, in English.

February 17, 1953

Dear Friend,

Both Nabokov and I were worried at having no news from you. In the meantime I was asked to inform the publishers about our plans. Thus we discussed them, Nabokov and I, and both of us hope that you will agree with our schedule. All three of us will be editors with equal responsibility. The royalties will be accordingly distributed in three equal parts. I will, however, ask the publishers whether Nabokov's translation could not be renumerated additionally.

The book will contain Nabokov's translation published parallel with my reconstruction of the original text of the Slovo. . . . There will follow a critical edition of the Slovo with footnotes giving the spelling variants and the explanation of emendations. . . . All this will be followed by a long commentary to the Slovo, telling first all that we know about the manuscript and its history, briefly characterizing the history of the research on the Slovo, and then introducing the Slovo itself against the background of Russian and international literature, oral tradition, art, thought and the whole culture of the late 12th century. . . .

You are supposed to write the whole historical part of this scholia and pass it on to me so that I can incorporate [it] into the other parts of this commentary. . . .

Now the final and most responsible question—to what date can you commit yourself to deliver the whole material expected from you? May I suggest the end of the summer vacation, so that I could do the final job during the winter semester. The question is very important.

Yours as ever,
Roman Jakobson

11. *Marc Szeftel to Roman Jakobson*
    Typed, in English.

Dear Friend,

I have received your detailed letter of February 17, and certainly agree with the idea outlined by you. . . .

It seems to me that right here in my study I have practically all important works published on the Slovo since La Geste appeared. . . . However, if you have been keeping the bibliography of the Slovo-up-to-date, and you have been much better equipped for it at Columbia and Harvard, than myself here at Cornell, I would greatly appreciate your communication of it to me. It would greatly help me to go over it, and thus to be sure not to miss anything, and maybe get from Harvard the material I lack.

I congratulate you again on your success with the Bollingen Series. The book as you have planned it will be a new triumph for the Slovo, this time in the English-speaking world, and I will be happy to participate in it.

Yours as ever,

Marc Szeftel

12. Roman Jakobson to Marc Szeftel, with a copy to Vladimir Nabokov
On Harvard University stationery, typed, in English.

March 9, 1953

Dear Friend,

I visited the Bollingen Foundation and on the basis of your and Nabokov's instructions, I discussed with them in detail our publication and the technicalities of our contract. Here are the basic results. The first edition of our book is to appear in 3,000 copies. It is to contain about 500 large pages and 48 illustrations, partly in color, if we find suitable colored miniatures, etc. Our plan was fully accepted. . . .

The contract will be sent to us for signature not later than April. Nabokov will receive for his literary contribution (translation of the Slovo and possibly Zadons[h]c[h]ina[8] and his translator's notes) $1000, of which $500, or one half, upon the signing of the contract and the other not later than at the beginning of 1954. You and I will receive for our contribution $500 each, the first half at the signing of the contract and the second not later than the beginning of 1954. As editors all three of us (Nabokov, concerned with the English style of the whole book) will receive 10% of the royalties. . . . Both Nabokov and I, and I am sure you too, consider this contract as very favorable. The manuscript is expected by the publisher in the Spring of 1954, and is to appear a few months later. . . .

I am happy to resume our literary cooperation, which was so fruitful in the past. . . .

Yours as ever,

Roman Jakobson

3. Marc Szeftel to Roman Jakobson
   Typed, in English

March 29, 1953

Dear Friend,

I have received your letter of March 9, and must congratulate the three of us on the good conditions you have been able to obtain from the Bollingen Foundation. It seems to me also that the Zadons[h]c[h]ina will greatly increase the value of our Slovo publication. As to the suggested appendix on the Slovo in Russian and world culture, you did not express in your letter your own feeling on the subject.

Would it not be preferable to have three articles by specialists on comparative literature, painting and music, should we accept this idea? We plan a highly scholarly publication, and it means that everywhere a high level of competence would be desirable. Frankly, I am not too enthusiastic with regard to this suggestion under different conditions.[9]

I gladly agree with you and Nabokov that the contract offered to us is very favorable, and look forward to its signature. The deadline of Spring 1954 for the manuscript seems to be quite realistic. I start working on it at once. . . .

Yours as ever,
Marc Szeftel

14. Marc Szeftel to Roman Jakobson
   Typed, in English

March 28, 1954

Dear Friend:

I have been really frustrated the last two months, while working on Igor in my spare time, not to be able to exchange *viva voce* opinions and ideas with you, as we did it in New York City with such a fruitful result. Writing is different, and requires much time, and this explains the lack of my letters, although I have had much to communicate. . . .

I really am sorry not to have met the deadline of April 1. I hope not to exceed it considerably, and anyway to have everything ready by July, as the ultimate deadline, and if it is only possible, much sooner. . . .

I have seen Nabokov very little lately. All our contact with regard to Igor is represented by two telephone conversations due to my initiative. I know he is very busy, meeting deadlines, but I do not know much of his work on Igor. We have a tentative appointment in the beginning of May to discuss the Igor problems.

The Nabokov translation and the Igor text in Poggioli's edition show certain differences, if compared with the text of *La Geste*, obviously due to your work on the text at Harvard.[10] I can explain to myself these differences, but here again the lack of personal contact is a frustration. One of the reasons of my proposing a meeting to Nabokov was the desire to get more clarity on these changes. . . .

Affectionately yours,
Marc Szeftel

15. *Roman Jakobson to Marc Szeftel*
On Harvard University stationery, typed, in English.

April 14, 1954

Dear Friend,

. . . . I have a very heavy program this semester, but in my seminar devoted primarily to the Slovo, and in my private studies. . . . I have seriously continued my research on the Slovo and Zadonshchina. Moreover, . . . I was lucky enough to have interested in our work such a unique expert in medieval art as Andre Grabar, who agreed to contribute to our volume a paper on the Slovo in connection with the Russian and Byzantine art of the 12th century.[11] He delivered a fascinating lecture on this subject here at Harvard, and he writes me from France that he succeeded in making a few new discoveries in this direction. . . .

Yours as ever,
Roman Jakobson

16. *Roman Jakobson to Marc Szeftel*
On Harvard University stationery, typed, in Russian.

January 1, 1958

Dear Marc!

Happy and Successful New Year! . . . I beg you, please, get the materials for our volume ready. We have to deliver it this summer.[12] It will be a real shame if we don't do it. I am working on Slovo and Zadonshchina. When will we see each other?

Truly yours,
Roman

17. Roman Jakobson to Marc Szeftel
  On Harvard University stationery, typed, in English.

27th January 1960

Dear Marc,

. . . . I had very pleasant talks with the people of Bol[l]inger Foundation. I am looking forward to the delivery of our whole manuscript before the end of 1960. I am looking forward to discussing with you a number of technicalities and other current questions. . . .

Yours as ever,
Roman Jakobson

18. Marc Szeftel to Roman Jakobson
  Typed, in English.

December 1, 1965

Dear Roman:

It has been a pleasure to all of us to have listened to Dr. Pritsak's report about his findings concerning Igor's Tale.[13] Although I do not agree with all of them it has been most interesting and stimulating.

This brings me again to the problem of our common publication, which has been pending so long. With the revival of the controversy concerning the Tale of Igor, especially in Moscow, it would be most desirable to have our book published within the nearest future.[14] When I saw you in Paris you told me that you will be working at it, but time marches on and I wonder whether something could be done to speed up the process of publication. . . .

Yours sincerely,
Marc M. Szeftel

19. Roman Jakobson to Marc Szeftel
  On "The Salk Institute for Biological Studies (San Diego, California)"
  stationery, typed, in English.

29th June, 1966

Dear Marc:

. . . . I had a phone call from Bol[l]inger Foundation and stopped for a couple of hours in New York to talk over its representatives questions of our joint volume. I promised them to have the volume delivered in 1967–8. As soon as I hear from you I shall be happy to discuss with you some further details of our book in progress. . . .

> Yours affectionately,
> Roman Jakobson

20. *Marc Szeftel to Roman Jakobson*
     Typed, in English.

July 7, 1966

Dear Roman:

. . . . I really am happy to know that you promised to the Bol[l]inger Foundation to have the volume delivered during the next academic year. My cooperation to this effect is completely assured to you.

> Yours affectionately,
> Marc M. Szeftel

21. *Roman Jakobson to Marc Szeftel*
     Handwritten, in Russian.

2–19–78

My Dear Friend (*Druzhishche*),

I am going back to Cambridge soon and then will try to get from Pritsak, who is recovering from a serious operation, your commentary to the Slovo, which I gave him at some point in order to solicit his comments. . . . [15]

> Yours, Roman Jakobson

Appendix 3
Nabokov in Szeftel's Diaries

Szeftel's numerous diaries belong mostly to the Seattle period of his life, although there is one notebook containing entries that cover the period from 1952 to 1960. It is not clear whether Szeftel kept other diaries through the 1940s and 1950s. If he did, he probably destroyed them, for they are not among his papers at the archive, and Kitty Szeftel has no other materials of this nature in her possession. It is quite likely that Szeftel's diary-writing intensified greatly upon his arrival in Seattle, since he felt even more lonely and isolated than he had at Cornell. The most detailed and exhaustive diaries, which contain virtually daily notes, belong to the period of 1968 to 1980. By then Szeftel had developed a rule of at least "100 words . . . every day."[1]

Most of his entries are in English or Russian, but occasional entries are in French or Polish. Szeftel tends to use Russian as his "personal" language to reminisce about his past and his childhood or to describe his emotions, feelings, and everyday events. "Russian," he wrote in 1969, "is my first language, as well as the language of my parents, and when I discuss intimate subjects, it is easier for me to do so in Russian."[2] His usage is not totally consistent, though, and some of the more intimate subjects, such as his feelings about his family or approaching old age, are also discussed in English. Toward the end of his life, however, Russian begins to predominate as the general language for all his entries.

The entries about Nabokov occur in both languages. The emphases throughout are Szeftel's. There are many more entries on Nabokov than given here, but they tend to be repetitive. I have also tried to limit this appendix to entries of general interest that have not been discussed or quoted in the main text. Some names have been replaced by initials, while others have been spelled out when only initialized in Szeftel's text.

1968

January 8, in English
Conversation with [Yuri] Ivask a few days ago on *Russian literature.* Adamovich's appraisal of Nabokov as a greatly talented "clown."[3] Still, he

considers Nabokov as the most outstanding writer of the Russian emigration (the most outstanding poet is Boris Poplavsky who died in 1936).[4] Boris Poplavsky was a "poète maudit"; the early death was the result of his way of life (drugs). Both Vera & Vladimir Nabokov told to Ivask: *My byli k Poplavskomu nespravedlivy* [We were unfair to Poplavsky]. The name of P. brought back Marina Tsvetaeva's excited complaint about his rudeness (this was told in Antwerp, privately organized lecture by M[arina] T[svetaeva], 1932?). She talked with admiration about Nicholas II's charm & then told that P. reacted to one of her remarks about Nicholas['s] death: *Nu, khorosho, chto ubili* [So? It's a good thing that they killed him!].[5]

January 20, in English
Friday afternoon, two guests at a coffee-hour, organized by Ivask: [Igor] Chinnov, a historian of *Russian literature* (in Paris from 1947 to 1953; now teacher at Kansas), and [S.], a Polish poet from London. Chinnov on [Ivan] Bunin's *Vospominaniia* [Memoirs]: grossly unfair, *svodil schety* [took revenge]; I have mentioned another example of unfair criticism: Nabokov on Tolstoi: Vera & Vladimir pointed out to me, years ago at Cornell, that it is strange to see no mention of literature in "War & Peace"; "is it possible that Pierre did not read Pushkin?" But "War & Peace" ends in 1812, while P. did not come to public attention before 1818! Other example concerning "Anna Karenina": N.'s remark . . . on Vronsky's playing tennis immediately after returning from *skachki* [races] (or *okhota* [hunting]) *priamo v shporakh v tennis igrat*! [to play tennis without taking off your spurs!] Did Tolstoi have to mention that Vronsky tidied himself up in a bathroom, and may be even took off the *shpory* [spurs]? Anyway, I said, for N. Russian literature counts only 5 or may be 6 great writers (one of them N. himself, naturally). And (I will add here) the world literature has for N. 20 or at most 25 acceptable names: I hope that my estimate is not overly optimistic.
   A question may be raised. Reading Tolstoy's diary and correspondence, and that of Flaubert, one is struck at the amount of suffering their writing involved. . . . Is there any suffering in Nabokov's creativeness? Is the butterfly only the final product of a painful growth (N. is an entomologist, and all his dedications are usually accompanied by a drawing of a butterfly!)? And then, I have noticed that clowns (and there is much clownery in Nabokov's manner) usually cover up basic melancholy. None is evident in this case, but still it may exist, deeper, at the bottom!
   Whether because I have known Nabokov at close hand or because of my

interest in his creative process, he seems to fascinate me as a person and a writer, although his writing leaves me cold, in spite of all its virtuosity and even beauty.

1969

February 24, in English

The diary gives me freedom, as if it were conversation, and I need this written monologue. Monologue? Is there any monologue without audience? There is none in front of me, but still I address myself to someone who is different from me (as a writer). To *another* myself? The one who watches and judges? I found myself suddenly in the midst of the "motive of the double," the Nabokov motive who calls it *zerkal'noe otrazhenie* [mirror reflection]. When I told to him that I saw this motive in his "Lolita" (Humbert-Humbert: two *identical* components of this name, and the whole Humbert-Quilty relationship), he agreed in saying that there always is, there must be, the "mirror" device. May be, my children, *another* part of my self, different from myself in time and space, but still *continuing* myself? Who knows? May be, if they are interested . . .

September 12, in Russian

I am literally *leading an existence,* day after day, instead of *living.* One should live inspiringly, systematically creating, building, constructing, just like Nabokov (he is, after all, older than I am but he is still working—and doing it so well) . . .[6]

November 6, in Russian

What am I? A Jew, a Russian, a Pole? Belgian, French, American? All of the above . . . or simply a human being? . . . About ten years ago I got an idea which my late friend V. B. Stankevich liked so much—to write a book, entitled *My Four Cultures* . . . as they get reflected in me, as if I were a prism. . . . The cultures are what's important, not me. . . . Will this book ever be written? It does not appear so. I could have written it earlier if I did not have these debilitating worries and all this shifting from place to place which leads to inactivity or little activity. Or it leads to spreading oneself too thin. One hundred topics instead of one! Likewise I will probably never write my commentary to Tolstoy's *War and Peace* which I had planned even earlier. I told V. V. Nabokov about it back then. He remarked: "It will take seven years!" Seven years have come and gone but I was busy with other things.

Marc Szeftel's diary entries, with English and Russian typically mixed, from 1970s (Courtesy of *Division of Manuscripts and University Archives at Suzzallo and Allen Libraries, University of Washington*)

December 9, in English

Michat K. Pawlikowski gave to V. Nabokov (in *Wiadomosci*) the dignity of the "greatest living writer"![7] There are so many writers in so many countries, whose greatness is either hidden or simply cannot be assessed because of lack of perspective. There is no doubt that N. has been an immense commercial success since the publication of "Lolita." Had M. P. been of the same opinion before this publication, by the way, as he is now? It would be interesting to check it. There is no doubt either that N. is an astonishing literary virtuoso, who performs amazing verbal pirouettes, and plays around with great style and much sparkling. I am afraid, however, that it is no more than a most impressive circus. Is circus the highest form of theatre? A less versatile, but more stirring drama, is certainly at least one floor above the circus. N. can do amazing things with words and images, but often one asks oneself whether there is an internal necessity in all of it. One feels that there is little earnestness behind all this glitter, and one would readily surmise that for N. writing is hardly suffering as it was for Flaubert or Tolstoy. A virtuoso of great talent but a novelist whose novels like [lack?] force and construction. An artist, certainly, but less than a virtuoso. That's why in reading N. one cannot forget oneself. One cannot see in his story a greater reality than reality itself as it is in Tolstoy's case. One can admire and enjoy it, but it is difficult to be carried away. At least this has been my feeling, both regarding his Russian novels, and his much more contrived English novels. No love, no suffering, no identification with things described! So why "the greatest"? A talented, self-centered, coquettish clown playing before a mirror. Treasuring his own words as if there [they] were precious jewels (often they are!), and impressing admirers of words for their own sake not by power of his expression, but by its elegant extravagance. I am sorry, but I prefer Kazantzakis. Would P. place K. above N., if K. were still alive? . . . As to N. I have read and reread "Lolita." I have read N.'s Russian novels and I liked some of them (the "Defense," for instance I did like very much). But I do not see the sign of real greatness, of stirring power, of literary magic . . . the blood of the nightingale's heart made the rose so beautiful in Wilde's beautiful tale about "The Rose and the Nightingale"! This is not N.'s art, N.'s cerebral art, which will not touch anyone's heart. . . . There are exceptions. The final scene of "Lolita" is one, and one is touched by it, to the bottom of one's heart. They are, however, exceptions. The rest is only playing [with] words. That's how I do feel. I may be wrong, but so may be also M. P., and Nina Berberova, and Mary McCarthy, and others who place N. at the very pinnacle. . . . Nabokov does not think that Stendahl was a writer! Does M. P. place N. above Stendhal? above Balzac? above Proust? The last two names are not great names, either, for N.[8] So much arrogance is not a proof of genius; modesty might have been.

December 10, in English

I have told [Oleg] Maslennikov about M. P[awlikowski]'s opinion of *Nabokov*.[9] He answered: *Na bezryb'i i rak ryba*! [lit.: in the absence of a real fish, even a crawfish is a fish]. A graduate student who was with us told [us] that she heard on the T.V. an interview with N. Among the questions there was one concerning his rating of writers. He placed James Joyce above everyone, and then Andrei Belyi. As to Dostoevsky, he constantly berates him as a second rater ("our native Pinkerton with mystical dressing"). I had a story to tell how, at Cornell, Langbaum, after listening to my talk on Lolita at the "Book and Bowl" commented on the Nabokov-Dostoevsky relationship. Actually, one can spot many a common topic or motive between the two of them, as I observed. To that, Langbaum answered that there [it?] would be quite valid to write an article on "Dostoevsky in Nabokov." N. would be furious, but matter would not lack. And I enumerated to-day before Maslennikov the common points: 1) the motive of the double; 2) life as a game (The Defense; King, Queen and Knave . . .); 3) love for a pubescent girl (Dostoevsky's "Stavrogin's Confession"). That much so far . . . Dostoevsky did not polish his prose, Nabokov does it very carefully, but D. had no time, he had to write for living. D. had a message, a deep moral and religious message to communicate, a vision of life based on pity for suffering. N. considers any message as dead wood in literature, but in spite of himself here and there pity for suffering rears his head also in his novels. This is not surprising, for both N. and D. derive from the same source, from Gogol. D. directly, N. through Belyi. Both are in the Gogol line of Russ. literature, which stressed the other side of life, beyond reality, the reflection of life in "krivoe zerkalo" [distorted mirror] of imagination. As Berberova said speaking of N. "life with the lining turned upside down." For N. this is only a game, which he plays very ski[ll]fully. For D. this was a glimpse of higher reality, a reversal of all values around the Christian concept of suffering. It seems to me that D. went farther, that he completed (retrospectively) what N. only sketched. This is my sketch of the N.-D. article!

One thing is surprising. It is the absence of St. Petersburg as a motive in N.'s work. Pushkin, Gogol, Dostoevsky, Blok, Belyi: all of them have the imperial city as a motive, as a personage. Not N.! His childhood memories, or adolescent memories, are connected with the various family estates, but not with St. Petersburg. . . .

December 15, in English

I have bought Nabokov's "Ada or Ardor." A big brick of a volume, which for the time being I have neither time nor courage to attack, but as [I] have so much material on N. already I wanted [it] to be more or less complete. May be, sometime I will write an essay on N. (not a book, this would be too much!). The pun is considered as the lowest form of humor, but N., obviously, enjoys it, as the title of this book shows in itself. "Lolita" is full of puns: "Humbert, Hamburg, Homburg . . . ," for example. It fits N.'s histrionic, somehow childish, verbal creativeness. [Is] Joyce, whom N. considers as the greatest writer of our century, as much full of puns as N.? May be he is that great, but my classically inclined taste never carr[ied] me farther than two pages of "Ulysses."[10] Classical! "Ulysses" is a classical title. . . . Obviously, no one can escape the impact of classical antiquity, at least not in Europe or America. . . .

December 24, in English

. . . . [There is] the warmth of Pnin, and the amazingly compassionate paragraph about all the unhappy Lolitas towards the end of the book. There is human heart in N., but he covers it up with so much tinsel and so many verbal stunts that it is hardly visible to the naked eye. . . .

1970

August 27, in Russian

After many years, Russian media has become interested in Nabokov. It's difficult to say whether this is the result of his Russian translation of *Lolita* or his popularity in general.[11] The translation, done by the author himself, was very harmful to the novel. In many places it reads quite crudely. English language, it appears, hid much of that due to the author's finesse. He managed to do it in English precisely because it is not his native language and he writes in it with certain artificiality which has some charm. The crudity of the translation was first brought to my attention by Ivask, and then I had a chance to verify it for myself. . . .

Articles about the novel appeared in both émigré and Soviet publications. . . . It is interesting that the evaluation of the novel is similar in both, even though the reasons for it . . . do not coincide[.] The topic is judged as immoral both here and there, and *Lolita* is considered a pornographic novel. I heard this opinion earlier as well in the Russian communities of both New York and Paris. Nabokov himself told me that he had nothing in common with the New York Russian circles, neither with the new émigrés nor the old.[12] He even quoted for me a phrase which someone relayed to him: "On the one hand, we have a saint, on the other, *Lolita*. . . . The saint is Boris Leonidovich [Pasternak]!"

August 29, in English
I gave talk on "Lolita" to the Cornell "Book and Bowl" (in 1958, I believe) at P. Abraham's [*sic*] home.[13] N. wanted to come, but I thought it may become embarrassing both for him and myself, for the talk, though full of praise, was not a panegyric, while the Nabokovs are very sensitive even to the mildest criticism. . . .

"Lolita" became a best seller simultaneously with Pasternak's "Dr. Zhivago." . . . And I saw N. at the Cornell University Library, in the Periodicals Rooms, looking at the weekly "NY Times Book Review" list of best sellers. The two books ran neck in neck, but, as N. pointed out himself, he was outdistanced by Pasternak that particular week. There was no bitterness, and even not a shade of resentment in N.'s remark, though he obviously paid attention to this race. We talked and the conversation touched on N.'s previous works. For me, "The Defense" was the best of his Russian novels, and I said it. N. did not agree. "The Defense" for him still suffered from the "émigré approach," as he put it. He considered as his best book (prior to "Lolita") the "Invitation to an Execution."[14]

October 7, in English
I have fingered through Nabokov's thick "Ada." On every page Russian and French phrases, or quotations of rhymes. It is almost entirely made of puns, as if it were reprehensible to talk simply. Such things as G. de Montparnasse for G. de Maupassant display a lack of taste. No, I do not like the book. It is simply boring to wade through so many contortions, though some of them show much artistic skill. N. is seventy, and such productivity is remarkable. I do not know whether he will undertake another volume, but I hope he will. A simple, graceful novel, like "Luzhin's Defense" [i.e., *Defense*] would be a better parting shot than this "Ada," a brick of a book all in knots

and puzzles. . . . [Something] [f]ull of gentle humour, like "Pnin," and without clowning at all.

1971

November 8, in English

. . . . Vera infallibly accompanied N. to his lectures, and, while he was busy in reading to the students his lectures, she, at the mention of a name, was writing it on the blackboard (to relieve V. V. of this drudgery, and to allow him uninterrupted performance). The students considered it as funny, but the performance was of the highest level and, although much of it must have been above their heads, N.'s lectures were popular. Vera was then reading the examination papers of the big class, in another selfless show of devotion. Still, N. must have had a hand in it, for he explained me once his system of grading and added that he arrived at knowing every student's work. The system of grading consisted in giving the grade of 50, to begin with, to every student, and then in adding 5 points for each of the ten questions, if well answered (less, if not answered that well). And once he told me an amazing story. It was the end of the year, when final degrees were given. One of his students, a senior, failed N.'s examination, and there were not enough credits for a B.A. degree because of that. A long-distance call then reached N. from Texas. "I speak to you as a father to a father." And he explained that, not having had himself a college education, he has deprived himself to give one to his son, and now this son cannot get the degree! And the son is in tears, crying: "You can hear him crying over the phone." N. never [had] changed a grade, but on this occasion, following his friend Morris Bishop's advice . . . , he gave in, yielding to tears, fatherly solicitations and the American college mythology.

November 13, in English

Again Nabokov, a topic which often returns to my mind. Unfortunately, without any system, and I am afraid to repeat what I have written already. Tant pis! In the "New York Review of Books" (Oct. 3 issue) there is "Nabokov on Nabokov," his review of a book on N. by [W. W.] Rowe.[15] A magnificent performance! N. dealt exclusively with R.'s chapter on N.'s "sexual symbols," taking it apart so thoroughly that the whole asinine inanity of applying Freudian symbolism to interpretation of literature, in N.'s case especially, becomes as evident as the light of the day. If literary critics must unburden themselves of their obsession with sexuality, one wonders why should it be done at other people's expense . . . ? This placing obscene labels on perfectly simple and decent matters is both tasteless, absurd and repulsive.

November 23, in English

I have read vol. 1 of N.'s "Lolita" first (in the Olympus [sic] Press), and vol. 2 only some time afterwards (I could not get it from Avgusta Jaryc at once). I had with N. about this book several conversations. . . . N. (like Wittlin and other writers) does not make his process of writing subject of conversation, when writing is being done, and it is understandable, for this interferes with it.[16] The matter ("facture") dissipates in the conversation, and artistic concentration is jeopardized by it. I have met N., again at the Library, after I have read volume 1. I have told him about it. He was almost chagrined that I have not had volume 2, much more important, he said than volume [1], but he would not lend me his own copy. No[t] much was said by me about the book. I only asked N. whether there is no motive of the double in it . . . N. agreed saying: "Oh yes! there was a mirror reflection. . . . " I have finally read volume 2, and then we talked about the novel again, about the whole of it, and then about Quilty's assassination by H.-H. N. agreed with me in my interpretation of "Lolita" as a book on destiny, the destructive destiny located within the man himself. As to the murder episode he said: "The uncanny effect comes from double inebriation. Quilty is under the action of a narcotic . . . , while H.-H. is "drunk." And then N. added: "How I love this book!" A legitimate feeling of a parent toward his child, the last and the youngest child!

1972

April 2, in English

Nabokov has been a Russian writer (*was* a Russian writer, to say it better, until 1940), and then he *changed* to English. At the present time, almost all of his Russian writing has been translated into English, but most of it by others. It is true, that several of them were translated by his son, Dmitry, under N.'s supervision, but this is not the same thing as authentic translation by the author. N. told me that such a translation is an ordeal for him, for he feels a different reader, with another frame of reference, and his natural tendency would be to rewrite the book, actually to write a different book on the same topic.

1975

January 8, in English

[A.] has climbed quite highly academically. . . . In this he did surpass his teacher, for I have never held any important administrative position. He has been also drawing higher salaries than mine. When I mentioned it to Nabokov [i.e., at Cornell] his comment was: "*Eta dubina!* [This blockhead!]" (he repeated it). This judgment was based on [A.'s] surmise that Pobedonostsev had influence on A. Blok.[17] [A.] was writing a thesis on Pobedonostsev, and Nabokov, hearing from him about it, quoted Blok's *Pobedonostsev nad Rossiei proster sovinyia kryla!* [Pobedonostsev has spread out owl's wings over Russia!][18] [A.] then said: "So, P. had influence on Blok?"

March 21, in English

. . . . It is late in the day, and dusk is closing in! Not darkness (this will be later), but lightly grey dusk when, as the Russians say it, "all cats are grey" . . . Dusk outside, dusk inside . . . Does ever Nabokov, the eternally young Nabokov, have this feeling of pervasive greyness[?] I have read an excellent article about him in the last *National Observer* by A. Tyler: "The Nabokov act returns, dazzling us with mirrors." About his newest book "Tyrants destroyed and other stories," 12 stories written between 1924 and 1939 and now translated by Dmitri. Is *Volshebnik* [*The Enchanter*] among them? This seems to be the case, for Anne Tyler says about one of the stories (she does not give its title) that "Humbert Humbert has a walk-on role some 30 years before *Lolita*."[19] I will watch for it, for I would like to read it. Nabokov never gave it to me (he promised!), and then told me when *Lolita* was published that he worked it in completely into *Lolita*. Did he? The great mystifier, the master of the hoax, with his eternal mirror games. To quote himself [i.e., him, Nabokov] about *Lolita* "*Vsegda est' zerkal'noe otrazhenie!* [There is always a mirror reflection!]" Anne Tyler says that "even at his simplest he is more convoluted that 12 other writers combined." This reminds me of Nabokov's observation in one of my seminars at Cornell in answer to a Czech student's idealizing the Russians as "Slavs" . . . : "The Russians are liars. That's why they are such good actors." Nabokov himself is an excellent actor! I would not like to imply that, also being a Russian, he did characterize himself in this remark, or almost. Anyway, as a writer he is always performing an act, and well. Still better were Gogol's acts (Nabokov is being compared to Gogol), but at the cost of a much unhappier life than

Nabokov's who, on the whole, has been a very lucky person. Exceptionally lucky! And, on the whole (so far as one knows) a well balanced life. How different from that of Gogol!

April 21, in English

A pleasant and interesting evening with the Waughs. Mrs. Demkova and her husband [were there] . . . [20] My conversation was mostly with the Demkovs, in Russian, which they characterized as "old-fashioned" (what else could it be at my age?). Demkov has read Nabokov's both autobiographies, the English and the Russian ones, his short stories and *tried* to read "Ada" but could not. Awfully complicated, ridden with puns and traps for the reader at every step. Also a very *recherché* language. It is amazing that almost every person, educated person I mean, who comes from there, has read Nabokov. Obviously, the official discredit did not harm his reputation (may be the opposite?). It made [it] dangerous reading him but in spite of it people do read him, whether in Russian and, especially, in English. He sure deserves this attention in the land of his birth and his ancestry.

June 22, in English

I have (more or less) read a book about "Lolita" by Carl Proffer, and then Nabokov's own "Strong Opinions" (mainly interviews of himself, very outspoken in his *written* answers).[21] More or less, for such reading is not easy at all, neither from the point of view of form (so many unknown words!) nor from that of content (oversophisticated both in images and ideas). Certainly, I could have cracked all of it, but I do not feel free (time!) not [i.e., "nor"] interested enough to make out of it an object of systematic study. This is not meant to deny Nabokov's amazing linguistic inventiveness, and the great originality of his thought. Just the opposite! But I do prefer simplicity, both of language and ideas. May be this century of complexities, more and more so, is a difficult milieu to adjust oneself for someone like myself, who is attracted most of all by the 18th-century style.

1976

November 10, in Russian

I remember a friend in Antwerp . . . once telling me that in music for him exists only two categories: "quiet" and "loud." Nabokov, too, once said something similar about himself. When I looked surprised and asked him whether it ran in the family, he said it did not. His father liked to sing, and his mother was an excellent pianist but he was quite a different story. I had to believe him (why would he make it up?), although it was hard to reconcile it with the musicality of Nabokov's writing and, of course, his poems. . . .

1977

January 2, in Russian

I was friends with Wittlin for 34 years, and did not allow our friendship to fade.[22] How much moral support I got from him! He was an important writer and a decent, kind man. It was not easy for him to write, and he left us relatively few works, but they all are of the highest quality. Nabokov finds it easy to write, and has written much more, but I place Wittlin, as a writer, higher than Nabokov. In Wittlin everything is genuine . . . without a shadow of Nabokov's self-admiration and without Nabokov's coquettish posemaking (*koketlivogo krivlianiia*). Nabokov is both "enfant gâté" and "enfant terrible." Everything works out for him, and everything is easy. Wittlin, on the other hand, lived, as he told me, "surrounded by demons." He was extremely strict toward himself, and, as a result, gave us less than he could have. I fully realize how talented Nabokov is, but I am lukewarm about his talent. I think he is a great storyteller and a virtuoso in language, but he touches me only when he reveals his heart, as in *Pnin,* and, especially, in *Speak, Memory,* his autobiography. . . . When N. was at Cornell, Avgusta Jaryc (his fan) once asked me: "What do you think, does Nabokov have a soul?" Of course, he does, and it shows itself when one least expects it, as in the end of *Lolita.* But Nabokov tries to hide it as much as he can with all the strength of his complex talent. How much simpler and more humanistic is Wittlin's *Salt of the Earth*"!

Nabokov was my colleague at Cornell University, and there we met frequently. We had a very good relationship, but we never had an intimate friendship. Nabokov avoids that kind of friendship; having Vera is enough for him, and it also contradicts his essential ego-centricity. Having left Cornell he has not written me at all. I was thinking of writing an article about Lolita, and sent him a letter to Switzerland asking him to send me the screenplay (for a comparison). I received a letter from Vera with a refusal: he probably wants to publish it with time and is afraid to *déflorer* it. There has been no contact since then . . . and, I suspect, there will not be one. *Telle était la fin de l'épisode Nabokoff dans ma vie.*

Our friendship was not to be. Whenever I told him that we almost never saw each other, he would respond: "But we know what we are working on (or 'what we are doing')!" From his point of view, it seems a contact was not necessary.

January 3, in Russian

The day has started poorly: the same morning depression. Trying to combat it, I started looking through my correspondence trying to find letters of my late friend Wittlin, and I put everything I could find in a separate file with his last name on it. Even I am amazed at my lack of organization, but I have always easily tired of paperwork. I apparently do not have Akakii Akakievich's soul, despite a large volume of timidity.[23] Akakii Akakievich is, in fact, a saint, as is Nabokov's Pnin . . . , if by sainthood one understands first of all humility.

January 5, in Russian

I tell Jewish jokes very rarely and never imitate the Jewish accent . . . but Harry Caplan, my colleague at Cornell, loved jokes in general, and Jewish jokes, in particular. He would tell them like an actor, with a proper accent (not only Jewish, but also Irish, German, etc., as a joke required). He was very proud of his Jewishness, and he obviously did not intend to present Jews as caricatures. But V. V. Nabokov, who grew up as a Russian liberal, told me that Caplan's jokes rubbed him the wrong way. He even considered, when he first had heard them, whether he should get up and demonstratively walk out. Nabokov is married to a Jewish woman, who never hides her Jewishness. . . . Nabokov is very strict about it. We talked about [K], a Ukrainian who . . . taught Russian. Nabokov was present at one of his 'performances' and then told me about what happened. K. was a rather primitive man. . . . Telling his students in Russian how he and his father had fled the USSR, he said that his father had paid to 'a *zhidok*' [derogatory for a Jew] to arrange one leg of their escape. Nabokov then told him, in front of the whole class: "Be careful in your choice of words!"

February 5, in Russian

Having read the previous page I realized that in English my text is quite clumsy (especially when I write on personal, rather than general, topics!) It's better to stick to my native Russian. Only Nabokov writes in English as freely as he does in Russian. At least that is what he says, and it is possible although not totally convincing: Nabokov's English prose is much more *artificial* than Russian.

February 16, in Russian

I spent the whole day calculating last year's expenses: preparation for the annual tax declaration for Internal Revenue Service. It's a boring occupation, but I am on my own in this: K[itty] and bills are incompatible. I remember how Vera Nabokov used to complain about this boring necessity, saying that she tried to do it as fast as she could. When I told her that this way they could be losing money, she responded: "Yes, I know that we are losing money but . . . it's so boring!"

July 8, in English

Nabokov's sudden death on July 2 in Switzerland! I have learned about it from a column on Nabokov in "Christian Science Monitor." . . . How did it happen? No news in the local papers: it is, obviously, not a newsworthy event for their readers. We are far away from the main roads of civilization! We have drifted apart completely since N. left Ithaca, but we were pretty closely connected before, and I will have to write a letter to Vera (as soon as I will read more about it in the "New York Times").

Thus people of my generation disappear one after another (he was 78). I wonder when my turn will come: 75 and 78 are close numbers.

July 15, in English

As to *Nabokov*, obituaries praising him as a genius have been appearing more or less everywhere. . . . It seems that he has been carried away by a recurrent virus infection (he spent a month in the hospital last year laid up with a virus pneumonia). It is surprising to me, for I have always considered Nabokov as physically indestructible. May be because of his athletic ways and talents, persisting into his Cornell period.

1978

September 14, in English

I have much fewer problems with French [than with English], and Nabokov's praise is there to prove it: he liked my commentary of the Igor Slovo not only because of its content, but also because of the writing (*khorosho napisano!* [well written!]).

November 10, in English

I remember Nabokov telling me that Vera considered the five years he spent on his translation [of *Eugene Onegin*] as a great waste of precious time, and may be she was right, I think, regarding the text of the translation itself, which has not been a success. But there is also a commentary, and it is pure Nabokov, i.e., interesting as such, probably the only valuable part of this four volume edition.

1979

October 30, in English

I have bought a copy of "Nabokov-Wilson Letters, 1940–1971" (they were writing to each other!) and in the index found my name: Nabokov's mention of my historical commentary to the *Slovo* as "admirable" (no, the work as a whole is called this way: "Szeftel's and Jakobson's studies being especially brilliant," p. 214).[24] And I have been thinking that en somme my scholarly contribution has been especially notable in three instances: this commentary, the book on the old Russian codes of charters . . . and the recent book on the 1906 constitution.

Appendix 4

Szeftel's Papers on *Lolita*

Included here are: a copy (probably a draft) of Szeftel's talk on Nabokov for the Book and Bowl, notes from 1960 on a study of *Lolita*, and the text of "Lolita at Cornell," which appeared in the *Cornell Alumni News* in November 1980.

1. LOLITA. BOOK & BOWL, 13.XI.1958

Typed, with occasional deletions and handwritten additions. This is one of the earliest lengthy samples of Szeftel's English prose now available, but one should bear in mind that it was a draft for a talk, and so was much less polished than were Szeftel's pieces intended for publication.

Tremendous success, 11 weeks first on the best seller list. Even the Marine Corps read it, & children know about it (Community Center book shop, 13 year old boy; the Halloween Parade—4 year old "Lolita"). Reasons analogous to the appeal of all forbidden fruit (it was, and still is, such a fruit) and to the great expectations of readers, who under other circumstances and for the same reason would be attracted rather by Micky Spillane than by Nabokov. I would like to know how far are they able to stay with the book, and how much do they understand from it. I would bet that many of them would be put hard to recognize their usual sex talk under Nabokov sophisticated story. The story is extremely well told, and even, if it were read only for literary reasons, it would deserve, and it would have had, many readers, and maybe, ~~still~~ a place on the best seller list.

Still, as a novel, it is not perfect. There is thinness, and prolixity at the same time, in its texture. It contains too much for a story (short), and not enough for a novel—I have in mind the main story. Otherwise, the book is rich, but much weight was ~~to~~ given to extraneous happenings, many of which seem to have been added to the story expressly (on purpose). ~~And it is not surprising~~ it makes the impression of an expanded short story, and actually it is one. "Volshebnik" ["The Enchanter"] written and read to

136

Aldanov 20 years ago (my own conversation with Aldanov and Nabokov); it was a short story. See L. pp. 313–314.

Film? Is there enough yarn for a film? Hollywood will not be embarrassed to add and to expand. A picaresque novel? Nabokov's opinion on Don Quixote.

Is it an analytical novel? In a way it is, but it is an analysis of a ph[y]siological, much more than of a psychological drama. One may object, that there is no firm distinction between the physiology and the psychology of love. However, from the point of view of drama, distinction there is. Physiology is monotonous, and repetitious, and we see it in "Lolita"; it cannot be compared as dramatic development to "Anna Karenina" or even "Madam Bovary,["] and it lacks the unity of Benjamin Constant's "Adolphe" (on the other hand). So, it does not strike the reader either as a drama of sentiment or as a drama of a structured series of events. From the latter point of view, certain episodes seem to be adventitious: what is the relevance of the Rita episode in H. H.'s main story? It is an interesting digression, to be sure, but the novel could live without it. This criticism having been made, "Lolita," whether happily or unhappily composed as a novel, is an extremely happy piece of artistic writing, full of jewels of invention and form, and above all, intelligent in its every word. Is it a product of heart, or mainly that of the mind? It is rather the latter, but in its cerebrality it transcends intellect into ~~splendid~~ imagination (most creative). ([In Szeftel's hand] However, this creativeness bears much more on details than on the whole. Not only does "Lolita" remain a novellette inspite of its volume, but it is flat and not three dimensional. The world in which it moved and this includes Nabokov's picture of America / recalls a theatrical decoration without any depth of background.)

Who [is] the hero, who himself told his story? H. H. "a salad of racial genes" (Swiss, of mixed French and Austrian descent), born in 1910. Hotel on the Riviera. Lycée in Lyon (1923–1927?). College in Paris and London (English literature—special field). Interprets French literature for English-speaking students and vice versa (a manual of French literature in English in 4 vv., finished by the time of his arrest). Territory of action—France in his youth (mostly), then from 1939 U.S.A. 1914—the key experience: love for Annabel Leigh, a "nymphet," unfulfilled (prefiguration of Lolita). Sexual life in Paris and marriage to Valeria (1935–1939). New York—advertising of his uncle's perfumes and writing the manual of literature ($7000 of yearly income ~~lo~~ left to him by his uncle!), then two mental breakdowns with long stays in sanatoriums, and a job [o]f "recorder of psychic reactions" with an arctic expedition. In 1947 H. H. looking for a quiet place to write his manual came to Ramsdale, N.H., and became a roomer in Mrs. Haze's house (Charlotte) for the only reason that he saw there Lolita. Marriage to Charlotte and her death. On the r[oa]d with Lolita 1948. Beardley High School (one year), then again the road in Summer 1949. Lolita's abduction in Nov. 1949. Rita— 1950–1952 (New York). Letter from Lolita Schiller, some 800 m. from NYC—needs a sizable sum of money. Trip to Lolita, and Quilty's murder. Died Nov 16, 1952 of coronary t[h]rombosis, in jail, a few days before the trial. Memoir published after Lolita's death.

The mot~ivef~ of all-devouring passion. Cfr Anna Karenina, normal passion. Here abnormal passion, still more devastating. Homosexual cured by this novel![1] Moral or immoral impact? "Madame Bovary" on trial 100 years ago.

Why abnormal passion as topic? Still more tyrannical than the normal one: 1) takes the meaning of inexorable destiny; 2) removes still more from reality. Passion: more than sex, love (Trilling). Cfr the "Carment" motive, p. 280.

The mot~ivef~ of destiny. Mot~ivef~ existing in other writings of Nabokov. "Zashchita Luzhina"—the chess-play destiny. In "Conclusive Evidence" (the Russian version)—"the visible signs of invisible destiny" in Gener. Kuropatkin's matches.

H. H. carried his destiny within himself, ~fought~ evaded it even by normal conn[ec]tions, but finally had to follow it. Everything played into his ~hano~ hands: Charlotte's love, her sudden death, Lolita's early depravation. See in this connection pp. 64–65.

The mot~ivef~ of evasion from reality. See again Luzhin. World as seen from *another* point of view: another clue to the choice as topic of abnormal passion. Wittlin on Gogol. Cfr another novel by Sirin: "Camera Obscura"— passion of a middle aged man for a trollop and blindness (destiny and otherworldness). The shifting, vertiginously, scenery of the road with its endless motels. Disregarding of all rules of traffic after Quilty's murder (pp. 308–309). Quilty's murder itself (H. H. is drunk, Quilty is drugged: grotesqueness of the murder), pp. 304–305.

The mot~ivef~ of the double (the mirror, the crooked mirror). H. H. (the name itself is double and sounds like a joke, or rather a grimace in a mirror) and Quilty: the latter's presence in "The Enchanted Hunters" simultaneously with H. H. and Lolita, pp. 128–129 (the hotel has the same name as one of Q's plays). Still earlier, Q. on p. 71 (his portrait next to that of H. H.) On the other hand, Quilty and Trapp, pp. 220–1. Strange coincidence: both Valeria and Lolita die in childbirth (pp. 32 and 6). (Annabel's name is Leigh, Poe's Annabel Leigh: "~~kingdom~~ princedom by the sea," p. 11).

The evasion from reality and the ghost of *the double* makes the reader often ask himself what in the story really happened to its abnormal ~~author~~ teller and what is the product of his sickly imagination. And, especially, is the American scene passing before his eyes what Nabokov saw with his own eyes, or what he made see H. H.? It certainly is not Kafka's America, it is a picture full of realistic traits, wittily observed and brilliantly presented by an intelligent foreign observer. Camp, small New England community, the Haze suburban residence, Beardsley High School and B. Col[l]ege, the motels, the roads, the department store, a church convention at "The Enchanted Hunters," etc. It is neither a picture of love (Mizener) nor (Slonim) a ~~satirical~~ caricature; "neither for nor against" (Mrs Nabokov). It is, however, a delightful assemblage of sketches. E.g., the farmer on his wife, p. 166; the 4 D's: pp. 179–180; pp. 195–199; the hotel-room noise on pp. 131–132 and 134; the motels on pp. 147–149. Dr. Quilty (the dentist) on pp. 293–294; pp. 32–33: experiment.

It is, on the whole, inspite of its scintillating brilliancy, a story which one does not read like one eats a pie (Carl Becker's expression *re* Carl Stephenson's little book on *Mediaeval Feudalism*). H. H.'s obsession with his desire for the nymphet impresses with monotony neighboring on gloom, and the sexual mechanism revealed in the process, though verbally perfect in Nabokov's telling story, is so indiscrete that some readers could not continue (M. Bishop). And then, like in a Scottish ballad, almost everybody is destroyed. Charlotte's death, Quilty's murder, ~~Va~~ H. H.'s death, Lolita's death. Even Valeria and her second husband die (is it again a double for Charlotte?). Yes, Annabel's early death, parallel to that of Lolita! and Jean Farlow carried away by cancer. . . .

One is however rewarded for ~~having~~ not having discontinued: otherwise one would have missed the best of the story, which is its second part. And at the very end, all ghastly char[a]cter disappears in an intense ray of light shifting the reader to another nobler reality, on pp. 309–310, when H. H. condemns himself for his passion (indirectly). *Time Magazine* spoke even in this connection of God discovered at the very end by H. H. and Nabokov . . . [The rest is written by hand.] This is too far-fetched: Nabokov, in this respect, certainly is not following Dostoevsky's footsteps. I pronounced the name of a writer, for whom N. does not have much respect ... and still something in (Langbaum, Slonim) common.

Still what Dostoevsky vigorously projected as dramatic development, is only ~~hinted~~ traced by Nabokov in final point without any previous development, than [unclear] hints. Here, I must say, Dostoevsky's art is more impressive.

On the other hand, Lolita's childhood at the moment of H. H.'s becoming her lover was already not very much of a childhood: it was after Charlie!

Is it a great book? Inspite of all its sparkling brilliancy, it is not, for it does not contain any meaningful revelation. It does not reveal any depth of human soul, like Dostoevsky, and it does not offer us any vision transfigurating the external world, like Gogol. At most does it have the value of a clinical study of an abnormal sexual case, all along with witticisms of charming, but not too deep a character. ([In Szeftel's hand] And even as such a study, it reveals little if one discounts the psychoanalysis of H. H.'s passion for nymphets: the mechanism of H. H.'s love for Lolita does not differ, in its description, from any erotical mechanism involving a powerful sexual desire. It would not be different, if Lolita were an adult. The most original portrature is, may be, that of Lolita ...) And I am afraid, Balsac will overlive it ...

2. NOTES FOR A STUDY OF LOLITA. 1960S
Typed, in English.

Nabokov
What do I have on him?

1) N.'s review (The NY Review, April 30, 1964) of Eugene Onegin's translation by Walter Arndt (A Dutton paperback). A pitiless, scathing appraisal of a rival translation.

2) A review of Nabokov's *Pale Fire* in "The Time Magazine," June 1, 1963, p. 84 s.t. The Russian Box Trick—N. is called in it it "the greatest verbal prestidigitator of his time."

3) A review of N.'s *The Gift* in the same magazine, July 14, 1963, p. 102, where N. is called "magician of words[.]"

4) Nabokov's interview by "Playboy," anniversary issue, Jan. 1964, pp. 35–45. Very revealing, in spite of what the preface to the interview says.

5) A review of N.'s *The Gift* in the New Yorker, April 25, 1964, pp. 198–205, by Donald Malcolm.

6) Excerpt from *Research at Cornell,* 1958–1959, p. 11, where *Lolita* is called[d] "the literary achievement of the year, of this and perhaps any other year by a Cornell writer" and credited to the research in the humanities as "an extraordinary successful novel[.]"

7) Notes on Berberova's review of *Lolita* (Nabokov and his "Lolita.") *Novyi Z[h]urnal,* t. [vol.] 57, 1960:[2] "in 1955, Lolita fulfilled Nabokov's promise."

8) My own paper on *Lolita,* delivered to "The Book and Bowl" of Cornell University on Novem[be]r 13, 1958: substantial notes. At the time I was offered by Mc Closkey [i.e., James McConkey] to have the paper published in "The Epoch" (he gave me 3000 words).[3] I did not accept the offer: N. was my colleague at Cornell. Question—should I prepare it now for publication, six years after the event? May be I should: the book is of lasting value, and by 1959 (end 1959) reviewing of it was "imperceptive" (to quote Research at Cornell). My paper, on the other hand, was praised at the time as unusually "perceptive" and as the first balanced review given to the book.

Another question—should I write an essay on "Lolita" (for it is still a literary issue), or an essay on Nabokov. The latter would require additional reading and much more work, for which time would have to be found. The latter is a problem, for there are other things to be done. But I am tempted.

I think the answer may be to write, first, an essay on "Lolita," and to see what will be the reaction. I am afraid, I will have to postpone until Seattle even that.[4]

3. LOLITA AT CORNELL

Published in the *Cornell Alumni News* (now *Cornell Magazine*) in November 1980. Reproduced here with their permission.

I was not surprised when, chancing to meet him at the university Library in 1951 (or perhaps 1952) Vladimir Nabokov told me he was in the process of writing the American version of "The Magician" ("Volshebnik").[5] I had never read that Russian novella, but the eminent Russian émigré novelist M. A. Aldanov had described its plot in details to me in 1942 and had called it "a masterpiece"—though "unpublishable" because of its highly erotic content. (In 1939 Aldanov had heard Nabokov read the story to a small group in Paris).[6]

When Nabokov became my colleague at Cornell in 1948, I had asked him to lend me the manuscript. He had promised he would, remarking in an expressive tone and with a side-glance, "Remember, it is not for kids!" But I never received it and somehow I did not insist. Now, he was telling me that "The Magician" was to become a two-volume novel to be called *Lolita,* with action in the US and the heroine an American teenager (he insisted on her being "an *American* girl").

Three or four years later the novel was out in France, and a few copies were sent to colleagues at Cornell on the author's instruction. I did not get one, but I did manage to borrow a copy. Certainly it was erotic and the topic scandalous, but I was not shocked. By 1955 eroticism in literature had become commonplace, and against the background, *Lolita* rather struck the reader by the discretion of its language: whatever the situation, there was not a single obscene word used to describe it.

But such a salacious topic for a novel written by someone teaching in a coeducational college aroused fears of a scandal—with ominous consequences for Nabokov—in a certain colleague who had brought Nabokov to Cornell and felt some responsibility for him. Prof. Morris Bishop, referring to the more explicit erotic passages in *Lolita,* was afraid that the magazines (he mentioned *Life* and *Time*) might blow up the whole thing and create a sensation that might endanger Nabokov's academic position. "I would not like to have to defend him in that," he told me, and added, "Would you?" Had it been even five years earlier Bishop's fears might have proven well-founded, but in 1955 things did not develop that way.

Three years later Putnam published the novel in the US, and it became an immense commercial—and literary—success. There *were* interviews in the magazines, in *Life* as well as in *Time,* but they only contributed to Nabokov's glory. And although the matter was not completely resolved, it seemed to me that Nabokov had weathered the storm, and I told him so on one of our library encounters. He replied, "It is not yet sure! People might still comment on *Lolita* perverting coed's purity. Ah! the pure coeds! An American myth!" But the University Report of 1958 did mention *Lolita* as an academic achievement, and all danger to Nabokov's position was over, with no lingering doubt.

Putnam's announcement of the publication of *Lolita* in a magazine (its title escapes me) was brought to my attention by Nabokov himself in the library's periodicals room during one of our chance encounters. It was a full-page ad; quite impressive. But the context was also impressive: on the opposite page there was an advertisement for Ralph Ginsburg's *An Unhurried View of Erotica.* When I pointed it out to Nabokov, he covered that page with his hand, not withdrawing the magazine, however. I thought of the ragpicker's remark in Jean Giraudoux's *The Madwoman of Chaillot*, that "Nowadays, everything must have its pimps"—though I did not repeat this to Nabokov. Still, both of us must have had the same reflection: how does one sell these days even the bestseller? Of course, the juxtaposition may have been quite accidental.

On the book market at that time *Lolita* was running neck-and-neck with Pasternak's *Dr. Zhivago,* and I once saw Nabokov in the same periodicals room bent over the *New York Times* bestsellers list comparing the weekly scores of the two books (we are all human). When I went over to shake hands with him, he said, "This week he is ahead of me!" But independent of this competitive aspect, Nabokov did not like Dr. Zhivago as a novel on literary grounds and was quite explicit about it.

Around the same time he saw me in front of the library, talking with Harry Caplan, a professor of classics. Pointing his thumb downward Roman-style, Nabokov said quite theatrically, '*delendam esse* Zhivago,' and then repeated it a few steps farther on (paraphrasing Cato's famous call for the destruction of Carthage).

At any rate, competition or no, *Lolita* became a spectacular bestseller. One month after its publication by Putnam, I heard from Nabokov himself that more copies of *Lolita* had already been sold than of all his previous writings together in both Russian and English. Then came the two paperback contracts, one for England and the other for the US, and, finally, a contract for a film. All this together meant considerable income.

Having read in the New York City Russian daily *Novoye Russkoe Slovo* about the sale of the film rights (for close to $150,000, I believe), I remarked upon it to Nabokov and pointed out "Now you are free to leave teaching." He replied, however, that this might still be dangerous, and he added, "I love Cornell." But it was only a question of time.

When I returned from a sabbatical in 1960 I learned of his resignation. *Lolita's* spectacular success focussed the publisher's attention on Nabokov's Russian novels, and they began to appear in English translation, one after the other. Numerous translations of *Lolita* were also published, and soon Nabokov's not too princely salary at Cornell could easily be foregone. Our mutual friend Morris Bishop allowed himself a quip in connection with this material abundance that followed *Lolita's* success: "Vladimir, at your age are you not ashamed to live off a girl like Lolita?" He told me that Vladimir had not liked his remark at all.

It is not surprising that such a sensational event as the publication of *Lolita* became the subject of much conversation at Cornell—and a controversial subject, as well. The peculiar topic of the novel had shocked some of my acquaintances on moral grounds, and some of them refused on principle to read such a "scabrous" book. This attitude was by no means restricted to Cornell, and I encountered it among people of Russian heritage, refugees I met at that time at the New York Public Library Slavonic Room.

Nabokov was aware of this hostility, and when I asked him whether he went often to New York City, he answered that he avoided the New York Russians, for they expressed their attitude to him quite clearly, saying that "On the one hand, there is a saint, while on the other hand . . . " (He did not finish the sentence, not wanting to quote the condemnation of his book as "pornography.") "The saint," he said, "is Boris Leonidovich"—i.e., Pasternak.

This attitude especially offended Vera Nabokov, who emphasized in a conversation with me the human side of the novel and, above all, Lolita's "complete loneliness in the whole world" after her mother's accidental death. She referred with anger to a Soviet monthly having reported that *Lolita* was a novel on "the defloration of an early teenager."

As for Nabokov, he simply mentioned (this was a month after the American publication of *Lolita*) that he had received a letter from a homosexual telling him that reading *Lolita* had cured him of his condition! The novel's impact in this connection seemed "moral" to him. This led me to express some ideas I had about the novel.

Nabokov agreed with my views that its theme was primarily destiny and that one of its motifs was the double ("There is always in my writing a mirror reflection," he said). I ventured to draw Nabokov's attention to the "throb of ecstasy" episode at the end of Volume I, Chapter 13, the erotic explicitness of which had so shocked Morris Bishop. The answer I elicited was: "Yes, but this I had to do!" (obviously, for reasons of artistic truth).

But if the theme of destiny explains *Lolita*'s topic in general, people were still looking for an answer as to why the author chose this unusual obsession as the theme for his novel, and, especially, why he revived and expanded that particular topic after a lapse of so many years since "Volshebnik" was read to a group of Russian friends in pre-war Paris. To that there could be no full answer, but in a conversation about it with Morris Bishop I told him about a friend of mind, a great Polish writer who, approaching old age, complained of the unexpected physical attraction he suddenly felt for his teenage daughter's girl friends.[7] But he brushed the attraction aside, I said, without transferring it to a novel. This was not necessarily Nabokov's case, but the story was suggestive, and it struck Bishop as a "little revelation."

No matter how they felt about the topic, both Cornell's faculty and its students acknowledged the novel as a remarkable literary performance. Some of the students had read it in Europe before it was published in the US, and Nabokov told me that after his class on European literature a student had come to him with an Olympia Press copy of *Lolita* in hand and, pointing to the book, had bowed deeply to him. Among our colleagues there was much talk about the novel, and people offered various opinions.

Arthur Mizener, professor of American literature, saw in the novel's artistically beautiful description of the American scene an expression of the author's love for his adopted country. Mizener obviously liked the novel very much, for he told me that Nabokov had the makings of "the greatest American writer." Not everyone was so enthusiastic. Gunther Thaer, a German writer, living in Ithaca, even characterized the novel as "an inflated novelette." English professor Mike Abrams, though greatly impressed by the performance, felt that from the point of view of construction, as a novel it was rather "sprawled."

Along the same line of appreciation, French professor Jean-Jacques Demorest, a very fine judge of literature, thought that it would have been most appropriate to add to the novel's second volume the subtitle "*A la maniere de Nabokov,*" while German professor Eric Blackall's comment was that the novel would have been artistically better if it had not gone on beyond the first part, with its ironic, most telling ending.

Others had reservations about the plot. In philosophy professor George Sabine's opinion, an American girl would not have passively submitted to Humbert Humbert's captivity as Lolita had, but would have looked for help, for example, by contacting the police. This comment was an attack on the heroine's authenticity that Nabokov so often stressed in his conversations with me.

Nabokov was still at Cornell when, in 1958 (or 1959), the Book and Bowl literary society asked me for a talk, and I chose *Lolita* as my subject.[8] We gathered at the home of Mike Abrams, whose wife showed me a copy of the Putnam edition with a butterfly drawn by the author, as was his custom on inscriptions. The Nabokovs learned about the talk, and wanted to come, but Mike Abrams did not encourage them, probably to save me embarrassment. This was probably the proper course, for my presentation did not avoid some criticism, and the Nabokovs were very sensitive to anything but praise.

But I do regret now that they did not have this opportunity, for my remarks inevitably would have encouraged Nabokov to talk about himself and his writing of *Lolita*. At any rate, my talk aroused much interest.

At that time few of Nabokov's Russian novels had been translated, and my analysis of *Lolita* was done against the background of Nabokov's previous writing, for the sake of illustrating the novel's three main motifs: destiny, the double, and the game. Jim McConkey, who was editor of the Cornell literary quarterly, *Epoch,* offered to publish the talk in 3,000 words, but I did not feel that I could publish it while Nabokov was still my colleague at Cornell. Vera Nabokov told me afterward that she and Nabokov had heard about my interesting talk and expressed disappointment that its content remained a mystery to them.

Four years later, already at the University of Washington, I thought of finally writing a study of *Lolita*. Nabokov was at that time in retirement in Montreux. I felt, however, that I could not proceed without the script of the film that had been produced in the meantime. I wrote to Nabokov about the matter and received a reply from Vera Nabokov, who said that he could not lend it to me. I understood the reason for it much later, when Nabokov published the screenplay as a separate volume in 1974. So I did not write the study, and this was our last contact before Nabokov's death in 1977.

Notes

INTRODUCTION

1. Some now doubt the veracity of Field's account, given the state of the index cards on which this and similar information had been jotted. Field's Nabokov archive has been recently auctioned, and a thorough study of his notes may eventually shed further light on the episode. I am grateful to Brian Boyd for sharing his observations with me concerning both the incident and Field's records of it. See Andrew Field, *VN: The Life and Art of Vladimir Nabokov* (New York: Crown, 1986), p. 291. See also Brian Boyd, *Vladimir Nabokov: The American Years* (Princeton: Princeton University Press, 1991), p. 288.

2. Some who knew Szeftel would disagree with this characterization. Vera S. Dunham, who was a good friend of Szeftel's before the war, when both studied under Alexander Eck in Brussels, describes the young Szeftel as both "imaginative" and "creative" (letter to the author, August 22, 1993).

3. Vladimir Nabokov and Edmund Wilson, *The Nabokov-Wilson Letters, 1940–1971*, ed. Simon Karlinsky (New York: Harper, 1979), p. 214.

4. Peter Kahn, letter to the author, August 16, 1993.

5. *The Nabokov-Wilson Letters*, pp. 36, 39.

6. Vladimir Nabokov, *Strong Opinions* (New York: McGraw-Hill, 1973), p. 106.

7. Vladimir Nabokov, *Pnin* (New York: Doubleday, 1984), p. 15. All subsequent citations are to this edition and will be incorporated into the text.

8. *Strong Opinions*, p. ix.

9. Although in later years he envied Nabokov his health, Szeftel outlived him. When he died in 1985, Szeftel had lived five years longer than had Nabokov.

10. Marc Szeftel to Vladimir Nabokov, letters, July 2, 1963. In Marc Szeftel Archive, Suzzallo and Allen Libraries, University of Washington (from now on identified as "SzA").

11. *My Poor Pnin* was the original working title for the novel.

12. In SzA, letters, July 16, 1963.

13. In *Phantom of Fact: A Guide to Nabokov's* Pnin (Ann Arbor: Ardis, 1989), Gennadi Barabtarlo, for example, spoke rather harshly of Andrew Field's very brief attempt to link Szeftel and Pnin (see *VN*, pp. 291–93), complaining that it was "[t]he

usual sort of thing: let but a man have plausibility, a knot, and a point of contact with the author, and he risks being drafted. These . . . conjectures, even if convincing, do not engage me in the least" (p. 44).

14. Some critics, among them André Mazon, John L. Fennell, and A. A. Zimin, have believed that the epic is a much later work and thus a "fake." Like Roman Jakobson, with whom he collaborated on several studies of the epic, Szeftel never doubted the work's authenticity and for many years fiercely argued with the "detractors." The general consensus on the epic is summed up by Dean S. Worth: "Attacks on the authenticity of [*The Lay*] have always come from amateurs, while its defenders have been philologists with professional competence in 12th-century Russian language and culture" (in *Handbook of Russian Literature,* ed. Victor Terras [New Haven: Yale University Press, 1985], p. 425).

15. Szeftel's widow, Kitty Szeftel, concurs in this opinion: "He took the idea of Marc as an immigrant professor having a hard time getting jobs and so forth . . . and then he really made up his own character" (personal interview, November 13, 1992). To a certain degree, this experience of a Russian émigré finding it hard to penetrate the American academe was, also, of course, shared by Nabokov himself. For more on that, see chapter 3 of the present study.

16. In Boyd, *American Years,* p. 289. In addition to making Nabokov laugh by imitating Szeftel's way of speaking, Appel also appears to have tried to reproduce Szeftel's English in the fictional Pnin's letter which he published in 1970 when guest-editing the *TriQuarterly* issue devoted to Nabokov and occasioned by Nabokov's seventieth birthday (reprinted in *Nabokov: Criticism, Reminiscences, Translations and Tributes,* ed. Alfred Appel, Jr., and Charles Newman [Evanston: Northwestern University Press, 1970], pp. 366–71). In the early years of his life in the United States, Szeftel, who had spent more than fifteen years prior to the war in Belgium, spoke English with a very strong accent that was, apparently, part Russian and part French. This was exactly the effect that Appel was trying to re-create when, in Pnin's letter, he used both heavy Russianisms and French spellings. Kitty Szeftel and Szeftel's son, Marc Watson, who have read Appel's piece, strongly deny that Marc Szeftel's English was ever as bad or as funny as the "Pninese" featured there. (Personal interview with Kitty Szeftel and Marc Watson Szeftel, July 15, 1993.) It should be noted, of course, that Szeftel was not the only émigré who spoke English with a combination of French and Russian accents, since many spent pre-war years in France or spoke French as their second language in Russia. It is also worth mentioning that Szeftel, while not perfect in English, spoke several other European languages quite well, and his French and Polish were, apparently, nearly flawless. For further discussion of Szeftel's English as remembered by his family, colleagues, and students, see chapters 2 and 3 of the present study.

17. Field, *VN*, p. 292.

18. Kitty Szeftel, personal interview, August 13, 1992.

19. Daniel C. Matuszewski, letter to the author, September 1, 1993.

20. SzA, diaries, April 2, 1970. The full statement reads: "[Nabokov], certainly, has a soul, but he carefully hides it in his writings. Not always successfully, for here and there, it shows itself, in 'Luzhin's Defense' [i.e. *Defense;* Szeftel uses here the translation of the Russian title of the novel], in 'Pnin' (very much so), and even in 'Lolita.' " One of Nabokov's and Szeftel's Cornell colleagues, James McConkey, remembers voicing a similar appreciation of the humanism in *Pnin* to its author who, much to McConkey's surprise, appeared to have been insulted by such a reaction to his novel: "Feeling the need to say something, an impulse I should have resisted, I told him that I had just read *Pnin,* which I had liked very much. He . . . asked 'Why?' I told him (and it was a truthful remark) that I liked it for the compassion I found within it. He abruptly turned away, as if I had slapped his face." (James McConkey, "Nabokov and 'The Windows of the Mint'," in *The Achievements of Vladimir Nabokov: Essays, Studies, Reminiscences, and Stories,* ed. George Gibian and Stephen Jan Parker [Ithaca: Cornell University Press, 1984], pp. 30–31.)

21. SzA, diaries, January 3, 1977; in Russian.

22. See, for example, SzA, diaries, December 4, 1977: "I do not think that mine has been a rather unusual spiritual road, not devoid of interest, especially for Americans. . . . [T]here is here a legacy to leave for the next generation. I am sure that *someone* will respond to my experience" (his emphasis).

23. Willis Konick, personal interview, November 10, 1993.

24. In 1958, Nabokov recommended Ivask as one of three possible readers who could evaluate his *Eugene Onegin* for Cornell University Press. He told the editor that his personal contacts with Ivask had been "very limited" but that he believed Ivask was an "honest scholar" (Vladimir Nabokov to John E. Simmons, April 8, 1958; in *Selected Letters, 1940–1977,* ed. Dmitri Nabokov and Matthew J. Bruccoli [New York: Harcourt, Brace, Jovanovich, 1989], pp. 254–55.

25. Konick, personal interview, February 12, 1993. The routine was also mentioned to me by, among others, Charles Timberlake, Professor of Russian History at the University of Missouri and a student of Szeftel's in 1961–66 at the University of Washington: "I remember that one of my contemporaries in Szeftel's courses . . . once told me 'Szeftel says that [Yuri] Ivask was the model for Pnin; Ivask says that it was Szeftel' " (letter to the author, January 13, 1994).

26. SzA, diaries, June 5, 1970; in Russian; SzA.

27. Field, *VN*, p. 291.

28. Arthur Mizener, "Professor Nabokov," in the *Cornell Alumni News,* September 1977, p. 56.

29. Robert M. Adams, letter to the author, August 2, 1993.

30. Harry Levin, letter to the author, August 11, 1993.

31. Peter Kahn, letter to the author, August 16, 1993.

32. M. H. Abrams, letter to the author, July 27, 1993.

33. Ross Wetzsteon, "Nabokov as Teacher," and Julian Moynahan, "*Lolita* and Related Memories," in *Nabokov: Criticism, Reminiscences,* pp. 246, 250–51.

34. Ambrose Gordon, in *Nabokov: The Man and His Work,* ed. L. S. Dembo (Madison: University of Wisconsin Press, 1967), pp. 144–56.

35. Vladimir Nabokov to Pascal Covici, February 3, 1954; in *Selected Letters,* p. 143.

36. In Russian, Szeftel—like Nabokov and many other émigré Russians of their generation—uses the old, pre-revolutionary orthography, which differs slightly from the modern orthography I use in my transliteration.

1 / MARC SZEFTEL'S ODYSSEY: AN ALIEN AND AN EXILE

1. Unless otherwise specified or cited, the biographical information used in this chapter is taken from Marc Szeftel's diaries, his "Intellectual Autobiography," numerous curriculi vitae, and interviews with the members of his family.

2. The numbers are those of the official census of 1897, cited in Salo W. Baron, *The Russian Jew under Tsars and Soviets* (New York: Schocken Books, 1987), p. 63. The 1897 census and its evaluation of the Russian Jewish population are also discussed in Alexander Orbach's article, "The Development of the Russian Jewish Community, 1881–1903," which appears in *Pogroms: Anti-Jewish Violence in Modern Russian History,* ed. John D. Klier and Shlomo Lambroza (Cambridge: Cambridge University Press, 1992), pp. 137–63. The numbers can be somewhat misleading, though, for as John D. Klier points out in "Russian Jewry on the Eve of the Pogroms," "[t]here was always an indeterminate number of Jews living illegally outside the Pale" (in *Pogroms,* p. 5).

3. The official emblem for the city, adopted in 1796, even incorporated a six-pointed star. See *Gorodskie poseleniia v Rossiskoi imperii* (Urban settlements in the Russian empire) (St. Petersburg: Obshchestvennaia Pol'za, 1860), v. 1, p. 404. The same publication, which was an official document of the Russian Ministry of Domestic Affairs, states that Starokonstantinov was upgraded from a *mestechko* (a Russian word for a settlement—*shtetl* in Yiddish) to a town in 1796 (ibid.).

4. According to the census of 1858, the town had only 10,000 citizens. The number is given in *Gorodskie poseleniia v Rossiiskoi imperii,* v. 1, p. 405.

5. For more on the two men, see, for example, *The Golden Tradition: Jewish Life and Thought in Eastern Europe,* ed. Lucy S. Dawidowicz (Boston: Beacon Press, 1967), pp. 113–18 and 321–26. About Goldfarben, who died in New York in 1908, see also Irving Howe, *World of Our Fathers* (New York: Harcourt Brace Jovanovich, 1976), pp. 461–93, and the "Theater" section of *How We Lived: A Documentary of Immigrant Jews in America, 1880–1930,* ed. Irving Howe and Kenneth Libo (New York: New American Library, 1979), pp. 237–76.

6. From a letter written to Szeftel probably in 1982, by Esfir B. Verkhnyatskaya, who read about his 80th birthday in *Novoe Russkoe Slovo,* a Russian émigré newspaper published in New York. In Russian; SzA.

7. Marc Szeftel, "Intellectual Autobiography." For the text of this document see Appendix 1, pp. 000–000.

8. In Irving Howe, *World of Our Fathers,* p. 11.

9. Marc Szeftel, "Intellectual Autobiography."

10. Szeftel describes his Hebrew back then as good enough to read "the Bible . . . , the beginning of the Mishna . . . , [and] also modern Hebrew literature (Bialik's lyrics and his epic on the Cossack massacre of Nemirov, Fikhman's poetry, D. Frishman's essays . . .) without difficulty and necessity to use the dictionary" (SzA, diaries, July 29, 1975).

11. Andreev, incidentally, became quite a hero among Russian Jews in 1915, when he joined Maxim Gorky, Alexander Rimsky-Korsakov, and several other non-Jewish artists and intellectuals in issuing the "Appeal for the Jews," which demanded the end of discrimination. For more on that, see, among others, Salo Baron, *The Russian Jew Under Tsars and Soviets,* pp. 162–67.

12. See *Pogroms,* pp. 228, 230. For an interesting discussion of some of the reasons for the violence against Jews and the social make-up of the attackers, see also "Policing the Riotous City" in Daniel R. Brower's *The Russian City between Tradition and Modernity, 1850–1900* (Berkeley: University of California Press, 1990), pp. 188–221.

13. SzA, diaries, November 7, 1969; in Russian.

14. Flora Sheffield, letter to the author, July 24, 1993.

15. This figure is taken from the tables printed in *Evreiskii mir* (The Jewish world), an annual publication of the Association des Intellectuels Juifs de Russie à Paris, 1 (1939): 379.

16. For more on the history of pogroms in Poland, see, for example, Michael Ochs, "Tsarist Officialdom and Anti-Jewish Pogroms in Poland," in *Pogroms,* pp. 164–89;

and Stephen D. Corrsin "Warsaw: Poles and Jews in a Conquered City," in *The City in Late Imperial Russia*, ed. Michael F. Hamm (Bloomington: Indiana University Press, 1986), pp. 123–51. For a general history of the Jewish-Polish relationship around the time of Szeftel's childhood, see Magdalena Opalski and Israel Bartal, *Poles and Jews: A Failed Brotherhood* (Hanover: University Press of New England, 1992).

17. Marc Szeftel, "Intellectual Autobiography"; SzA.

18. The two weeks in Smolensk were the only time Szeftel spent in Russia proper, as opposed to the Russian Empire. He never visited either Moscow or St. Petersburg, which he later felt was a huge detriment to him as a Russian historian.

19. Marc Szeftel, who was only thirteen, of course, did not then know Marc Chagall. Their only meeting took place at the house of Jakob Frumkin in New York in 1943. In his diaries, Szeftel remembers that Chagall impressed him "as a simple, direct, definitely Jewish and juvenile (in spite of his age) personality. His great glory did not seem to influence at all his external behavior" (SzA, diaries, July 27, 1975). Jakob Frumkin, who became a good friend of Marc Szeftel, was the same man who, three years earlier, had been instrumental in bringing the Nabokovs to New York. See note 53, this chapter.

20. Marc Chagall, *My Life*, trans. Elisabeth Abbott (New York: Orion Press, 1960), p. 119.

21. Marc Chagall, *Angel nad kryshami* (Angel above the roofs) (Moscow: Sovremennik, 1989), p. 72.

22. Marc Szeftel, "Intellectual Autobiography."

23. In his diary Szeftel lamented that during his fourteen years in Poland, "I was never invited, not even once, to a Polish Christian household, despite the fact that both in the gymnasium, and later at the University, I had Polish *copains* [pals]" (SzA, diaries, August 28, 1976; in Russian. "Copains" is in French and underlined).

24. SzA, diaries, September 29, 1969.

25. SzA, diaries, November 25, 1969; in Russian.

26. Kitty Szeftel, personal interview, August 13, 1992.

27. This could have been the earliest instance of Nabokov's and Szeftel's being in the same country after they had left Russia and before their arrival in the United States, provided that Szeftel's trip took place after June of that year, when Nabokov arrived in Berlin upon his graduation from Cambridge. Later instances of Nabokov's and Szeftel's being within the same borders included Szeftel's two trips to France (at the time when Nabokov was already residing there), one in 1937 to attend a convention and another in 1939 to do research in Paris. Nabokov, likewise, visited Szeftel's home territory: in January of 1937 he spent three days in Brussels as a guest of Zinaida Shakhovskaia and her husband. He read a lecture on Pushkin (the first version of his

essay "Pouchkine, ou le vrai et le vraisemblable" to be published later that year in the *Nouvelle Revue Française*) at the Brussels Palais des Beaux-Arts on January 21 (see Brian Boyd, *Vladimir Nabokov: The Russian Years,* [Princeton: Princeton University Press, 1990], p. 432). Since Szeftel, who was at the time a student at Brussels' Université Libre, never mentions the event, it is probably safe to assume that he was not in the audience that evening.

28. Flora Sheffield, phone interview, December 23, 1993.

29. Kitty Szeftel, personal interview, August 13, 1992.

30. In letters sent to Polish officials, Szeftel estimates that he lived in the household of his parents-in-law for three and a half years, and in the household of his sister-in-law for two and a half years (SzA, letters; in Polish and Hebrew).

31. Ryfka Szeftel apparently remained there at least until the war, and would have very likely perished in a concentration camp during the war, being both a Jew and a mental patient.

32. The Carkes family appears to have held Szeftel responsible for Ryfka's illness. A cousin of Szeftel's mother, Nadezhda Kovner, who still lived in Poland at the time and was asked by the Szeftels to consult lawyers and rabbis on Marc's behalf as well as to negotiate with the Carkes family, wrote (in an undated letter) that the Carkeses believed they had "substantial proof that [Ryfka] got sick because of M[arc]" (SzA, letters; in Russian). Interestingly enough, at the time when the negotiations with Ryfka's family were taking place, Marc and his family were also trying to find another potential match for him. The same Nadezhda Kovner informs the Szeftels in one of her letters that the parents of the young woman Marc inquired after regard him as a "wonderful match" but do not want her to leave Poland for Belgium (SzA, letters, undated; in Russian).

33. Nadezhda Kovner mentions the change of faith as a possibility in one of her letters to the Szeftels (in SzA). The same possibility is also discussed in a letter by Marc's distant relative, Jacques Scheftel, a French lawyer whom Marc consulted regarding Belgian laws on divorce. "The change of faith," Jacques Scheftel stated there, "does not affect the questions of marriage in the countries where the system of laws is based on the principles of religious tolerance or on the separation of religion and the state" (SzA, letters, June 10, 1931; in Russian).

34. SzA, diaries, November 22, 1977.

35. William Nemerever, phone interview, January 6, 1994.

36. Flora Sheffield, phone interview, December 23, 1993.

37. SzA, diaries, September 14, 1978.

38. Flora Sheffield, phone interview, December 23, 1993.

39. Flora Sheffield identifies the girl in question as the governess of her cousin

(phone interview, December 23, 1993). It appears that, once again, Szeftel may have toyed with the idea of changing his faith.

40. Kitty Szeftel, personal interview, August 13, 1992.

41. Vera S. Dunham, letter to the author, September 21, 1993. Her emphasis.

42. Marc Szeftel, "Alexandre Eck, 1876–1953. In Memoriam," in *The Russian Review* (October 1956): 272–73.

43. Vera S. Dunham, letter to the author, October 16, 1993.

44. That may have been at least one reason why, already after the war, when invited by Eck to come back to Brussels and resume his teaching there, Szeftel decided to stay at Cornell. In his diary he also notes "the danger, which was quite real at the time, that I may find myself under the Soviet power," which implies that he believed after the war that most of Europe could be invaded by the Soviet Union (SzA, diaries, September 13, 1976; in Russian). In a later entry (November 15–16, 1978), Szeftel describes Eck's reaction to his decision to stay at Cornell as follows: "Eck understood my decision as 'treason' and wiped me out of his mind afterwards."

45. SzA, diaries, March 21, 1968.

46. I am using as a reference here Ron Chernow's book about the Warburg family—*The Warburgs: The Twentieth-Century Odyssey of a Remarkable Jewish Family* (New York: Random House, 1993), p. 466. According to Chernow's study of this influential German and American banking family, a Vienna cousin of the Warburgs was one of those who committed suicide the day Hitler entered Austria by leaping to his death from the third-floor window of his home. For a more general history of European Jews during the Second World War, see among others, Raul Hillberg's *The Destruction of the European Jews* (New York: Holmes & Meier, 1985).

47. Vera S. Dunham, letter to the author, September 21, 1993.

48. SzA, diaries, September 9, 1976; in Russian ("*Nepriiatnoe bol'no vspominat', a ego bylo mnogo*").

49. Flora Sheffield, phone interview, December 23, 1993.

50. Uriel Szeftel apparently had cancer of the throat. He was seventy years old when he died—see SzA, diaries, September 13–14, 1969.

51. Flora Sheffield, phone interview, December 23, 1993.

52. Kitty Szeftel, personal interview, August 13, 1992. It is quite likely that Arthur Szeftel had actually assured his brother that their parents were coming with him and Flora. The probable reason one of the bus tickets remained unused is that Arthur had bought four bus tickets, intending to give one ticket to Marc and the other three to the family of Flora's aunt. When his parents were late on the day of the departure, and the other people were already seated in the taxi, it probably became very difficult, given the high stakes involved, to convince Flora's aunt and her family that

they should vacate the seats. In his diary, Marc Szeftel recounts yet another contemporaneous incident on the border involving a car: "[M]y best friend from Antwerp whom I met on the French-Belgian border in May 1940, keeping guard over a car in which his family could escape to France, neither offered me a place in this car [n]or asked me how I plan to manage without car and without money. He was rich, but he refrained from this question. Years afterwards[,] both of us in New York City[,] he referred himself to this encounter, saying that seeing me leaving on *foot* he thought that he will never see me again" (SzA, diaries, December 7, 1969; his emphasis). This description also raises a question of whether Szeftel ever used the bus ticket that Arthur had given him or whether he crossed the border on foot. The mention of the lack of money is likewise somewhat confusing, since Flora Sheffield clearly remembers that Arthur had given his brother money prior to Marc's departure (phone interview, December 23, 1993).

53. The director of HIAS (Hebrew Immigrant Aid Society), the organization that chartered the ship, was Jakob Frumkin, who later became a friend and frequent correspondent of Marc Szeftel. According to Brian Boyd, Frumkin was very helpful to the Nabokovs in their attempt to flee France: "Yakov Frumkin [was] an old friend of Nabokov's father, who like many other Russian Jews was glad to be able to repay the dead man for his bold stands against the Kishinyov pogroms and the Beilis trial by now offering his son a cabin for half fare" (Boyd, *Russian Years*, p. 521). In his diary, Szeftel remembers that Frumkin indeed always admired V. D. Nabokov's attitude and actions toward Jews (see SzA, diaries, January 5, 1977).

54. SzA, letters, March 2, 1961.

55. In his diary, Szeftel does mention "[m]y Polish friend, lieutenant Wojcik . . . who knew of my origins [while] the others did not." (SzA, diaries, January 4, 1977; in Russian.)

56. Daniel Crouse, phone interview, August 11, 1993. Szeftel appears to be responding to his stepson's and similar entreaties to write about his war experiences when he says in his diary that the two years in France "produced what people were calling 'a war story,' my own war story, lived but not written, for why should one revive these heart-squeezing experiences? Once is enough" (SzA, diaries, February 9, 1978).

58. Once they crossed the mountains into Spain, refugees were far from being assured of immediate safety. Thus, around the same time, Walter Benjamin, a famous literary critic and the author of *Illuminations,* who was also Jewish, crossed the Pyrenees with other refugees only to be refused entry into Spain. Convinced that he would now be sent back to France to face the Gestapo, Benjamin committed suicide. The very next morning, however, the decision was reversed, and the rest of the group was allowed to stay.

58. Szeftel's Polish, which he did not learn until he was already a teenager, was apparently accent-free—"all Poles I have been meeting express their amazements at the correctness of my language after so many years outside Poland . . . , and at the lack of all foreign accent" (SzA, diaries, Sept. 15, 1978).

59. Kitty Szeftel, phone interview, December 28, 1993.

60. SzA, diaries, February 8, 1970; his emphasis. Szeftel recounts this incident several times throughout his diaries—as, for example, in the entry for December 22–23, 1971, where his description of Father Perrin's response is somewhat more dramatic: "Then, with a vibrating voice, he gave me the answer: 'No. It will not be sinful, for the law is iniquitous. If a thief is punished for stealing, Jew or Christian, this is just. But if he is punished only because he is Jewish, this is unjust. Let alone the punishment of an innocent man.' And he quoted from St. Bernard: 'Those who insult the Jews strike Jesus himself on his cheek in his mother's person.' "

61. See SzA, diaries, February 9 and 11, 1970. It appears that here, yet once again, Marc Szeftel may have contemplated converting to Catholicism. Ironically, later in life, Szeftel showed very little tolerance when his daughter and son were considering converting to other faiths (Sophie Tatiana, who was raised by her mother as an Episcopalian, to Judaism, and Marc Watson, to Buddhism), telling them that he did not believe in conversions, and that "everyone should stay in the religion that they were born into" (Sophie Tatiana Keller, personal interview, July 28, 1993).

62. Flora Sheffield, phone interview, December 23, 1993.

63. Kitty Szeftel, phone interview, December 28, 1993.

2 / COLLEAGUES AND COLLABORATORS: SZEFTEL AND NABOKOV AT CORNELL

1. See also Introduction, note 14, p. 148. Edmund Wilson, in a letter to Nabokov, relates an interesting incident he himself witnessed while visiting the École Libre in 1943 for a discussion on the epic: "Vernadsky read a paper, in which he remarked that the French, not content with having destroyed the text at the time of Napoleon's invasion, seemed now to want to deprive Russia of the honor of having produced the poem [i.e., André Mazon]. . . . He was replied to by a French or Belgian Byzantologist [i.e., Henri Grégoire, who was a Belgian] . . . who tried to show, in a patronizing way, that the *Slovo* was a fraud. Roman Jakobson could not contain himself and made tumultuous interruptions. Finally, monsieur Byzantologist said: 'M. Jakobson, c'est un monstre' " (December 2, 1948; in *Nabokov-Wilson Letters*, pp. 216–17). In a shorter but more contemporaneous version of the event, Wilson, in a letter to

Nabokov on April 1, 1943, described the evening as follows: "[It was] the first of a series of lectures devoted to rescuing the *Slovo o polku Igore[v]e* from the aspersions of André Mazon—a matter, I gathered, of patriotic duty. Vernadsky said that the French, not content with having burned the manuscript in Moscow, were now trying to deprive them of the poem itself. The French Byzantologist Grégoire, who presided, seemed to get a little nettled by the Russians and the session ended with a debate which became, I thought, rather acrimonious" (in *Nabokov-Wilson Letters*, p. 99). Whatever Grégoire's true views may have been, both on the epic and on Jakobson, they did not prevent his becoming a co-editor of *La Geste Du Prince Igor'*.

2. *La Geste Du Prince Igor': Épopée Russe du Douzième Siècle,* ed. Michel Rostovtzeff, Henri Grégoire, Roman Jakobson, and Marc Szeftel (New York: Rausen Brothers, 1948).

3. SzA, diaries, March 22, 1972.

4. Roman Jakobson and Marc Szeftel, "The Vseslav Epos," in *Memoirs of the American Folklore Society* ("Russian Epic Studies"), ed. R. Jakobson and E. J. Simmons, 42 (1947): 13–86.

5. Jack Haney, personal interview, July 12, 1994. Szeftel's complaint that Jakobson was often given credit for the work Szeftel had done was not mere paranoia. Thus in "Roman Jakobson: The Master Linguist," Joseph Frank states: "[D]uring his first years in this country [Jakobson] labored at a new edition of *The Lay of the Host of Igor*, the twelfth-century Russian epic . . . of which Jakobson produced a restored text with a historical commentary of enormous erudition" (in Joseph Frank, *Through the Russian Prism: Essays on Literature and Culture* [Princeton: Princeton University Press, 1990], p. 10). Frank is obviously talking about *La Geste Du Prince Igor'* here, where the fifty-page-long historical commentary ("Commentaire Historique Au Texte Du Slovo") was contributed by Marc Szeftel. The only other historical piece in the volume—a brief essay entitled "La Geste D'Igor' Au Point de Vue Historique"— was likewise not written by Jakobson, but by Vernadsky.

6. SzA, diaries, February 20, 1978.

7. Mikhail Karpovich to Marc Szeftel, April 24, 1943; SzA.

8. SzA, diaries, November 15–16, 1978. The topic of his planned dissertation— "The Social Classes of Kievan Russia"—clearly suggests how superficial Szeftel's transformation from a historian to a sociologist was going to be.

9. This three-page typewritten document, found in SzA and dated May 10, 1944, is entitled "Contemporary American Sociology."

10. Incidentally, Mosely played an interesting role in Nabokov's academic history. A long-time fan of Sirin-Nabokov, he apparently was the first person to mention Nabokov to Bishop, as early as 1941, as someone Cornell "ought to get" (see Morris

Bishop, "Nabokov at Cornell," in *Nabokov: Criticism, Reminiscences*, p. 234). A year later Mosely wrote a glowing letter of recommendation for Nabokov which allowed the writer to obtain a series of guest lectureships. "Mr. Nabokov," Mosely wrote, "is already the greatest Russian novelist writing today, and contains infinite promise of ever greater achievement" (quoted in Boyd, *American Years*, p. 43).

11. Frederick George Marcham Archive, Cornell University.

12. Marcham Archive. Marcham describes a long visit with Day in Day's office, where the president was trying to convince him to persuade his colleagues in the history department to change their recommendation.

13. Paul Gates Archive, Cornell University.

14. For more on the practices at other Ivy-League schools, see, for example, Dan A. Oren, *Joining the Club: A History of Jews and Yale* (New Haven: Yale University Press, 1985); and Stephen Steinberg, *The Academic Melting Pot: Catholics and Jews in American Higher Education* (New York: McGraw-Hill, 1975).

15. Morris Bishop, *A History of Cornell* (Ithaca: Cornell University Press, 1962), pp. 194, 340. There were other interesting early examples of similar attempts (all largely unsuccessful) to move towards a wider acceptance of Jews at Cornell. In 1874, for example, when a rich New York financier, Joseph Seligman, volunteered to pay the salary of Felix Adler if Cornell appointed Adler as professor of Hebrew and Oriental literature, Cornell was brave enough to agree. According to Morris Bishop, Adler became an instant success among the students and townspeople, who called him "Young Eagle" and packed his lectures. His popularity with some of his colleagues was not quite so great, though, and soon rumors and complaints began to circulate that "many students, the cream of the professors, and some eminent citizens were getting 'gloriously drunk' on the fine old wines proffered by Adler." In other words, the professor of Hebrew was displaying the kind of un-Christian behavior one could easily expect from a Jew. Adler was silently let go after two years, despite Seligman's protests and threats (*History*, 192–93). The same "good intentions—poor results" pattern was followed once again in 1885, when John Frankenheimer, one of the very few Jewish graduates, was nominated as an alumni trustee. On the one hand, Cornell's president Andrew D. White fully endorsed Frankenheimer, who assured him that during his stay at Cornell he had never felt any anti-Semitism. On the other, the Syracuse *Standard* newspaper immediately accused Cornell alumni of being bad Christians, and Frankenheimer was never elected (*History*, 247–48).

16. *History*, 404. The anti-Jewish bias at Cornell fraternities apparently continued well into the 1960s. James Augerot, now a Professor of Slavic Linguistics at the University of Washington, remembers how in autumn of 1962, while at Syracuse, he was invited by a friend to come to his Phi Delta Theta Homecoming celebration at

Cornell and bring a date. Augerot "asked a woman, Joan Ross, from New York to go with me. It involved spending the night at the Phi Delta Theta fraternity house. When I advised my friend whom I invited, he reacted in a strange way and finally let me know that the woman I had invited was Jewish and that we couldn't stay at the fraternity house.... Joan and I spent the weekend otherwise. This was my first experience up close with discrimination" (personal communication, July 16, 1994).

17. The bias appears to have been particularly strong in the humanities. Oren addresses this issue in *Joining the Club:* "[I]n the humanities the aspiring Jewish academic knew that no matter how prolific a writer, how dynamic a teacher, how sparkling a person one was, one could have no control over one's fate" (p. 119). There were notable exceptions, however, as in the case of Harry Wolfson, Harvard's preeminent Hebraist and philosopher, who grew up in a succession of Polish and Ukrainian "shtetls" within the Pale of Settlement. For more on him, see Leo W. Schwartz, *Wolfson of Harvard: Portrait of a Scholar* (Philadelphia: The Jewish Publication Society of America, 1978).

18. Paul Gates Archive, Cornell University. Samuel Flagg Bemis to Cornilus deKiewiet, March 17, 1945. Ephim Fogel, a late professor of English literature hired by Cornell in 1949, received an even blunter reminder of the academic practices at the time when his friend from Lafayette College warned him in 1947 that at his college "self-righteous Presbyterianism reigns: in other words, no Jews, no negroes, no dogs allowed—it's the same old story" (Ephim Fogel Archive, Cornell University; Hal E. Gerber to Ephim Fogel, March 10, 1947).

19. SzA, diaries, December 31, 1971.

20. M. H. Abrams, personal interview, September 16, 1993. There is also the example of Harry Caplan, who came from a prominent Jewish family in Albany and was destined to become one of Szeftel's rare friends on campus. He freely told Jewish jokes, was a very popular Professor of Classics as well as a brilliant conversationalist, and was apparently widely accepted and esteemed at Cornell. According to Naomi Pascal, Associate Director and Editor-in-Chief of the University of Washington Press, and her husband, Paul Pascal, Professor Emeritus of Classics at the University of Washington, Caplan told them he was the first Jewish faculty member to be hired by Cornell. In the 1960s the Pascals saw Caplan occasionally in Seattle, where he would come to visit his brother. Naomi Pascal remembers him as being "soft-spoken but very self-confident (at least when we knew him in his later years); proud of being Jewish but not defensive or arrogant; and probably very skilled at turning aside any slur with a joke" (personal interview, August 1, 1996; e-mail communication, August 2, 1996).

21. SzA, diaries, December 31, 1971.

22. Knight Biggerstaff, personal interview, September 14, 1993.

23. Marcham Archive, Cornell University. Charlotte Fogel, the widow of Ephim Fogel who knew Szeftel, puts it more bluntly: "To them Szeftel was 'this little person.' He was an embarrassment and inconvenience" (personal interview, September 13, 1993).

24. Marcham Archive, Cornell University.

25. Gould P. Colman, personal interview, September 13, 1993.

26. Colman, personal interview, September 13, 1993; Biggerstaff, personal interview, September 14, 1993.

27. Beatrice MacLeod, personal interview, September 16, 1993.

28. Gates Archive, Cornell University. The courses are mentioned in Paul Gates's letter to David Joravsky (March 21, 1952), who was going to replace Szeftel while he was on sabbatical the following year.

29. Marcham Archive, Cornell University.

30. Frank Walker, letter to the author, July 27, 1993.

31. Milton Barnett, phone interview, September 15, 1993.

32. To give just one more example of former students' responses, here is one from John C. Cairns: "I sat in on a couple of his courses and greatly enjoyed them. Like anyone who knew Professor Szeftel a little in those days (1947–51) I was fascinated by him, admired his intensely professional, no-nonsense approach, was amused, as students always are, by his various little tics" (letter to the author, September 27, 1993). Szeftel's own thoughts on his teaching seem to support the view that some students may have found him an interesting lecturer. Thus he wrote once, in a rather Pninian English, "I enjoy my teaching, especially lecturing, and there are also contacts with students outside of the class I do enjoy, another type of lecturing, informal this time and spontaneous. They do listen, sometime spellbound, and myself I am stimulated to improvised colored reflection" (SzA, diaries, January 25, 1968).

33. Kitty Szeftel, personal interview, August 13, 1992.

34. Sophie Tatiana Keller, personal interview, July 28, 1993. Szeftel's hostility to American football, described to me also by Kitty Szeftel, was not shared—and was even resented—by the family he had married into. The Crouses, including Kitty and her son, Daniel, were avid fans and held season tickets. (Kitty Szeftel, personal interview, August 13, 1992).

35. Morris Bishop to Marc Szeftel, August 27, 1947, SzA.

36. Bishop Archive, Cornell University; Morris Bishop to Blanche Knopf, August 16, 1947. Knopf's response, where she stated: "I know no one in Russian literature at the moment" is dated August 21, 1947 (also in Bishop Archive).

37. Quoted in Brian Boyd, "Nabokov at Cornell," in Gibian and Parker, eds., *The Achievements of Vladimir Nabokov*, p. 123.

38. See Boyd, *American Years*, p. 123; and Field, *VN*, p. 26.

39. Milton Cowan, personal interview, September 15, 1993. In the same interview Cowan stated that it was also he, and not Bishop, who found the first house for the Nabokovs to rent in Ithaca. The house was at 957 East State Street, and the Nabokovs would rent it again, several years later, from the new owners, the MacLeods.

40. Nabokov first visited Cornell in May of 1944 when he was invited by Peter Pertzoff, professor of Russian who later moved to Columbia with Simmons, to read one of his stories ("A Forgotten Poet") at the Book and Bowl Club. Neither Szeftel, who would not be hired by Cornell till a year later, nor Bishop, who was away at the time, met him then (see Brian Boyd, "Nabokov at Cornell," in *Achievements of Vladimir Nabokov*, p. 126; and *American Years*, p. 72.).

41. William Townbridge Merrifield Forbes Archive, Cornell University; Vladimir Nabokov to William Forbes, February 2, 1948. (The letter is reproduced in Nabokov's *Selected Letters*, pp. 80–81, but in an edited version, with the omission of Nabokov's reference to chairing the Russian department.) We also know that he even ordered stationery that identified him as Chair of the Russian Department at Cornell—see Boyd, *American Years*, pp. 134, 167.

42. *Cornell Directory of Faculty and Staff, 1948–1949* and *Cornell Directory of Faculty and Staff, 1949–1950*, pp. 71, 81 respectively.

43. In the 1950 *Directory* the listing was somewhat modified to "Assoc. Prof. Russian Literature" (*Cornell Directory of Faculty and Staff, 1950–1951*, p. 79).

44. See Marc Szeftel to Vladimir Nabokov, February 26, 1948; and Vladimir Nabokov to Marc Szeftel, March 2, 1948 and March 21, 1948. SzA. The March 2 letter is also quoted in Brian Boyd, "Nabokov at Cornell," in *Achievements of Vladimir Nabokov*, p. 128. Nabokov wrote a letter to deKiewiet as well, discussing the courses he wanted to teach. In it he reiterated the same notion that he had conveyed to Szeftel earlier: "Russian literature (both theory and practice of it) is my special field and I feel sure that this is the field in which students would profit most from my lectures." In response to deKiewiet's suggestion that Nabokov should serve on some committees in the College of Arts, of which deKiewiet was still the dean, Nabokov informs him that he is "a poor organizer . . . entirely lacking in administrative talents" (Vladimir Nabokov to Dean C. W. deKiewiet, March 21, 1948; in *Selected Letters*, p. 83).

45. Roman Jakobson to Marc Szeftel, March 26, 1948: "What is your relationship with Nabokov? Should I send you a copy for forwarding to him? What do you think?" (SzA, in Russian).

46. Vladimir Nabokov to Marc Szeftel, April 15, 1948; SzA.

47. Mark Aldanov to Vladimir Nabokov, August 13, 1948; in *Oktiabr'* 1 (1996): 138.

48. Gardner Clark, personal interview, September 11, 1993.

49. Milton Cowan, personal interview, September 15, 1993.

50. Morris Bishop, "Nabokov at Cornell," in *Nabokov: Criticism, Reminiscences,* p. 235.

51. Milton Cowan, personal interview, September 15, 1993.

52. One of James McConkey's favorite Nabokov stories, which he had told Brian Boyd and repeated to me, is of Véra Nabokov giving her husband a poke upon seeing McConkey, as the Nabokovs were walking down the hall, "a real sharp [one], I didn't know she would do things like that. . . . She had a very sharp little elbow, and she poked him just like that, into his ribs . . . , and he knew what that meant so he raised his head and looked me straight in the eye and gave me this dazzling, vacant smile and then proceeded down the hall. I thought 'Oh, my, I have arrived' " (personal interview, September 14, 1993).

53. As Brian Boyd points out, many at Cornell were struck by what they perceived as "the subservient role" Véra Nabokov played in the relationship (*American Years,* p. 133). I encountered similar puzzlement during my interviews. Gardner Clark remembers seeing the couple during one of their frequent moves when Nabokov was carrying a light chess set and an almost weightless lamp, while his rather fragile wife carried two heavy suitcases (personal interview, September 11, 1993). Another interesting vignette was offered to me by Dorothy Staller, the wife of Cornell professor George Staller. She once saw Véra Nabokov come out of a grocery store with two heavy shopping bags and head for the car, where Vladimir Nabokov was sitting in the passenger seat. Véra apparently could not find her keys, so she had to put the bags down to look for them. Having located her keys, she opened the trunk, lifted the heavy bags again and put them in. Her husband did not stir (phone interview, September 16, 1993). See also Stacey Schiff, "The Genius and Mrs. Genius: The Very Nabokovian Marriage of Vladimir and Véra," in *The New Yorker,* Feb. 10, 1997, pp. 41–47.

54. SzA, diaries, November 8, 1971.

55. Peter Kahn, personal interview, September 15, 1993.

56. Ross Wetzsteon, "Nabokov as Teacher," in *Achievements of Vladimir Nabokov,* p. 245. Even after Nabokov left Cornell, there were still "horror" stories rampant among graduate students there that Nabokov's questions were being used in Ph.D. comprehensive exams. According to Lee Croft, professor of Russian at Arizona State University who studied at Cornell during 1969–1973, one of the graduate students used that fear to play a practical joke on his friends by circulating a photocopy of a topic that asked the candidate "to name all manner of obscure dogs [in] Russian literature. Everyone who saw it was terrified . . . and none, given its requirement of picayune detail, doubted that it was Nabokov's work" (letter to the author, Septem-

ber 2, 1993). The joke was probably based on Ephim Fogel's anecdote about Nabo-kov's asking Fogel whether he ever examined his students on the names of King Lear's dogs—see Fogel's reminiscences in *Achievements of Vladimir Nabokov,* p. 231.

57. This question, based on Jane Austen's *Mansfield Park,* is quoted by Stephen Jan Parker in his 1969 Cornell doctoral dissertation, "Vladimir Nabokov-Sirin as Teacher: Russian Novels," p. 6. The answer, according to Parker, was supposed to be "cold pork bones and mustard."

58. Parker, "Vladimir Nabokov-Sirin as Teacher: Russian Novels," p. 5.

59. As is well known, Nabokov did not care for Dostoevsky as a writer with a sole exception of *The Double,* which he considered a masterpiece. The best story on Dostoevsky, Nabokov, and Cornell students comes from Herbert Gold, who substi-tuted for Nabokov in the 1950s when Nabokov was on leave: "[Nabokov] used to say, 'Dostoevsky is not a Russian writer.' By which he meant, of course, that he didn't write what he considered a good Russian style. I had a student who had had the first half of the class with him, and she asked me if Dostoevsky was a Swede, because she knew he wasn't a Russian writer because Professor Nabokov had said it so many times, but since he was so gloomy, she thought he might be a Swede" (Herbert Gold, "Nabokov Remembered: A Slight Case of Poshlost," in *Achievements of Vladimir Nabokov,* p. 54).

60. James McConkey, personal interview, September 14, 1993. The chairman at the time was David Daiches, another Cornell professor who occasionally published light verse in *The New Yorker* in the 1950s. McConkey also recalls this episode in "Nabokov and 'The Widows of the Mint' " (in *Achievements of Vladimir Nabokov,* p. 30). The incident is further described by Brian Boyd in *American Years,* where Boyd identifies the young man in question as "a star student, one of the brasher young fiction writers in the Cornell creative program," and gives the following picture of the student and Nabokov's post-episode relationship: "Often reluctant to credit the intelligence of those who disagreed with him, Nabokov for the remainder of the term noted in his diary whether the 'idiot' was present or not in class: only six times out of twenty. The young man . . . received an F on the exam. He went to Arthur Mizener and M. H. Abrams to complain. Convinced that Nabokov was overreacting, they asked him to reconsider the grade. He would not" (p. 308).

61. SzA, diaries, January 5, 1977; in Russian. Szeftel also records Nabokov as having told him that during their conversation Cowan behaved "'like an Irish peasant" ("*kak irlandskii muzhik*"). Szeftel does not give any date for the Nabokov-Cowan "sharp conversation," but Boyd, relying on Nabokov's diary, dates it back to 1951—see *American Years,* p. 199. Nabokov never ceased complaining about Fairbanks, protest-ing as late as 1958 that "[T]he head of the Russian Language Dept., Prof. G. Fair-

banks, does not have any Russian. He cannot speak it, he cannot write it" (quoted in Boyd, *American Years,* p. 369).

62. Edward L. Krawitt, letter to the editor, *The New York Times Book Review,* December 3, 1995, p. 4.

63. SzA, diaries, November 7, 1971, where he also states: "As to Nabokov's oral style, I have heard him delivering year after year, in my seminar at Cornell, the same lecture . . . on 'The author, the critic and the reader in 19th century Russia.' . . . When not anymore a Cornell professor, he was invited to inaugurate the Cornell Festival with a lecture, it was still the same lecture, and I have heard people commenting on it: 'he *is* an actor!' " (Szeftel's emphasis). The lecture is published as "Russian Writers, Censors, and Readers" in Vladimir Nabokov, *Lectures on Russian Literature,* ed. Fredson Bowers (New York: Harcourt Brace Jovanovich, 1981), pp. 1–12.

64. Milton Cowan, personal interview, September 15, 1993.

65. Robert M. Adams, "The Wizard of Lake Cayuga," in *The New York Review of Books,* January 30, 1992, p. 3.

66. M. H. Abrams, personal interview, September 16, 1993.

67. James McConkey, personal interview, September 14, 1993.

68. SzA, diaries, January 2, 1977.

69. SzA, diaries, April 2, 1970, and again, January 2, 1977. Like Szeftel, Avgusta (her first name was also often spelled as "Augusta") Jaryc was a Russian Jew from the "provinces"—in her case, Kiev. Her family left Russia after the revolution and settled in France, from whence she fled, like the Nabokovs, on the eve of the German occupation. She began teaching at Cornell a year later than Szeftel. She appears to have been closer to the Nabokovs than was Szeftel, but was in no way their intimate friend. When I was in Ithaca in 1993, I went to visit her in a convalescent home, but her physical and mental states were already such that no interview was possible. She died on March 29, 1994 at the age of 88. I am grateful to Gardner Clark, who forwarded me a copy of her obituary in the *Ithaca Journal,* April 2, 1994.

70. Szeftel apparently came close to marrying someone earlier in New York. A letter from his former New York landlady, dated October 18, 1948, states, among other things, that he should not regret "the emptiness of his personal life" because it was better than marrying someone who they all thought was not right for him. (SzA; the letter is in Russian; the name of the correspondent is illegible.)

71. Gardner Clark, personal interview, September 11, 1993.

72. See Boyd, *American Years,* p. 140.

73. Daniel Crouse, personal interview, August 11, 1993.

74. See Boyd, *American Years,* p. 136. Nabokov also mentions his translation of the epic in a letter to Edmund Wilson, November 1, 1948: "I have been translating a good

deal lately. For instance, I am making a new translation of *Slovo o polku I[goreve]*" (in *The Nabokov-Wilson Letters*, p. 209).

75. Roman Jakobson to Marc Szeftel, October 18, 1948; SzA.

76. Roman Jakobson to Marc Szeftel, October 28, 1948; SzA.

77. Roman Jakobson to Marc Szeftel, November 22, 1948; SzA.

78. The letter is dated November 21, 1948; in *The Nabokov-Wilson Letters*, p. 214.

79. Ibid., p. 216.

80. Roman Jakobson to Marc Szeftel, January 28, 1949; SzA.

81. Boyd, *American Years*, pp. 136, 686–87.

82. Later that year Nabokov tried to have his piece published in *Partisan Review*. He wrote to Philip Rahv, who was the editor: "I have written a piece—half-essay half-review—on the famous Russian epic 'La Geste d'Igor' and on the latest translation of it into several languages. It is about 3,500 words long" (Vladimir Nabokov to Philip Rahv, May 21, 1949, in *Selected Letters*, p. 93). Rahv declined the offer.

83. See Roman Jakobson to Marc Szeftel, October 24, 1950: "push Nabokov to complete his translation of the *Slovo* which we could publish with your and my revised commentary" (SzA).

84. On Nabokov's visits to Harvard and his teaching there in 1952 see Boyd, *American Years*, pp. 196, 214–17. See also Roman Jakobson to Marc Szeftel, January 31, 1952: "after a discussion with Nabokov I will write you all my questions and suggestions concerning our planned book," and Roman Jakobson to Marc Szeftel, February 17, 1953: "Both Nabokov and I were worried at having no news from you. . . . Nabokov and I . . . discussed [our plans] and both of us hope that you will agree with our schedule" (SzA).

85. Roman Jakobson to Vladimir Nabokov and Marc Szeftel, December 10, 1952; SzA.

86. Roman Jakobson to Marc Szeftel, February 17, 1953; SzA. See also Roman Jakobson to Marc Szeftel, March 9, 1953: "Nabokov will receive for his literary contribution . . . $1000. . . . You and I will receive for our contributions $500 each" (SzA).

87. Vladimir Nabokov to Harry Levin, May 2, 1953; in *Selected Letters*, p. 137.

88. Vaun Gillmor (assistant secretary, Bollingen Foundation) to Marc Szeftel, July 21, 1953; Szeftel's handwritten notes on the details of the contract are on the back of the same letter; SzA.

89. Marc Szeftel to Roman Jakobson, March 24, 1954; SzA.

90. SzA, diaries, November 12–13, 1974.

91. See "Nabokov's Translation—observations concerning his draft," a two-page document detailing Szeftel's corrections and comments; SzA.

92. SzA, diaries, November 29, 1971: "He sent to me his translation to read, and to check from the point of view of historical data. When I have suggested (in writing) changes he accepted them readily." Szeftel describes his corrections and Nabokov's reaction to them again in his entry on November 12–13, 1974.

93. In Boyd, *American Years*, pp. 167–68.

94. See the same incident described in Boyd, *American Years*, pp. 302–03. Andrew Field also relates the episode in *VN*, pp. 238–39, but for some reason dates it as having happened eleven years earlier, in 1946, at which point Jakobson was actually still teaching at the École Libre des Hautes Études and at Columbia. (He started teaching at Harvard on a permanent basis in 1949.) Both Field and Boyd give the same version, which differs somewhat from Szeftel's version of Jakobson's statement: "Gentlemen, even if one allows that he is an important writer, are we next to invite an elephant to be Professor of Zoology?"

95. Szeftel is inaccurate here. McCarthy died in 1957, and his influence had declined sharply since 1954, when he was denounced by the Senate for his witch-hunting tactics. It has to be noted, however, that at Cornell Nabokov had a reputation of someone who was cavalier with accusations of "Bolshevism" even in the midst of McCarthyism. Thus M. H. Abrams remembers that in the early fifties Nabokov vocally complained against a colleague who edited a textbook of modern Russian and included therein a section of the Soviet Constitution as an example of "official prose" (personal interview, September 16, 1993; the colleague was Gordon Fairbanks, the author of *Russian Area Reader*. The incident is also described in Boyd, *American Years*, p. 199). Nabokov was apparently quite happy with his "McCarthyist" reputation, for, according to Boyd, "[a]t a time when university faculties were hostile to the search for Communists on their campuses, Nabokov befriended the FBI agent assigned to Cornell and declared he would be proud to have his son join the FBI in that role" (*American Years*, p. 311).

96. Szeftel, on the other hand, liked Karpovich, whom he once called "the fairest of men" (SzA, diaries, October 13, 1980).

97. This quote, as well as the quotes and information used in the preceding paragraph, are all taken from the same diary entry, November 29, 1971; SzA. The whole affair left a very sour aftertaste for Szeftel. He ends the entry remarking: "All this makes me think that great talent does not make necessarily for great people, in the human sense of the epithet. This goes both for N. and J."

98. Vladimir Nabokov to Roman Jakobson, April 14, 1957, in *Selected Letters*, p. 216. Bollingen, with whom he later published *Eugene Onegin*, apparently did not demand the return of Nabokov's share of the advance payment—see Boyd, *American Years*, p. 311.

99. Brian Boyd does not make a connection between Nabokov's letter and the incident at Harvard either. He thinks that "Nabokov was in fact convinced that Jakobson was a Communist agent," and that this conviction made it "impossible for him to work alongside Jakobson" (*American Years,* p. 311). Nabokov's possible belief that Jakobson was indeed an agent does not, however, explain the precise timing of the letter, since Jakobson's trip to Russia had taken place a whole year before the letter was written.

100. See Jakobson's letters in Szeftel's archive, the last one dated February 19, 1978, and still bearing references to their projected volume. The letter, written in Russian, also bears a touching declaration of friendship from the eighty-one-year-old Jakobson to the seventy-six-year-old Szeftel: "My loyal, friendly feelings for you are not lessening, but, to the contrary, have strengthened with the years, so that the years we spent together working on Igor and Vseslav are now for me full of invigorating (*bodriashchikh*) memories."

101. *The Song of Igor's Campaign: An Epic of the Twelfth Century* (New York: Random House, 1960). In this edition, featuring the much-revised translation of the work, Nabokov challenged Jakobson's view on the epic's authenticity only halfway, by outlining the grounds for skepticism. He also took another swipe at Jakobson himself: "In [my] first version I followed uncritically Roman Jakobson's recension as published in *La Geste Du Prince Igor.* Later, however, I grew dissatisfied not only with my own—much too 'readable'—translation but also with Jakobson's views" (p. 82).

102. For Szeftel's reaction to the omission of any acknowledgment of his or Jakobson's help, see SzA, diaries, November 12–13, 1974, where he writes: "Nabokov's translation was published as a separate volume without any acknowledgment either to Jakobson's elucidation of the text (of which Nabokov took advantage) nor of my corrections."

3 / PNIN

1. Gennadi Barabtarlo, *Phantom of Fact,* p. 57.

2. Brian Boyd, *American Years,* p. 272. A similar suggestion was made by William Carroll, "Nabokov's Signs and Symbols," in *A Book of Things About Vladimir Nabokov,* ed. Carl Proffer (Ann Arbor: Ardis, 1974), p. 204.

3. Vladimir Nabokov and Elena Sikorskaia, *Perepiska s sestroi* (Ann Arbor: Ardis, 1985), p. 5; in Russian.

4. Julian Connolly, "A Note on the Name 'Pnin'," in *Vladimir Nabokov Research Letter* 6 (1981): 32–33.

5. Andrew Field, *VN*, p. 295.

6. Barabtarlo, *Phantom of Fact*, p. 204.

7. Ibid., p. 56.

8. Here is what Nabokov, in his commentary to *Eugene Onegin* (Bollingen Foundation, 1964) has to say about Alexander Radishchev, an important political activist and writer of the late eighteenth century: "Aleksandr Radishchev (1749–1802), the liberal-minded author of *A Journey from St. Petersburg to Moscow*, printed on his private press, a work for which he was banished to Siberia by Catherine the Great for the rest of her reign, but which Alexander I allowed to be published in 1810. The *Journey* is a clumsily worded but fiery piece of eighteenth-century prose directed against oppression and slavery. Pushkin, who condemned its style . . . knew it well" (volume 2, part 2, p. 274).

9. Vladimir Orlov's *Russkie prosvetiteli 1790–1800–kh godov* (Moscow: Goslitizdat, 1950), pp. 63–177.

10. Cornell, according to the records of its libraries' acquisitions, did not purchase Orlov's book either in 1950 or in 1953, when a second edition came out.

11. *Selected Letters*, p. 135. For a description of the intensity and scope of his research, see also Boyd, *American Years*, pp. 222–23.

12. SzA, diaries, November 10, 1971.

13. That Nabokov was familir with the link between the two names becomes obvious when one encounters 'Dr. Olga Repnin' in *Look at the Harlequins*.

14. Orlov does not specify whether Ivan Pnin's son did or did not have children of his own.

15. Vladimir Nabokov to Katharine White, September 29, 1953, in *Selected Letters*, p. 140.

16. Vladimir Nabokov to Katharine White, September 29, 1953: "*Conclusive Evidence* and *Pnin* have been brief sunny escapes from [*Lolita*'s] intolerable spell" (*Selected Letters*, p. 140).

17. See Boyd, *American Years*, p. 225.

18. SzA, diaries, August 29, 1970. See also February 4, 1972, where Szeftel adds that Nabokov told him he received "800 dollars for each story."

19. Vladimir Nabokov to Katharine White, July 26, 1953, in Boyd, *American Years*, p. 225; Boyd, ibid.

20. *Strong Opinions*, p. 84.

21. See, for example, Richard Stern's review, where he called the book "formless . . . a group of sketches which the author has hardly tried to make into a novel" ("Pnin and the Dust Jacket," *Prairie Schooner* 31 [1957]: 161). Even one of Nabokov's most ardent fans, John Updike, still believes today that *Pnin* is a "quasi novel,"

consisting of "collected . . . short stories about the touching Russian émigré professor" ("A Jeweler's Eye," in *The New York Times Book Review,* October 29, 1995, p. 7). Pascal Covici, the editor at Viking Press, which at first was interested in publishing *Pnin* but then turned it down, seems to have anticipated these critical opinions of the book when he suggested to Nabokov in 1955 that *Pnin* was "not a novel." "I do not know if it is or not. . . ," Nabokov responded, brimming with irritation. "All I know is that PNIN is not a collection of sketches. I do not write sketches" (*Selected Letters,* p. 179).

22. Since the original manuscript of the novel has apparently been lost or misplaced, we will probably never know for sure how the novel evolved. It should be noted, however, that most critics who have written about *Pnin* are much less skeptical about Nabokov's statement than I am, despite the fact that Nabokov changed the ending of the book late in the game. Gennadi Barabtarlo even suggests that Nabokov may have intended Pnin to survive all along and was merely "pulling . . . legs" of his editors to keep them in suspense (*Phantom of Fact,* p. 41).

23. *The New Yorker,* June 20, 1953, p. 32.

24. *The New Yorker,* May 7, 1955, p. 48.

25. Eugene Kinkead, "Profiles: The Tiny Landscape," in *The New Yorker,* July 9, 1955, p. 32.

26. *The New Yorker,* November 28, 1953, pp. 42, 44.

27. *The New Yorker,* November 28, 1953, p. 46.

28. In Nabokov's "Notes for Pnin's Life," kept at the Library of Congress, Nabokov's original notation for chapter 3 has the month (February), the year (1953) and the day (Tuesday). The number 15 is then added with the help of an insertion mark. This could suggest that the date was inserted at a later point, thus explaining why the discrepancy between the day of the week and the actual date may have escaped Nabokov's notice. I am grateful to Dmitri Nabokov for allowing me to review Nabokov's "Notes," a page-and-a-half document which deals almost exclusively with the dates in the novel. These dates include the death of Pnin's parents (1917), Pnin's graduation from Prague University (1925), his separation from Liza (1938), and the beginning of his teaching at Waindell (1945). The document itself has no date on it, but given that the dates it lists coincide with those in the novel, as opposed to *The New Yorker* version of the chapters, it was probably written in 1955.

29. For other discussions of this calendar "slip" in *Pnin,* see Fred Moody's "At *Pnin*'s Center" (in *Russian Literature TriQuarterly* 14 [1976]: 76–77), and Barabtarlo, *Phantom of Fact,* p. 122, as well as in his *Aerial View: Essays on Nabokov's Art and Metaphysics* (New York: Peter Lang, 1993), where Barabtarlo strengthens his suggestion that the mistake was deliberate because it brought the date of Pushkin's death

(i.e., February 10) into the picture (p. 145). Tony Sharpe also addresses the issue of the wrong day in his 1991 monograph *Vladimir Nabokov* (London: Edward Arnold, 1991), where, following Moody, he suggests that the slip is "intentional, designed to be hard evidence of Vladimir Vladimirovich's unrealiability" (p. 51). It is worth noting that at the end of the book, which takes place in 1955, Pnin is leaving Waindell on his birthday, February 15, which is said (this time correctly) to have been a Tuesday (*Pnin*, 186). For a general discussion of what he calls "Fatidic Dates" in Nabokov, see Pekka Tammi, *Problems of Nabokov's Poetics: A Narratological Analysis* (Helsinki: Suomalainen Tiedeakatemia, 1985), pp. 327–29.

30. Kitty Szeftel, personal interview, November 13, 1992.

31. Vladimir Nabokov to Katharine White, August 11, 1954, in *Selected Letters*, p. 150.

32. Vladimir Nabokov to Pascal Covici, February 3, 1954, in *Selected Letters*, pp. 143–44.

33. *The New Yorker*, April 23, 1955, p. 31.

34. Pascal Covici of Viking Press, for example, argued with Nabokov in 1954 that "killing" Pnin would be a mistake. It is doubtful, however, that Covici's opinion alone could be instrumental in Nabokov's change of heart, since he rarely acted on editors' suggestions unless he had his own reasons to alter things. For more on Covici's reaction, see Boyd, *American Years*, pp. 256–47.

35. Vladimir Nabokov to Cass Canfield, December 8, 1955, in *Selected Letters*, p. 182.

36. David H. Richter, "Narrative Entrapment in *Pnin* and 'Signs and Symbols'," in *Papers on Language and Literature: A Journal for Scholars and Critics of Language and Literature* 4 (Fall 1984): 424.

37. Review of Nabokov's *Pnin* in *Spectator*, September 27, 1957, p. 403. Reprinted in *Nabokov: The Critical Heritage*, ed. Norman Page (London: Routledge and Kegan Paul, 1982), p. 111.

38. Marc Szeftel was similarly hostile to Freudian thought and especially its literary applications. "If literary critics must unburden themselves of their obsession with sexuality," he wrote in 1971, "one wonders why should it be done at other people's expense . . . ?" (See SzA, diaries, November 13, 1971. A fuller version of this anti-Freudian tirade is reproduced in Appendix 3 of the present volume.)

39. Reprinted in Joseph Frank, *Through the Russian Prism*, p. 49.

40. Field, *VN*, p. 289.

41. Donald Morton is one of the critics who observes that "Pnin's life parallels in broad outline that of Nabokov"—see *Vladimir Nabokov* (New York: Ungar, 1974), p. 85.

42. In 1950, the year his teeth were removed, Nabokov reportedly told Szeftel: "Now I don't have a single tooth of my own. They were all replaced by two very

expensive dental plates. It's scary: if I drop one, it's several hundreds of dollars right there!" (SzA, diaries, June 5, 1970; in Russian).

43. Following M. Bezrodnyi's suggestion, Alexander Dolinin believes the Komarovs are fictional representations of Nabokov's fellow-writer, Aleksei Remizov, and his wife Serafima, both of whom Nabokov knew and disliked in emigration. See Dolinin's commentaries to *Pnin* in Vladimir Nabokov, *Izbrannoe* (Selected Works), ed. N. A. Anastas'ev (Moscow: Raduga, 1990), p. 669.

44. Vladimir Nabokov, *The Gift* (New York: G. P. Putnam, 1963), p. 9.

45. Vladimir Nabokov to Pascal Covici, February 3, 1954, in *Selected Letters,* p. 143.

46. Vladimir Nabokov to Pascal Covici, September 29, 1955, in *Selected Letters,* p. 178.

47. Boyd, *American Years,* p. 277.

48. Charles Nicol, "Pnin's History," in *Critical Essays on Vladimir Nabokov,* ed. Phyllis A. Roth (Boston: G. K. Hall, 1984), p. 103.

49. Gennadi Barabtarlo is one of several critics who refuses to identify the narrator too closely with Nabokov because of VN's arrogance. He suggests that "N—'s snobbish and itching desire to point out and set off, at every step, even to the detriment of truth, his social . . . and intellectual superiority over Pnin" would set him quite apart from Nabokov (*Phantom of Fact,* p. 29).

50. In *American Years,* Boyd makes a similar point when he writes that in *Pnin* "Nabokov . . . suggests how far the easy images we make of each other fall short of the truth and become less than human" (p. 278). See also Corrinne Hales, "The Narrator in Nabokov's *Pnin,*" in *Russian Literature TriQuarterly* 22 (1989), where she notes: "The narrator's rather desperate chase after Pnin as he leaves is futile. He can never catch Pnin any more than Jack Cockerell can. . . . The real discrepancy was never between one version of Pnin or another. It was always between perception and the idea of 'factual reality' " (p. 180). Other critics disagree, though. Thus Page Stegner states, rather unequivocally, that "*Pnin* does not deal with questions of illusion and reality" (*Escape into Aesthetics: The Art of Vladimir Nabokov* [New York: Dial, 1966], p. 97).

51. *Selected Letters,* p. 182.

52. *Strong Opinions,* p. 85.

53. There are obvious dangers in injecting light jokes into a serious discussion, but this one I cannot resist. There actually exists an independent character whose name is a combination of VN's and Pnin's. It is V. V. Pnin, an "aristochien," or an aristocratic dog, created by Belgian painter Thierry Poncelet and writer Bruce McCall in *Sit!: The Dog Portraits of Thierry Poncelet* (New York, Workman, 1993). Like Pnin and VN, V. V. Pnin is an exile ("So often exiled to Siberia that his personal bowl and straw

mattress were kept in permanent reserve") and feels close to Pushkin (" 'Poor Pnin,' sighed his best friend Pushkin, 'always baying at the moon' "). It is not clear how the "humorless" Pnin would have reacted to this innocuous joke, but Nabokov probably would have appreciated it.

54. In "The List or Manifest of Alien Passengers for The United States Immigrant Inspector at Port of Arrival" from "Champlain," the ship on which the family arrived in the United States on May 27, 1940, the Nabokovs listed themselves as people "without nationality," since they were neither citizens of the Soviet Union nor of Germany or France. The list is kept among the Nabokov Papers at the Library of Congress. I am grateful to Brian Gross for sharing his copy with the subscribers of "Nabokv-L," the e-mail forum edited by D. Barton Johnson. For a general description of Nabokov Papers at the Library of Congress, see *The Vladimir Nabokov Research Newsletter* 4 (Spring 1980): 20–33.

55. As mentioned earlier, Nabokov became a citizen in 1945, having spent more than twenty-five years as a stateless person. His sponsor at the citizenship examination was Mikhail Karpovich, the "Al Cook" of *Pnin,* who at the time was still Nabokov's good friend. For more on that, see Boyd, *American Years,* p. 87.

56. David Cowart, "Art and Exile: Nabokov's *Pnin,*" in *Studies in American Fiction* 2 (Autumn 1982): 202. By mentioning "exorcising" here, Cowart is probably alluding to Dabney Stuart's assertion that, in the character of Pnin, "the narrator consciously objectifies part of himself in order to exorcise it"—see Stuart's article "Nabokov's *Pnin:* Floating and Singing," in *Makers of the Twentieth-Century Novel,* ed. Harry R. Garvin (Lewisburg: Bucknell University Press, 1977), p. 275.

57. In an August 11, 1954, letter to Katharine White, Nabokov identified the state as "New Hampshire." See *Selected Letters,* p. 150.

58. For more on Karpovich's summer house and the people who stayed there, see Andrew Field, *Nabokov: His Life in Part* (London: Hamish Hamilton, 1977), p. 234; Barabtarlo, *Phantom of Fact,* p. 197; and Boyd, *American Years,* pp. 14–16.

59. Boyd, *American Years,* p. 15.

60. Daniel was born in 1937, the Szeftels were married in 1949. Victor was born in 1940, and Liza's visit where she asks her ex-husband to take partial responsibility for her son's education and well-being occurs in 1952.

61. In Nabokov's "Notes to Pnin's Life," which, as discussed in note 28, this chapter, feature mostly the new dates for the final version of *Pnin,* there is a rare instance when a notation does not deal with any chronology but simply mentions Pnin's work in folklore. It is, therefore, quite possible that the original chapter 2, meant for *The New Yorker* and now apparently lost, did not even contain this

passage, which only strengthens my suspicion that *Pnin* did undergo heavy "Szefteli-zation" in its final form.

62. Boyd, *American Years,* p. 288.

63. See my Introduction, p. 0, where Abrams is quoted as stating that he heard from Nabokov that "Pnin was more Nabokov himself than any other person" (a letter to the author, July 27, 1993).

64. *Perepiska,* p. 41. In Russian, the last phrase is in French.

65. See Boyd, *American Years,* pp. 88–89. Being a non-Jew probably prolonged Sergei's life for he was neither gassed nor cremated, eventually succumbing to a stomach ailment brought on by malnutrition.

66. SzA, diaries, October 14, 1969; in Russian. Szeftel obviously assumes here that his mother was killed soon after she disappeared from her apartment in Lyon, which, given her age and state of health, is probably a reasonable conclusion.

67. Kitty Szeftel, personal interview, August 13, 1992.

68. See for example, an entry in Szeftel's diary from October 4, 1976, where he talks about his habit of "praying to Mother, asking her for help" (*"privychka . . . molit'sia materi, prosia pomoch' "*); SzA.

69. If purely coincidental, it is probably due to the fact that Nabokov may have had a similar, even if somewhat more sophisticated, sense of the "otherworld," as a place populated by the protective ghosts of loved ones. See, for example, his reference to "tender ghosts humoring a lucky mortal" at the end of chapter 6 of *Speak, Memory: An Autobiography Revisited* (New York: G. P. Putnam, 1966), p. 139. Here I disagree with Gennadi Barabtarlo, who suggests that the readers' sympathies are supposed to be with the more traditional religious sentiments expressed by another character, Professor Chateau, who, being "a practicing Greek Catholic," "deplored [Pnin's] agnostic attitude" (*Pnin,* 129; *Phantom of Fact,* p. 210).

70. Lucy Maddox, *Nabokov's Novels in English* (Athens: University of Georgia, 1983), p. 92.

71. Ibid., p. 89.

72. Michael Wood, *The Magician's Doubts: Nabokov and the Risks of Fiction* (London: Chatto & Windus, 1994), p. 164.

73. Ibid., pp. 167–68. Leona Toker is one critic who would probably disagree with Wood's assessment of Pnin's reliability. In *Nabokov: The Mystery of Literary Structures* (Ithaca: Cornell University Press, 1989), she writes: "[W]hat if Pnin himself is unreli-able? What if he is confusing the narrator with someone else? He is presented as liable to such confusion" (p. 25). Arthur Mizener is even more certain about the narrator's reliability "edge" over Pnin: "Pnin's character can be . . . subtly and beautifully defined

for us because the story's narrator, though he is deeply sympathetic with Pnin, is acutely aware of the realities of the world around him. However much he shares Pnin's feelings, he never shares Pnin's innocent self-confidence that only Pnin is in step. . . . [I]t is this narrator who—indirectly and therefore unobtrusively—suggests the larger meaning of Pnin's life, the meaning that Pnin can feel but never formulates." ("Seriousness of Vladimir Nabokov," in *Sewanee Review* 76 [1968]: 661, 662).

74. Andrew Field, *Nabokov: His Life in Art* (Boston: Little Brown, 1967), p. 132. Hazel Cohen uses Field's formulation in her article "*Pnin:* A Character in Flight from His Author," in *English Studies in Africa: A Journal of the Humanities* 1 (1986): 57–71.

75. Michael Long, *Marvell, Nabokov: Childhood and Arcadia* (Oxford: Oxford University Press, 1984), p. 60.

76. Julian W. Connolly, "*Pnin:* The Wonder of Recurrence and Transformation," in *Nabokov's Fifth Arc: Nabokov and Others on His Life and Work,* ed. J. E. Rivers and Charles Nicol (Austin: University of Texas Press, 1982), p. 209. For a comprehensive summary of different critical approaches to the relationship between the narrator and the protagonist in the novel, see Corrinne Hales's "The Narrator in Nabokov's *Pnin,*" pp. 169–81.

77. This point is made by, among others, Fred Moody in "At *Pnin*'s Center," (*Russian Literature TriQuarterly* 14 [1976]: 82); and J. H. Garrett-Goodyear in " 'The Rapture of Endless Approximation': The Role of the Narrator in *Pnin*" (*Journal of Narrative Technique,* 3 [Fall 1986]: 201). Garrett-Goodyear calls the combination of Cockerell and the breakfast he serves VN "the doom [the narrator] deserves."

78. Charles Nicol, "Pnin's History," in Roth, ed., *Critical Essays,* pp. 103, 104.

79. Paul Grams, "*Pnin:* The Biographer as Meddler," in A *Book of Things about Vladimir Nabokov,* p. 200.

80. *VN,* p. 292.

81. See, for example, SzA, diaries, April 25, 1968: "I remember an observation by a friend . . . who granted me all possible intellectual and moral qualities, except the gift of organization (according to him, the great gift of the Jews). I have thought since then quite often . . . that I really lack it: a strange flabbiness of will at the start, a kind of apprehension . . . of action, even decision, and fatalistic defeatism crippling even an easy enterprise."

82. Just to give one example which may simultaneously address the issues of lists and English (as well, perhaps, as Szeftel's Pnin-like naïveté), here is a 1952 entry in Szeftel's diary, where he is planning his sabbatical year: "One hour of *reading* without taking notes, just reading silently and thinking—every day. One day—poetry; the other day—a novel or an essay. Whatever is the daily task, one hour minimum of *writing:* letters, notes, drafts,—anything" (SzA, August 22, 1952; his emphasis).

83. SzA.

84. See Field, *VN*, p. 293. This legend was related to me as well by, among others, Peter Kahn and James McConkey, but it soon became clear that it was based on the same misinformation about Szeftel's professional history at Cornell.

85. The information about Szeftel's articles can be found in annual records of "Scholarly Production" in Szeftel's archive. The study on Vseslav Epos, mentioned also in chapter 2, came out in the "Memoirs of the American Folklore Society" series.

86. For an interesting discussion of the use of the Cinderella tale in *Pnin*, see Charles Nicol, "Pnin's History," in Roth, ed., *Critical Essays*, pp. 94–99.

87. Vladimir Nabokov, *Pale Fire* (New York: Berkley Books, 1962), p. 103.

88. Ibid.

89. Ibid., p. 153.

90. Ibid., pp. 189–90.

4 / SZEFTEL IN SEARCH OF SUCCESS: *LOLITA*

1. Vladimir Nabokov to Katharine White, December 23, 1953; in *Selected Letters*, p. 142.

2. Dorothy Parker, "Lolita," in *The New Yorker*, August 27, 1955, pp. 32–35.

3. This correspondence between Nabokov and White has not been published but can be found in the Berg Collection at the New York Public Library. I am grateful to Seth Roberts for bringing my attention to it. After Nabokov's *Lolita* was published, Dorothy Parker became one of its most vocal fans, calling the novel "a fine book, a distinguished book—all right, then—a great book" (from Parker's review in *Esquire;* also quoted in a full-page Putnam ad for *Lolita* which appeared in *The New York Times Book Review* on August 21, 1958). Nabokov, in turn, went on record in 1964 to state that he had been Dorothy Parker's "admiring reader . . . for many years" (Vladimir Nabokov to Byron Dobell, January 8, 1964; in *Selected Letters*, p. 352).

4. I am not aware of any work on Nabokov, including Boyd's and Field's biographies, which mentions this episode of *Lolita* history.

5. SzA, diaries, November 23, 1971. According to Szeftel, Mark Aldanov, a Russian émigré writer living in New York at the time, "had described [*Volshebnik's*] plot and details" to him in 1942 and "had called it 'a masterpiece'—though 'unpublishable' because of its highly erotic content." Aldanov himself apparently "had heard Nabokov read the story to a small group in Paris" in 1939 ("Lolita at Cornell," published in the *Cornell Alumni News* in 1980 and reprinted in Appendix 4 of the present volume).

Szeftel never got to read the story itself, however: "Nabokov only promised to give it to me to read, but never gave it" (February 1, 1979; SzA).

6. Quoted in Boyd, *American Years*, p. 295.

7. See SzA, diaries, November 23, 1971. Szeftel also kept records of most of the books he read. He has two contemporaneous notes related to *Lolita:* "1956. II. Nabokov. Lolita (I), Paris 1956," and "1957. IV. 16. Lolita (II)." (In his November 23, 1971, entry Szeftel explains that he got "vol. 2 only some time afterwards—I could not get it from Avgusta Jaryc at once." Unlike Szeftel, Jaryc probably was given her copy by the Nabokovs.)

8. SzA, diaries, April 2, 1970. Szeftel actually drew Nabokov's attention to the other ad, and it was at that point that Nabokov covered it with his hand smiling, according to Szeftel, "a modest, somewhat subdued, smile, surprisingly." See also his entry for August 28, 1970: "I see again before me N. discreetly covering with his hand [the other] ad, while showing to me . . . [the ad for] 'Lolita.' " For yet another description of this incident, see SzA, diaries, August 27, 1970.

9. *The Nabokov-Wilson Letters*, p. 298. The letter is dated February 29, 1956, and Nabokov is referring here to Harvey Breit's column in the February 10, 1956, issue of the *New York Times Book Review*. Harvey Breit was the critic who disclosed Nabokov's identity as the author of *Lolita* on March 11 of the same year. For more on that, see Boyd, *American Years*, p. 295.

10. SzA, diaries, August 27, 1970; in Russian. Szeftel describes her reaction in "Lolita at Cornell" as well.

11. *The Nabokov-Wilson Letters*, p. 288.

12. William Styron, "The Book on *Lolita*," *The New Yorker*, September 4, 1995, p. 33.

13. Sophie Tatiana Keller, personal interview, July 28, 1993. Kitty Szeftel claims it was all a joke, and she even told Nabokov about it: "I said, 'You know, Vladimir, we don't allow Tatiana to walk by your house anymore on the way to school.' He burst out laughing, but Marc was horrified" (Kitty Szeftel, personal interview, August 13, 1992).

14. M. H. Abrams, personal interview, September 16, 1993.

15. Alison Jolly, letter to the author, January 26, 1996.

16. SzA, diaries, August 27, 1970; Szeftel gives the same quote from Bishop in "Lolita at Cornell."

17. Morris Bishop to Alison Bishop, May 28, 1957. Morris Bishop Archive, Cornell University.

18. Milton Cowan, personal interview, September 15, 1993.

19. Morris Bishop to Alison Bishop, May 28, 1957. Morris Bishop Archive, Cornell University.

20. SzA, diaries, August 27, 1970. See also November 20, 1971: "Talking about

[*Lolita*] to Morris Bishop at the time of its appearance in the Olympus [sic] Press, I said to him that only the topic may raise objections, and not the writing itself which certainly is not pornographic. Bishop's reply was that I am mistaken, and he referred (with much gusto in his description, I must say) to the incident where Humbert Humbert holds Lolita on his knees, the 'bubble of happiness' incident." See also "Lolita at Cornell."

21. SzA, diaries, August 27, 1970; M. H. Abrams, personal interview, September 16, 1993. Marc Szeftel also quotes another close friend of Nabokov at the time, Harry Levin, as saying in a conversation with Szeftel that *Lolita* was "very hard reading." SzA, diaries, August 29, 1970. The April 17, 1970 entry quotes Levin as saying it was "a rather painful going (did he use the word 'tedious'?)"; SzA.

22. Alison Jolly, letters to the author, January 26, 1996, and February 11, 1996.

23. SzA, diaries, April 2, 1970; Field, *VN,* p. 302, where it reads "Delendum esse Zhivago!" thus making Zhivago into a neuter noun (rather than feminine, as in Szeftel's version) but still keeping the problematic infinitive form of the verb. The statement is also mentioned in *American Years* (drawn partially from "Lolita at Cornell"), where Boyd corrects Szeftel's (and Field's) Latin grammar by changing the phrase into "Delenda est Zhivago!" (p. 372). This way the phrase truly parallels Cato's "Carthago delenda est" which was, of course, Nabokov's intent. I am grateful to my former Latin teacher and now a colleague at the University of Washington, Professor James J. Clauss of the Department of Classics, for reminding me of the rudimentary grammatical rules in Latin which both Szeftel and Field violated. Szeftel quotes the phrase also in "Lolita at Cornell."

24. Herbert Gold, "Nabokov Remembered," p. 58.

25. SzA, diaries, August 27 (in Russian), and August 28, 1970. See also "Lolita at Cornell."

26. For the history of Book and Bowl, I am relying on the official log of Book and Bowl, kept at Cornell University Archives; an article by Emuson Hinchliff, published in the June 15, 1957, issue of the *Cornell Alumni News,* and valuable information given to me by past and current members of the organization at the Book and Bowl meeting held on Cornell campus on September 14, 1993. I would particularly like to thank Gould P. Colman for all his help both as Cornell University Archivist and as a member of Book and Bowl.

27. Quoted in Emuson Hinchliff, "Intelligence," the *Cornell Alumni News,* June 15, 1957, p. 638.

28. In the 1950s Bishop appears to have lost much of his enthusiasm for Book and Bowl. Thus he wrote to his friends, Richard and Lisa Robinson, on April 21, 1953: "I never go to the Book and Bowl any more. The gap has become too great." The "gap"

he is alluding to was probably that between faculty and students. Morris Bishop Archive, Cornell University.

29. Kitty Szeftel, personal interview, November 13, 1992.

30. The terms of joining the society are spelled out in a letter from Peter Detmold, Secretary, Book and Bowl, to Marc Szeftel, 6 December 1946; SzA. Unlike Nabokov, Szeftel liked to join clubs and societies on campus. Thus in 1947 he became a member of the Research Club of Cornell University and was invited to a talk by Professor F. M. Smock entitled "Some Contributions of Basic Research to the Fruit Industry" (See J. Douglas Hood, Secretary-Treasurer, The Research Club of Cornell University to Marc Szeftel, November 10, 1947; SzA). Since fruits were not among Szeftel's scholarly interests, we can probably assume that he did not attend that one. Throughout his stay at Cornell Szeftel was also a regular member of the Thursday Luncheon Group, founded and chaired by Professor Walter F. Willcox (see Walter F. Willcox's Memorandum to Members of the Thursday Luncheon Group, February 10, 1961 [Willcox was 100 years old at the time!], and Felix Reichmann to Marc Szeftel, October 16, 1962; both in SzA).

31. SzA, diaries, October 31, 1979.

32. M. H. Abrams, personal interview, September 16, 1993.

33. M. H. Abrams, personal interview, September 16, 1993. The incident was also described to me by several Book and Bowl members at the September 14, 1993, meeting I attended.

34. Peter Kahn, personal interview, September 15, 1994.

35. In *VN* (p. 305), Andrew Field erroneously lumps these two meetings together.

36. James McConkey is one of the people who remembers it this way; personal interview, September 14, 1993.

37. James McConkey, personal interview, September 14, 1993.

38. Field, *VN*, p. 305; M. H. Abrams, personal interview, September 16, 1993.

39. SzA, diaries, August 29, 1970. He voiced the same sentiment in "Lolita at Cornell": ". . . my presentation did not avoid some criticism, and the Nabokovs were very sensitive to anything but praise."

40. "Lolita, Book and Bowl, 13. XI. 1958"; SzA. The document is typed with some handwritten additions and numerous corrections. It may be a draft of the talk rather than its final copy.

41. James McConkey to Marc Szeftel, December 15, 1958; SzA.

42. "I was offered by Mc Closkey [sic] to have the paper published in 'The Epoch'. . . . I did not accept the offer: N. was my colleague at Cornell" ("Nabokov: What do I have on him?" no date; in SzA). See also "Lolita at Cornell": "Jim

McConkey . . . offered to publish the talk . . . but I did not feel that I could publish it while Nabokov was still my colleague at Cornell."

43. "Lolita at Cornell."

44. "Nabokov: What do I have on him?"; SzA.

45. For Szeftel, Gogol's Akakii Akakievich, the quintessential "little" humiliated man who nevertheless fought to defend his dignity, was, like Pnin, "a saint"—see SzA, diaries, January 3, 1977. Szeftel was not the only one to see the connection between the two protagonists. In *Vladimir Nabokov: America's Russian Novelist* (London: Marion Boyars, 1977), G. M. Hyde also draws a strong parallel between Pnin and Akakii Akakievich—see his chapter "A Debt to Gogol: *Pnin*," pp. 149–70.

46. SzA, diaries, December 10, 1969 (in English; "krivoe zerkalo" is written in Russian).

47. Nina Berberova, "Nabokov i ego 'Lolita'," *Novyi zhurnal* LVII (1959): 92–115. Berberova's article contains a number of highly arguable points, among them her statement that both *Pnin* and Nabokov's autobiography were somehow necessary for Nabokov but will prove totally "unnecessary" for his readers. About *Pnin* she wrote: "*Pnin* . . . is about twenty–twenty-five years too late. It should have been written in the era of Nabokov's first novel, *Mary*,—back then . . . there still existed absent-minded professors and young brilliant scholars who were ready to succeed them with such enthusiasm" (95). It is not clear who Berberova considers "a young brilliant scholar" in the book, since the narrator, who is shown to succeed Pnin, belongs to the same generation as the protagonist.

48. Szeftel means the treatment of the same topic in Nabokov's *Volshebnik* (*The Enchanter*).

49. "Nabokov. Lolita. Content & Form," no date; SzA.

50. See Roman Goul to Marc Szeftel, November 27, 1960; SzA.

51. Morris Bishop to Marc Szeftel, February 19, 1963; SzA.

52. Marc Szeftel to Vladimir Nabokov, July 2, 1963; SzA.

53. Véra Nabokov to Marc Szeftel, July 16, 1963; SzA.

54. See, for example, January 2, 1977: "I was thinking of writing an article about 'Lolita' and sent him a letter . . . asking him to send me the screenplay (for a comparison). I received a letter from Vera with a refusal: he probably wants to publish it with time and is afraid to *déflorer* it" (in Russian; *déflorer* is in French). Szeftel ends the entry by stating, in French: "*Telle était la fin de l'épisode Nabokoff dans ma vie*" ("Such was the end of the Nabokov episode in my life"; SzA). In "Lolita at Cornell" Szeftel gives the same reason for the refusal: "I wrote to Nabokov . . . and received a reply from Vera Nabokov, who said that he could not lend [the screen-

play] to me. I understood the reason for this refusal only much later, when Nabokov published the screenplay as a separate volume in 1974. So I did not write the study, and this was our last contact before Nabokov's death in 1977."

55. Sophie Tatiana Keller, personal interview, July 28, 1993.

56. SzA, diaries, August 28, 1970.

57. SzA, diaries, April 14, 1971; in Russian. The person who told him this was Yuri Ivask—see SzA, Yuri Ivask to Marc Szeftel, December (no day), 1970, where Ivask writes that earlier in the year he saw the Nabokovs in Montreux, and that Nabokov struck him as "*sovsem molodoi chelovek*"—i.e., the identical Russian phrase that Szeftel uses in his diary.

58. Marc Szeftel (*sous la direction initiale de Alexandre Eck*), *Documents De Droit Public Relatifs A La Russie Médiévale* (Brussels, Éditions de la Librairie Encyclopédique, 1963).

59. *Slavic Review* 4 (December 1964): 740–41.

60. *The American Historical Review* (April 1965): 844.

61. The review was written by Horace W. Dewey. In *Speculum: A Journal of Mediaeval Studies* (October 1964): 753–55.

62. Anonymous. *Voprosy istorii* 5 (1964): 210.

63. Marc Szeftel, *Russian Institutions and Culture up to Peter the Great*. Preface by Donald W. Treadgold (London: Variorum Reprints, 1975); Marc Szeftel, *The Russian Constitution of April 23, 1906: Political Institutions of the Duma Monarchy* (Brussels: Les Édtions de la Librairie Encyclopédique, 1976).

64. SzA, diaries, January 18, 1971.

65. Robert C. Howes, *The Tale of the Campaign of Igor: A Russian Epic Poem of the Twelfth Century* (New York: Norton, 1973), p. vii.

66. Robert C. Howes, *The Testaments of the Grand Princes of Moscow* (Ithaca: Cornell University Press, 1966), p. vii.

67. SzA, diaries, June 22, 1975. According to Jack Haney (personal interview, July 12, 1994), Szeftel saw Haney's copy of the book, sent to him by Howes before Szeftel had yet received his. (He did several weeks later—see SzA, diaries, July 11–13, 1975.)

68. SzA, diaries, March 21, 1975.

69. SzA. On small index cards with dates of publication.

70. SzA. A list of projected works; no date. The list also features a project that he talked about frequently in his last years, but never wrote—a book entitled *My Four Cultures*.

71. See SzA, Bill Harrison to Marc Szeftel, March 1, 1974, March 24, 1974, and April 22, 1974.

72. "Nabokov. Durham 1974"; SzA.

73. See SzA, for correspondence with the University of British Columbia, Allen Sinel to Marc Szeftel, May 11, 1977, and Allan Smith to Marc Szeftel, September 22, 1977; for correspondence with Seattle University, Robert D. Saltvig to Marc Szeftel, June 16, 1977; and for correspondence with the University of Washington, Richard J. Dunn to Marc Szeftel, July 14, 1977, and Donna Gerstenberger to Marc Szeftel, October 12, 1977. Szeftel mentions the talk he gave for Tatiana's book-reading group in SzA, diaries, January 8, 1977.

74. Sophie Tatiana Keller, personal interview, July 28, 1993.

75. SzA, diaries, July 15, 1977.

76. SzA, diaries, July 8, 1977.

77. SzA, diaries, July 10, 1977: "I have written to . . . Vera Nabokov (in connection with V. V.'s death)"; Véra and Dmitri Nabokov to Marc Szeftel, July 1977; SzA.

5 / LIFE AFTER NABOKOV

1. Alef's relationship with Szeftel soured in later years. Szeftel resented what he suspected was Alef's lack of respect for him as a historian and a human being, and Alef, indeed, thought of Szeftel as a scholar with "fixed ideas" and as an "arrogant man" with a "rather outsized opinion of his own importance" (letter to the author, July 23, 1993).

2. Donald W. Treadgold, personal interview, September 2, 1992.

3. Donald W. Treadgold to George Vernadsky, March 29, 1961 (files of the Department of History at the University of Washington). Treadgold first met Szeftel in 1950, at Stanford, when Szeftel was on sabbatical.—See a letter from the Warden of All Souls College, Oxford (name illegible) to Marc Szeftel, January 8, 1951, where he says he received Szeftel's letter of December 30 and is glad Szeftel had met Treadgold at Stanford; SzA.

4. Harry Caplan to W. Stull Holt, April 9, 1961 (files of the Department of History at the University of Washington).

5. Kitty Szeftel, personal interview, November 13, 1992; Gardner Clark, personal interview, September 11, 1993.

6. Marc Szeftel to W. Stull Holt, May 30, 1961 (files of the Department of History at the University of Washington). On May 18, 1961, Szeftel also got an offer from the University of California at Berkeley for a one-year visiting appointment, which he subsequently declined in favor of the permanent job in Seattle—see Lincoln Constance, Dean of College of Letters and Science, University of California at Berkeley, to Marc Szeftel, May 18, 1961; SzA. Constance mentions in this letter a similar visiting

appointment offer—and a proposed larger salary—which Szeftel got earlier from their sister campus at Davis.

    7. Donald W. Treadgold, personal interview, September 2, 1992.

    8. Knight Biggerstaff, personal interview, September 14, 1993.

    9. Paul W. Gates to Marc Szeftel, October 9, 1961; SzA.

    10. See for example, a response by a former colleague to one of Szeftel's letters which has not survived: "I am extremely sorry and chagrined that you have such a bad recollection of Cornell. It is surely not true that you were not appreciated; as a matter of fact, you are missed very much by the many friends you have on the faculty" (Felix Reichmann to Marc Szeftel, October 16, 1962; SzA).

    11. W. Stull Holt and George E. Taylor to Dean Solomon Katz, April 27, 1961; files of the Department of History.

    12. George E. Taylor to Marc Szeftel, May 15, 1961; and George E. Taylor to Marc Szeftel, May 19, 1961; files of the Department of History.

    13. Philip W. Cartwright to George E. Taylor, June 1, 1961. The letter read in part: "Firstly, you indicate that the summer salary will continue until retirement. . . . I do not see how the University can guarantee this. . . . Secondly, I know of no situation in which we have granted salary to cover additional medical expenses, whatever they may be, pursuant to Dr. Szeftel's leaving Cornell" (files of the Department of History).

    14. George E. Taylor to Dean Cartwright, June 5, 1961; files of the Department of History.

    15. The figures, which Szeftel looked up in the library, can be found in SzA. In 1964–65, for example, the top salary in the department (which was paid to W. Stull Holt) was $18,639, while Szeftel's salary was only $14,130.

    16. Imre Boba, personal interview, August 18, 1993.

    17. Marc Szeftel to Donald W. Treadgold, February 3, 1967; his emphasis; files of the Department of History.

    18. Peter Sugar, personal interview, October 17, 1995.

    19. Sophie Tatiana Keller, personal interview, July 28, 1993.

    20. Imre Boba, personal interview, August 18, 1993.

    21. Peter Sugar, personal interview, October 17, 1995.

    22. During my interview with him, Treadgold stated that, while disappointed that Szeftel had not published more during his tenure at the University of Washington, he still thought he and his department had made a proper choice: "There were not terribly many medievalists. . . . He was the best we could've done. He had class . . . , he had standards, and, academically, there was no question about his seriousness" (Donald W. Treadgold, personal interview, September 2, 1992). Peter Sugar, Treadgold's long-time colleague and friend at the university, believes, however, that

Treadgold did end up regretting the appointment but did not want to make his feelings about it public, partially because of his pity for Szeftel and respect for the family, and partially because his own high recommendation of Szeftel's scholarship had been decisive in Szeftel's hiring (Peter Sugar, personal interview, October 17, 1995).

23. Donald W. Treadgold to Robert Burke, Hellmut Wilhelm, and Dean Philip W. Cartwright, February 9, 1967; files of the Department of History.

24. Donald W. Treadgold to Otis Pease, Lyman Legters, and George Taylor. February 19, 1967; files of the Department of History.

25. SzA, diaries, October 7, 1969; his emphasis.

26. Peter Sugar, for example, believes that Szeftel was "arrogant," "felt superior to most of us," and "expected to be treated as the cat's meow" (Peter Sugar, personal interview, October 17, 1995).

27. SzA, diaries, September 13–14, 1969; in Russian; his emphasis.

28. SzA, diaries, September 29, 1969. Fleury's book was entitled *Nos grands médecins d'aujourd'hui* and was published in 1891 by Société d'Éditions Scientifiques (Paris).

29. Sophie Tatiana Keller, personal interview, July 28, 1993.

30. Donald W. Treadgold, personal interview, September 2, 1992.

31. Peter Sugar, personal interview, October 17, 1995.

32. Anonymous. Personal interview, October 14, 1995.

33. "He was much too moral to have affairs. Extremely straight-laced about men and women relationships" (Sophie Tatiana Keller, personal interview, July 28, 1993). Szeftel, indeed, could be quite intolerant on issues pertaining to sex, in general, and to homosexual sex, in particular. Thus in 1978 he was scandalized by finding, on "the new fiction shelf" of his local public library, a book entitled *The Joy of Lesbian Sex*. Having examined it in enough detail to describe some of the drawings in his diary, Szeftel took the book to a librarian and registered his complaint: "Do not you have any limits imposed by simple decency and good taste?" (SzA, diaries, October 28, 1978).

34. Donald W. Treadgold, personal interview, September 2, 1992.

35. SzA, Diaries, May 16, 1970; in Russian.

36. SzA, Diaries, May 14, 1970; in Russian.

37. Donald W. Treadgold, personal interview, September 2, 1992.

38. Sophie Tatiana Keller, personal interview, July 28, 1993.

39. Sophie Tatiana Keller, personal interview, July 28, 1993.

40. Imre Boba, personal interview, August 18, 1993.

41. SzA, Diaries, November 3, 1969; in Russian.

42. A copy of the certificate is in SzA. Szeftel was very happy to receive the award, presented to him in front of many Slavists at the banquet during an annual AAASS convention in Saint Louis—see his entry from October 19, 1976.

43. SzA, diaries, April 16, 1969.

44. SzA, diaries, August 9, 1978.

45. Charles Nicol to Marc Szeftel, January 17, 1979; SzA.

46. In Szeftel's hand on Nicol's January 17 letter: "Jan. 22: *Around "Lolita"*, 3000–4000 (within a month)"; SzA.

47. Charles Nicol to Marc Szeftel, January 26, 1979; SzA.

48. SzA, diaries, February 1, 1979.

49. Charles Nicol to Marc Szeftel, March 21, 1979; SzA.

50. Charles Nicol to Marc Szeftel, July 8, 1979; SzA.

51. Stephen Jan Parker to Marc Szeftel, April 2, 1979; SzA.

52. Stephen Jan Parker to Marc Szeftel, April 27, 1979; SzA.

53. Stephen Jan Parker to Marc Szeftel, September 20, 1979; SzA.

54. Stephen Jan Parker, letter to the author, September 14, 1993.

55. See SzA, diaries, September 28, 1979: "What he means by 'style and content,' I do not get: did he not ask me for recollections about N.?"

56. See SzA, Felix Reichmann to Marc Szeftel, December 3, 1979, where he also mentions Abrams' and Caplan's eagerness to help. Szeftel recorded in his diary that he had written letters both to Abrams and Caplan concerning the article (November 24, 1979). Harry Caplan died a year later (see SzA, diaries, December 11, 1980). See also SzA, James McConkey to Marc Szeftel, March 26, 1980, where McConkey mentions that Abrams forwarded him the manuscript and proceeds to soothe the old man's hurt ego: "Of course I remember your Book and Bowl talk, for I liked it very much. It included, as you know, more critical commentary that the present recollections—in particular, I recall your comments on the affinities between Nabokov and Dostoevsky, that writer he so despised, I wish it had been possible at the time for that talk of yours to have been published in *Epoch:* the issue would have become a collector's item."

57. "A very pleasant surprise: a check of $150 in the mail from the Cornell Alumni News for my 'Lolita at Cornell' " (SzA, diaries, September 29–30, 1980).

58. John Marcham to Marc Szeftel, September 24, 1980; SzA.

59. SzA. The top of the list reads as follows: "Nicol; myself; Ivask; Andreev; Abrams; F[lorence] Clark; Reichmann."

60. Marc Szeftel, "Lolita at Cornell," in the *Cornell Alumni News*, November 1980. Reprinted in Appendix 4 of this volume with the permission of *Cornell Magazine* (formerly *Cornell Alumni News*).

61. SzA, diaries, September 29–30, 1980; his emphasis.

62. SzA, diaries, April 14, 1980.

63. SzA, diaries, May 13, 1980. Ivask's letter is preserved in the archive. See Yuri Ivask to Marc Szeftel, May 1, 1980, where Ivask, who himself wrote poetry, complains that Nabokov, both as a poet and a prose writer, is too artificial (SzA). Ivask uses the words "an aesthete" and "an acrobat" in this letter which Szeftel is echoing here. Véra Nabokov mentioned *potustoronnost'*, or the otherworld, in her introduction to the 1979 Ardis edition of Nabokov's poems—*Stikhi* (Ann Arbor: Ardis, 1979), pp. 3– 4. For more on "the otherworld" in Nabokov, see Vladimir E. Alexandrov, *Nabokov's Otherworld* (Princeton: Princeton University Press, 1991). I tend to agree with John Updike who wrote that Nabokov had a "strictly nonsectarian fascination with a possible afterlife," as opposed to a more traditionally Christian belief ("A Jeweler's Eye," p. 7).

64. SzA, diaries, September 29–30, 1980; his emphasis.

65. SzA, diaries, December 29, 1980. Struve's letter, dated December 24, 1980, can be found in Szeftel's archive. Szeftel's accurately summarizes its contents. Struve also told him that in none of his reminiscences about Nabokov he ever had mentioned this episode for fear that it could hurt Véra Nabokov's feelings. According- ing to Brian Boyd, Nabokov actually denied having had an affair with Olga Gzovskaia in early 1920s in Berlin, even though Gaidarov was, indeed, suspicious and jealous, and almost challenged Nabokov to a duel—see Brian Boyd, *Russian Years*, p. 182.

66. SzA, diaries, August 31, September 1, and September 3, 1981. His emphasis. He learned that the library did not have his book from Kitty Szeftel, who had visited Ithaca that year.

67. SzA, diaries, December 29, 1981, his emphasis. "The Lectures of Professor Pnin," reprinted in *Through the Russian Prism*, pp. 49–53.

68. Frank's original letter is not in the archive, but he remembers his reaction to Szeftel's article in a later letter, written in response to Szeftel's appraisal of Frank's review of Roman Jakobson and Krystina Pomorska' *Dialogues*—"Roman Jakobson: The Master Linguist"—which appeared in the April 12, 1984 issue of *The New York Review of Books*. The review is also reprinted in *Through the Russian Prism*, pp. 3–17. See Joseph Frank to Marc Szeftel, May 27, 1984; SzA.

69. SzA, diaries, March 17, 1983; in Russian.

70. Sophie Tatiana Keller, personal interview, July 28, 1993.

71. SzA, diaries, March 17, 1983; in Russian.

72. SzA, diaries, October 9, 1983.

73. SzA, diaries, November 14, 1983, and January 31, 1984.

74. Sophie Tatiana Keller, personal interview, July 28, 1993; Kitty Szeftel, personal interview, August 13, 1992.

75. Kitty Szeftel to John Rogister, September 9, 1985; SzA.

76. The *Seattle Times*, June 20, 1985, p. D5.

77. Treadgold's typed copy of the obituary, which was presented to Kitty Szeftel, is kept in SzA. The obituary, minus those lines, was published in *Slavic Review* 3 (Fall 1985): 612–14, following the obituary for Gleb Struve, who died the same year.

APPENDIX 1 / SZEFTEL'S "INTELLECTUAL BIOGRAPHY"

1. September 27, 1976; both entries in Russian; his emphasis.

2. Szeftel is referring here to the "Famous Converts" subchapter in Salo W. Baron's *The Russian Jew under Tsars and Soviets*, pp. 133–36, where Kovner's Hebrew name "Abraham Uri" is used instead of "Albert." Kovner's famous letter to Dostoevsky (1877) is translated into English and published in L. S. Dawidowicz, ed., *The Golden Tradition: Jewish Life and Thought in Eastern Europe*, pp. 338–43.

APPENDIX 2 / CORRESPONDENCE WITH VLADIMIR NABOKOV AND ROMAN JAKOBSON

1. Thomas Bergin was the chairman of the Division of Literature at the time.

2. *La Geste Du Prince Igor'*.

3. According to Kitty Szeftel, Véra Nabokov came and examined their house with the view of renting it the following academic year, when the Szeftels were going to be in Europe on sabbatical leave. The Nabokovs eventually decided against renting the house. (Kitty Szeftel, personal interview, August 13, 1992.)

4. I.e., "The Vseslav Epos" in *Russian Epic Studies*.

5. I.e., "The Vseslav Epos."

6. Nabokov spent the spring term of 1952 at Harvard as Visiting Lecturer in Slavic Languages—see Brian Boyd, *American Years*, pp. 211–17. Boyd describes a dinner at the Levins' house with the Nabokovs and the Jakobsons, at which Nabokov "could not recall Jakobson's patronymic." Boyd suggests that this was yet another instance of Nabokov having "difficulty remembering the names of those he did not care for" (p. 215), but I have found no indications that, at this early point in their relationship, Nabokov already held a negative opinion of Jakobson.

7. Nabokov had eight months of leave from Cornell and came to Cambridge in early February to pursue research in Widener Library for his commentary on *Eugene Onegin*. He stayed until early April. See Boyd, *American Years*, pp. 222–23.

8. *Zadonshchina* is a 14th-century Russian epic with strong echoes of the *Slovo*. The proponents of the *Slovo*-as-a-late-fake theory usually assume that *Slovo* was fashioned after *Zadonshchina*, rather than the other way around. Jakobson obviously wanted to include *Zadonshchina* in part to debunk that theory.

9. Without referring to Nabokov by name, Szeftel is basically objecting here to Nabokov's being in charge of this part of the volume. Szeftel shared the widespread sentiment at Cornell that Nabokov was not, strictly speaking, a "scholar."

10. Szeftel is referring here to a bilingual Russian-Italian edition of the *Slovo* which came out that year and to which Roman Jakobson contributed critical annotations—*Cantare della gesta di Igor: epopea russa del XII secolo*, ed. Renato Poggioli (Rome: Einaudi, 1954). For his translation, Nabokov probably relied on the Russian text of the *Slovo* as it appeared in that volume, rather than on the somewhat different version published earlier in Jakobson's and Szeftel's *La Geste*.

11. André Grabar was a preeminent and prolific scholar of early Orthodox Christian and Byzantine art.

12. At this point, Hugh McLean, who got his Ph.D. from Harvard in 1956, was supposed to replace Nabokov as a literary editor and translator—see SzA, which contains several notes to this effect.

13. Omeljan Pritsak, a medieval Russian historian and a Turkologist, taught at Harvard at the time and also chaired their program in Ukrainian Studies. Pritsak was particularly interested in the Turkic vocabulary of the *Slovo*, and authored a number of articles on the subject. He also had his own theory on the date and place of the *Slovo*'s composition, and it was, perhaps, to that topic that he addressed himself in the talk to which Szeftel is referring here. (I am grateful to Dan Waugh, Marc Szeftel's successor as a Russian medieval historian at the University of Washington, for sharing with me his assessment of Pritsak's contribution to the *Slovo* research.)

14. The controversy was stirred this time by a talk given by a prominent Soviet historian, A. A. Zimin, back in Moscow, where he questioned the authenticity of the *Slovo* as a twelfth-century epic. Apparently unbeknownst to Zimin, the manuscript of his forthcoming book, which contained further elaboration on his findings, was smuggled to the West and found itself in Roman Jakobson's hands. Jakobson then proceeded to debunk Zimin's theory and to publish his own counter arguments before Zimin's book actually came out. Zimin was outraged at Jakobson's actions, which he considered both unethical and unprofessional (see A. A. Zimin to Marc Szeftel, October 30, 1967; SzA).

15. There is some mystery involving the true extent of Pritsak's participation in the project. In 1981, Marc Szeftel got a letter from William McGuire, Associate Editor of the Bollingen Series, who was writing a book about the Bollingen Foundation and wanted to know why Szeftel had left the project and had been replaced by Pritsak. This was news to Szeftel, who recorded in his diary: "Now, McGuire said in his letter that I... 'later withdrew... in favor of Omeljan Pritsak.' Well, I have never withdrawn! And, Jakobson never proposed to me to be replaced by Pritsak! This I have written to McGuire" (SzA, diaries, December 11, 1981). McGuire responded by saying that he was still puzzled as to what Pritsak's role was supposed to have been (both letters are in SzA). Upon receiving this second letter, Szeftel wrote to Jakobson "to tell [him] that, if he still wants to publish the book, I will be happy to cooperate" (SzA, diaries, December 29, 1981; the letter itself is not in SzA). Six and a half months later, Szeftel received the news of Jakobson's death.

APPENDIX 3 / NABOKOV IN SZEFTEL'S DIARIES

1. SzA, diaries, May 27, 1968.

2. SzA, diaries, November 30, 1969; in Russian.

3. Georgii Adamovich (1884–1972), an émigré critic who, together with Vladislav Khodasevich, was a major influence on Russian émigré literature in Europe in the 1920s and 1930s. Ivask knew Adamovich well and, in 1979, published his "Razgovory s Adamovichem (1958–1971)" (Conversations with Adamovich [1958–1971]) in Novyi zhurnal (New journal), an émigré periodical published in the United States.

4. Boris Poplavsky (1903–35), a controversial émigré poet, famous for his unruly but innovative mystical poetry as well as for his "decadent" lifestyle in Paris. Poplavsky was believed to have committed suicide in 1935, and some of its rumored particulars involving a love triangle were reflected in Iasha Chernyshevsky's suicidal pact with his friends in Nabokov's Dar (The Gift). Soon after his death, Poplavsky was hailed by Khodasevich, whose opinion Nabokov valued greatly, as "undoubtedly one of the most talented [poets] in the emigration, even, perhaps, the most talented." Adamovich, who rarely agreed with Khodasevich, did in this instance. He considered Poplavsky, as a poet, more gifted and interesting than Andrei Bely. For more on Poplavsky, his life and a critical assessment of his work, see Simon Karlinsky and Alfred Appel, Jr., eds., The Bitter Air of Exile: Russian Writers in the West, 1922–1972 (Berkeley: University of California Press, 1977), pp. 274–333.

5. A later entry the same year (May 26; in Russian) adds more information about Tsvetaeva's lecture: "I was reading yesterday about Tsvetaeva, who came back to

Russia . . . and committed suicide in Elabuga in 1941. Before the war (early thirties?) I spent a whole evening with her at my friends' house. She gave a talk on the subject of "The Poet and Our Times" [*Poet i sovremennost'*] (it was a rather disorganized talk) and afterwards she read her poems and simply talked. About contemporary French language she said a remarkable thing: 'It has gotten cut so short [*'ego tak obkarnali*]' since mediaeval times than only notions remain!' Her father was the director of the Museum of Alexander III and told his children about the amazing charm of Nicholas II ([Alexander] Kerensky says the same thing in his memoirs)."

6. Nabokov's *Ada* just appeared that year, and Nabokov's portrait, surrounded by pictures of his mother, St. Basil, Russian scrabble pieces, and, of course, a butterfly, was featured on the cover of the May 23, 1969, issue of *Time* magazine. The cover story compared him to Prospero and the Cheshire cat, and had the following to say about the difference between Nabokov and his character, Pnin: "It was not for Nabokov . . . to commit the hilarious gaffes of his comic creation, the émigré Professor Timofey Pnin. Years of having to conform with dignity as an outsider had marked his manner. Writer Janet Lewis, who was the widow of critic Yvor Winters, recalls that Nabokov would never kiss a woman's hand, as many other refugees did. 'If I were in Russia,' he once confided to her, 'I would kiss your hand' " (p. 89. The cover story was written by Martha Duffy and R. Z. Sheppard).

7. *Wiadomosci* was a Polish weekly émigré newspaper published in London.

8. Nabokov actually liked Proust, particularly the initial volumes of *Remembrance of Things Past*. It is true, however, that he did not care much for Balzac.

9. Oleg Maslennikov taught at that time in the Slavic Department of the University of California at Berkeley and was probably in Seattle giving a talk.

10. Joyce would say that Szeftel still read more of *Ulysses* than did Joyce's wife, Nora Barnacle Joyce, who, according to the writer, read two pages, *including* the cover.

11. The Russian *Lolita* was published in New York by Phaedra in 1967. It was translated by Nabokov with the help of his wife. For more on that, see Boyd, *American Years*, pp. 487–91.

12. In 1970 the "new" émigrés were still represented by the so-called second wave of emigration, i.e., the generation that had left Russia during or soon after the World War II. Several years later, with a new influx of predominantly Russian Jewish emigration to the West, the situation would change, and the so-called third wave of immigrants would inherit the title of the "new" émigrés.

13. The meeting took place in M. H. Abrams's house—see chapter 4 of the present study.

14. Szeftel is obviously referring here to *Invitation to a Beheading*, but he is translat-

ing the Russian title into English more literally than does the official English translation. The Russian title is *Priglashenie na kazn'*, where *kazn'* means *any* execution, not
just a beheading.

15. W. W. Rowe, *Nabokov's Deceptive World* (New York: New York University
Press, 1971). The review is reprinted in *Strong Opinions*, pp. 304–07.

16. See note 22, this section.

17. Konstantin Pobedonostsev, a famous jurist as well as Nicholas II's tutor,
became the Ober-Procurator of the Holy Sinod in 1880. He is often credited with
inciting and promoting extreme forms of reaction which led to political instability in
the country at the turn of the century.

18. The line is from the opening stanza of chapter 2 of Blok's unfinished verse epic
Vozmezdie (*Retribution*, 1910–1921): "*V te gody dal'nie, glukhie, / V serdtsakh tsarili son
i mgla: / Pobedonostsev nad Rossiei / Proster sovinye kryla / I ne bylo ni dnia, ni nochi, /
A tol'ko—ten' ogromnykh kryl . . .* etc. While Pobedonostsev obviously had no influence on Blok, he may have influenced the political views of some writers of the
previous generation. In *Vozmezdie*, Blok himself mentions Pobedonostsev's friendship with Dostoevsky (chapter 1, lines 618–23).

19. *The Enchanter* was, of course, not there. It was not published till 1986, a year
after Szeftel's death. The reviewer was referring to Nabokov's story "A Nursery Tale"
(*Skazka*). "I had not reread my 'Skazka' since 1930," Nabokov wrote in his introduction to the story, "and, when working now at its translation, was eerily startled to
meet a somewhat decrepit but unmistakable Humbert escorting his nymphet in the
story I wrote almost half-a-century ago" (*Tyrants Destroyed and Other Stories* [New
York: McGraw-Hill, 1975], p. 40).

20. Natal'ia Sergeevna Demkova was at the time a prominent Soviet literary
scholar who specialized in medieval Russian literature, and, in particular, literature
of the Old Belief. Her husband was a well-known physicist who was often invited to
the United States. Demkova, who joined him on that trip, gave a lecture at the
University of Washington on "Searching for Manuscripts in the Russian North." (I
am grateful to Dan Waugh, the host of the dinner that Szeftel is describing here, for
this information.)

21. I.e., *Keys to Lolita* (Bloomington: Indiana University Press, 1968).

22. Jozef Wittlin (1896–1976) was a Polish émigré writer and poet who lived in
Paris and New York. His anti-war novel *Salt of the Earth* (1936) was widely read in
Europe.

23. Akakii Akakievich, the hero of Gogol's "Overcoat," was a small clerk who
actually enjoyed performing seemingly mindless clerical errands.

24. One cannot help wondering what might have happened if Szeftel had known

about Nabokov's remark to Wilson at the time it was made, rather than over thirty years later. It is sadly ironic that, when Szeftel finally heard Nabokov say something he had always wanted to hear him say, the glow of the praise could no longer change either their relationship or Szeftel's basic feelings about himself as a scholar.

APPENDIX 4 / SZEFTEL'S PAPERS ON *LOLITA*

1. Szeftel is referring here to his memory of Nabokov's telling him that one reader had written to thank him because *Lolita* had supposedly cured him of homosexuality. See the diary entry for August 27, 1970, and "Lolita at Cornell."

2. Berberova's article—"*Nabokov i ego Lolita*'" (Nabokov and his "Lolita")—was published a year earlier than Szeftel states here. Szeftel's notes can be found in the archive.

3. In his letter of December 15, 1958, cited earlier, James McConkey informed Szeftel that: "*Epoch* has not published any sort of notice about *Lolita* or Nabokov, an omission we would like to remedy; at a recent editorial meeting I mentioned some of the comments which you had made during your talk, and was immediately commissioned by my fellow editors to approach you on the possibility of a review." He offered Szeftel "3,000 to 3,500 words" and promised that the review would be out "in mid-January, if all goes well. (It rarely does.)" (SzA).

4. Szeftel was in England at the time.

5. I.e., *The Enchanter.*

6. Nabokov himself described this group as follows: "I read the story one blue-papered wartime night to a group of friends—Mark Aldanov, two social revolutionaries and a woman doctor" (*Lolita*, 312). In his 1986 publication of the story, Dmitri Nabokov identified the "two social revolutionaries" as Vladimir Zenzinov and Ilya Fondaminsky, and the woman doctor as "Madame Kogan-Bernstein" (*The Enchanter*, 12).

7. Szeftel is referring to Wittlin here.

8. The meeting took place in November of 1958.

Bibliography

Adams, Robert M. "The Wizard of Lake Cayuga." *The New York Review of Books,* January 30, 1992.

Alexandrov, Vladimir. *Nabokov's Otherworld.* Princeton: Princeton University Press, 1991.

Appel, Alfred, Jr., and Charles Newman, eds. *Nabokov: Criticism, Reminiscences, Translations and Tributes.* Evanston: Northwestern University Press, 1970.

Barabtarlo, Gennadi. *Aerial View: Essays on Nabokov's Art and Metaphysics.* New York: Peter Lang, 1993.

———. *Phantom of Fact: A Guide to Nabokov's Pnin.* Ann Arbor: Ardis, 1989.

Baron, Salo W. *The Russian Jew Under Tsars and Soviets.* New York: Schoken Books, 1987.

Berberova, Nina. "Nabokov i ego 'Lolita.' " *Novyi zhurnal* LVII (1959).

Bishop, Morris. *A History of Cornell.* Ithaca: Cornell University Press, 1962.

Boyd, Brian. *Vladimir Nabokov: The American Years.* Princeton: Princeton University Press, 1991.

———. *Vladimir Nabokov: The Russian Years.* Princeton: Princeton University Press, 1990.

Brower, Daniel R. *The Russian City between Tradition and Modernity, 1850–1900.* Berkeley: University of California Press, 1990.

Chagall, Marc. *Angel nad kryshami.* Moscow: Sovremennik, 1989.

———. *My Life.* Trans. Elisabeth Abbott. New York: The Orion Press, 1960.

Chernow, Ron. *The Warburgs: The Twentieth-Century Odyssey of a Remarkable Jewish Family.* New York: Random House, 1993.

Cohen, Hazel. "*Pnin:* A Character in Flight from His Author." *English Studies in Africa: A Journal of the Humanities* 1 (1986).

Connolly, Julian. "A Note on the Name 'Pnin'." *Vladimir Nabokov Research Letter* 6 (1981).

Cornell Directory of Faculty and Staff. 1948–1949; 1949–1950; 1950–1951.

Cowart, David. "Art and Exile: Nabokov's *Pnin.*" *Studies in American Fiction* 2 (Autumn 1982).

Dawidowicz, Lucy S., ed. *The Golden Tradition: Jewish Life and Thought in Eastern Europe.* Boston: Beacon Press, 1967.

Dembo, L. S., ed. *Nabokov: The Man and His Work*. Madison: University of Wisconsin Press, 1967.

Dolinin, Alexander. "Primechaniia k romanu 'Pnin'." In Vladimir Nabokov, *Izbrannoe*, ed. N. A. Anastas'ev. Moscow: Raduga, 1990.

Field, Andrew. *Nabokov: His Life in Art*. Boston: Little Brown, 1967.

———. *Nabokov: His Life in Part*. London: Hamish Hamilton, 1977.

———. *VN: The Life and Art of Vladimir Nabokov*. New York: Crown, 1986.

Frank, Joseph. *Through the Russian Prism: Essays on Literature and Culture*. Princeton: Princeton University Press, 1990.

Garrett-Goodyear, J. H. " 'The Rapture of Endless Approximation': The Role of the Narrator in *Pnin*." *Journal of Narrative Technique* 3 (Fall 1986).

Garvin, Harry R., ed. *Makers of the Twentieth-Century Novel*. Lewisburg: Bucknell University Press, 1977.

Gibian, George, and Stephen Jan Parker, eds. *The Achievements of Vladimir Nabokov: Essays, Studies, Reminiscences and Stories*. Ithaca: Cornell University Press, 1984.

Gorodskie poseleniia v Rossiiskoi imperii. St. Petersburg: Obshchestvennaia Pol'za, 1860.

Hales, Corrinne. "The Narrator in Nabokov's *Pnin*." *Russian Literature TriQuarterly* 22 (1989).

Hillberg, Raul. *The Destruction of the European Jews*. New York: Holmes & Meier, 1985.

Hinchliff, Emuson. "Intelligence." *Cornell Alumni News,* June 15, 1957.

Howe, Irving. *World of Our Fathers*. New York: Harcourt Brace Jovanovich, 1967.

Howe, Irving, and Kenneth Libo. *How We Lived: A Documentary History of Immigrant Jews in America, 1880–1930*. New York: New American Library, 1979.

Howes, Robert C. *The Tale of the Campaign of Igor: A Russian Epic Poem of the Twelfth Century*. New York: Norton, 1973.

———. *The Testaments of the Grand Princes of Moscow*. Ithaca: Cornell University Press, 1966.

Hyde, G. M. *Vladimir Nabokov: America's Russian Novelist*. London: Marion Boyars, 1977.

Jakobson, Roman, and Marc Szeftel. "The Vseslav Epos." *Memoirs of the American Folklore Society*. 42 (1947).

Karlinsky, Simon, and Alfred Appel, Jr., eds. *The Bitter Air of Exile: Russian Writers in the West, 1922–1972*. Berkeley: University of California Press, 1977.

Kinkead, Eugene. "Profiles: The Tiny Landscape." *The New Yorker,* July 9, 1955.

———. "Profiles: Egg Is All." *The New Yorker,* June 20, 1953.

Klier, John D., and Shlomo Lambroza, eds. *Pogroms: Anti-Jewish Violence in Modern Russian History*. Cambridge: Cambridge University Press, 1992.

Lattimore, Richmond. "Omsk." *The New Yorker*, May 7, 1955.

Long, Michael. *Marvell, Nabokov: Childhood and Arcadia*. Oxford: Oxford University Press, 1984.

Maddox, Lucy. *Nabokov's Novels in English*. Athens: University of Georgia, 1983.

Mizener, Arthur. "Professor Nabokov." *Cornell Alumni News*, September, 1977.

————. "The Seriousness of Vladimir Nabokov." *Sewanee Review* 76 (1968).

Moody, Fred. "At *Pnin*'s Center." *Russian Literature TriQuarterly* 14 (1976).

Morton, Donald. *Vladimir Nabokov*. New York: Ungar, 1974.

Nabokov, Vladimir. *Bend Sinister*. New York: Time, 1964.

————. *The Defense*. Trans. Michael Scammel with Vladimir Nabokov. New York: Capricorn, 1964.

————. *The Enchanter*. Trans. Dmitri Nabokov. New York: G. P. Putnam, 1986.

————, trans. from Alexandr Pushkin, with commentary. *Eugene Onegin*. New York: Bollingen Foundation, 1964.

————. *The Gift*. Trans. Michael Scammell with Vladimir Nabokov. New York: G. P. Putnam, 1963.

————. *Invitation to a Beheading*. Trans. Dmitri Nabokov with Vladimir Nabokov. New York: G. P. Putnam, 1959.

————. *Lectures on Russian Literature*. Ed. Fredson Bowers. New York: Harcourt Brace Jovanovich, 1981.

————. *Lolita*. New York: G. P. Putnam, 1958.

————, and Edmund Wilson. *The Nabokov-Wilson Letters, 1940–1971*. Ed. Simon Karlinsky. New York: Harper, 1979.

————. *Pale Fire*. New York: Berkley Books, 1962.

————, and Elena Sikorskaia. *Perepiska s sestroi*. Ann Arbor: Ardis, 1985.

————. "Pnin." *The New Yorker*, November 28, 1953.

————. *Pnin*. New York: Doubleday, 1957.

————. "Pnin Gives a Party." *The New Yorker*, November 12, 1955.

————. "Pnin's Day." *The New Yorker*, April 23, 1955.

————. *Selected Letters, 1940–1977*. Eds. Dmitri Nabokov and Matthew J. Bruccoli. New York: Harcourt Brace Jovanovich, 1989.

————, trans. *The Song of Igor's Campaign: An Epic of the Twelfth Century*. New York: Random House, 1960.

————. *Speak, Memory: An Autobiography Revisited*. New York: G. P. Putnam, 1966.

————. *Stikhi*. Ann Arbor: Ardis, 1979.

————. *Strong Opinions.* New York: McGraw-Hill, 1973.

————. *Tyrants Destroyed and Other Stories.* Trans. Dmitri Nabokov with Vladimir Nabokov. New York: McGraw-Hill, 1975.

————. "Victor Meets Pnin." *The New Yorker,* October 15, 1955.

Opalski, Magdalena, and Israel Bartal. *Poles and Jews: A Failed Brotherhood.* Hanover: University Press of New England, 1992.

Oren, Dan A. *Joining the Club: A History of Jews and Yale.* New Haven: Yale University Press, 1962.

Orlov, Vladimir. *Russkie prosvetiteli 1790–1800–kh godov.* Moscow: Goslitizdat, 1950.

Page, Norman, ed. *Nabokov: The Critical Heritage.* London: Routledge and Kegan Paul, 1982.

Parker, Dorothy. "Lolita." *The New Yorker,* August 27, 1955.

Parker, Stephen Jan. "Vladimir Nabokov-Sirin as Teacher: Russian Novels." Ph.D. dissertation, Cornell University, 1969.

Poggioli, Renato, ed. *Cantare della gesta di Igor: epopea russa del XII secolo.* Rome: Einaudi, 1954.

Poncelet, Thierry, and Bruce McCall. *Sit!: The Dog Portraits of Thierry Poncelet.* New York: Workman, 1993.

Proffer, Carl, ed. *A Book of Things about Vladimir Nabokov.* Ann Arbor: Ardis, 1974.

————. *Keys to Lolita.* Bloomington: Indiana University Press, 1968.

Richter, David H. "Narrative Entrapment in *Pnin* and 'Signs and Symbols'." *Papers on Language and Literature: A Journal for Scholars and Critics of Language and Literature* 4 (Fall 1984).

Rivers, J. E, and Charles Nicol, eds. *Nabokov's Fifth Arc: Nabokov and Others on His Life and Work.* Austin: University of Texas Press, 1982.

Rostovtzeff, Michel, and Henri Grégoire, Roman Jakobson, Marc Szeftel, eds. *La Geste Du Prince Igor': Épopée Russe du Douzième Siècle.* New York: Rausen Brothers, 1948.

Roth, Phyllis A., ed. *Critical Essays on Vladimir Nabokov.* Boston: G. K. Hall, 1984.

Rowe, W. W. *Nabokov's Deceptive World.* New York: New York University Press, 1971.

Schiff, Stacy. "The Genius and Mrs. Genius: The Very Nabokovian Marriage of Vladimir and Véra." *The New Yorker,* February 10, 1997.

Schwartz, Leo W. *Wolfson of Harvard: Portrait of a Scholar.* Philadelphia: The Jewish Publication Society of America, 1978.

Sharpe, Tony. *Vladimir Nabokov.* London: Edward Arnold, 1991.

Stegner, Page. *Escape into Aesthetics: The Art of Vladimir Nabokov.* New York: Dial, 1966.

Steinberg, Stephen. *The Academic Melting Pot: Catholics and Jews in American Higher Education.* New York: McGraw-Hill, 1975.

Stern, Richard. "Pnin and the Dust Jacket." *Prairie Schooner* 31 (1957).

Styron, William. "The Book on *Lolita*." *The New Yorker,* September 4, 1995.

Szeftel, Marc. "Alexandre Eck, 1876–1953. In Memoriam." *The Russian Review,* October 1956.

————, sous la direction initiale de Alexandre Eck. *Documents De Droit Public Relatifs A La Russie Médiévale.* Brussels: Éditions de la Librairie Encyclopédique, 1963.

————. "Lolita at Cornell." *Cornell Alumni News,* November, 1980.

————. *The Russian Constitution of April 23, 1906: Political Institutions of the Duma Monarchy.* Brussels: Les Éditions de la Librairie Encyclopédique, 1976.

————. *Russian Institutions and Culture up to Peter the Great.* London: Variorum Reprints, 1975.

Tammi, Pekka. *Problems of Nabokov's Poetics: A Narratological Analysis.* Helsinki: Suomalainen Tiedeakatemia, 1985.

Terras, Victor, ed. *Handbook of Russian Literature.* New Haven: Yale University Press, 1985.

Toker, Leona. *Nabokov: The Mystery of Literary Structures.* Ithaca: Cornell University Press, 1989.

Treadgold, Donald W. "Marc Szeftel, 1902–1985. In Memoriam." *Slavic Review* 3 (Fall 1985).

Updike, John. "A Jeweler's Eye." *The New York Times Book Review,* October 29, 1995.

Wood, Michael. *The Magician's Doubts: Nabokov and the Risks of Fiction.* London: Chatto & Windus, 1994.

Index